TOURISM AND CULTURAL CHANGE 6
Series Editors: Mike Robinson and Alison Phipps

Histories of Tourism

Representation, Identity and Conflict

Edited by
John K. Walton

CHANNEL VIEW PUBLICATIONS
Clevedon • Buffalo • Toronto

Library of Congress Cataloging in Publication Data
Histories of Tourism: Representation, Identity and Conflict
Edited by John K. Walton.
Tourism and Cultural Change: 6
Includes bibliographical references.
1. Tourism–History. I. Walton, John K. II. Series.
G156.H57 2005
910'.9–dc22 2005009587

British Library Cataloguing in Publication Data
A catalogue entry for this book is available from the British Library.

ISBN 1-84541-032-7 / EAN 978-184541-032-2 (hbk)
ISBN 1-84541-031-9 / EAN 978-184541-031-5 (pbk)
ISBN 1-84541-033-5 / EAN 978-184541-033-9 (electronic)

Channel View Publications
An imprint of Multilingual Matters Ltd

UK: Frankfurt Lodge, Clevedon Hall, Victoria Road, Clevedon BS21 HHJ.
USA: 2250 Military Road, Tonawanda, NY 14150, USA.
Canada: 5201 Dufferin Street, North York, Ontario, Canada M3H 5T8.

Typeset by Saxon Graphics Ltd.
Printed and bound in Great Britain by Marston Book Services Limited, Didcot

Contents

The Contributors vii

Introduction
John K. Walton 1

1 Empires of Travel: British Guide Books and Cultural Imperialism in the 19th and 20th Centuries
John M. MacKenzie 19

2 'How and Where To Go': The Role of Travel Journalism in Britain and the Evolution of Foreign Tourism, 1840–1914
Jill Steward 39

3 Selling Air: Marketing the Intangible at British Resorts
John Beckerson and John K. Walton 55

4 Tourism in Augustan Society (44 BC–AD 69)
Loykie Lomine 71

5 A Century of Tourism in Northern Spain: The Development of High-quality Provision between 1815 and 1914
Carlos Larrinaga 88

6 Japanese Tea Party: Representations of Victorian Paradise and Playground in *The Geisha* (1896)
Yorimitsu Hashimoto 104

7 Radical Nationalism in an International Context: Strength through Joy and the Paradoxes of Nazi Tourism
Shelley Baranowski 125

8 'Travel in Merry Germany': Tourism in the Third Reich
Kristin Semmens 144

9 Coffee, Klimt and Climbing: Constructing an Austrian National Identity in Tourist Literature 1918–38
Corinna Peniston-Bird 162

10 Paradise Lost and Found: Tourists and Expatriates in El Terreno, Palma de Mallorca, from the 1920s to the 1950s
John K. Walton 179

11 '50 Places Rolled into 1': The Development of Domestic Tourism at Pleasure Grounds in Inter-war England
Helen Pussard 195

12 Public Beaches and Private Beach Huts: A Case Study of Inter-war Clacton and Frinton, Essex
Laura Chase 211

13 'The Most Magical Corner of England': Tourism, Preservation and the Development of the Lake District, 1919–39
Clifford O'Neill 228

The Contributors

Shelly Baranowski is Professor of History at the University of Akron, Ohio, and has published extensively on religion, rural identities and tourism in Weimar and Nazi Germany. Her most recent book is *Strength through Joy: Consumerism and Mass Tourism in the Third Reich* (Cambridge University Press, 2004).

John Beckerson has a PhD in the history of British tourism policy from the University of East Anglia and contributed to the new history of the Isle of Man (Liverpool Univeristy Press, ed. John Belchem). He is a curator at the Museum of St Albans.

Laura Chase completed her PhD on seaside environments and urban policy in inter-war Essex at the University of Essex, and now works for Essex County Council.

Yorimitsu Hashimoto teaches at Yokohama National University and is completing a PhD at Lancaster University. He has published on the idea of the 'yellow peril' in Britain at the turn of the 19th and 20th century.

Carlos Larrinaga teaches at the Universidad del País Vasco, based in San Sebastián. He has published extensively on various aspects of the economic history of the Basque Country in the 19th and 20th century.

Loykie Lomie is Senior Lecturer in Business Management at King Alfred's College, Winchester, and has a PhD in Sociology from the University of Essex.

John M. Mackenzie was for many years Professer of Imperial History at Lancaster University. He is the author of many books on themes involving imperialism, popular culture and environmental history, and edits the Manchester University Press series on Imperialism and Popular Culture. He is now attached to the University of St Andrews and is co-ordinating editor of the journal *Environment and History*.

Clifford O'Neill teaches History in the Faculty of Education, St Martin's College, Lancaster. He publishes on the 20th-century Lake District and on the teaching of history in schools.

Corinna Peniston-Bird is Lecturer in History at Lancaster University. She has published on inter-war Austria and on the Second World War, the Blitz, gender and the Home Guard in Britain.

Helen Pussard is Senior Lecturer in Sport and Exercise Science at Roehampton University, and is co-editor of *Leisure, Space and Visual Culture* (Eastbourne: Leisure Studies Association, 2004).

Kristin Semmens is Lecturer and Post-Doctoral Research Fellow in History at the University of Victoria, Canada. She has recently published *Seeing Hitler's Germany: Tourism in the Third Reich* (Palgrave Macmillan, 2005).

Jill Steward is Senior Lecturer in History of Art in the Division of Art, Design and Film, University of Northumbria, Newcastle-upon-Tyne. She has published extensively on tourism and gender in the Hapsburg Empire and on travel writing.

John K. Walton is Professor of Social History at the University of Central Lancashire, Preston, and founding president of the International Commission for the History of Travel and Tourism. He has published extensively on the social and cultural history of tourism, resorts, regions and identities, especially in Britain and Spain.

Introduction

JOHN K. WALTON

This collection of essays is intended as a response to, and a stimulus for, the growing visibility of the history of tourism as an essential component both of historical understanding and of the development of a grounded, humanistic dimension to the increasingly interdisciplinary ventures that come under the label of tourism studies (Baranowski & Furlough, 2001; Berghoff *et al.*, 2002; *Historia Contemporánea*, 2002; Tissot, 2003). It is clear that the history of tourism is (at last) developing as an exciting and dynamic field, and that (fittingly) it is advancing on a broad international front, as indicated by the formal constitution in 2002 of the International Commission for the History of Travel and Tourism as an accredited section of the International Commission for the Historical Sciences; by the emergence of a dedicated tourism history journal, published in Naples (*Storia del Turismo*); and by the increased interest in travel and tourism now being taken by the long-established *Journal of Transport History*. The importance of the contribution of history to the understanding of tourism as an outstandingly significant current phenomenon, the world's largest and most dynamic industry, a leading sector both in continuing globalisation and the generation of cultural resistance to its implications, with the capacity to create enormous environmental footprints and to transform cultures in ways that are hard to predict, is now beginning to gain recognition within tourism studies, which has been slow to accept that it needs to learn from historical studies, and within history, whose innate conservatism as a discipline has tended to relegate it to the margins of the allegedly inconsequential. This latter is an increasingly bizarre standpoint but professional inertia has made it disproportionately difficult to dispel. Where the agenda of historical studies is not dominated by high politics and international diplomacy, it still offers more legitimacy to the study of the coal, steel or cotton industries, or the examination of seemingly quantifiable aspects of living standards (wages, prices, demography and height), than to service industries (transport and banking apart) whose inescapable current importance should be drawing more attention to their neglected significance in the past (but see, for example, Hill, 2002).

Mutual recognition has probably been hindered by contrasting writing styles, as tourism studies (as opposed to cultural studies of tourism) has tended towards a social science paradigm with very formal reviews of the literature and overt statements of aims, objectives and methodology, while historians tend to write in a more fluid and literary style and (in this field at least, and especially since the growth of influences from cultural studies on the discipline) to use evidence in more allusive, indirect and cross-referential ways. Any such contrasts in approach should be turned to advantage, not least to enrich the student experience by inviting the critical comparison of approaches, rather than becoming an excuse for perpetual estrangement. Students also need to adjust for the multiplicity of mansions that make up the house that bears the tourism studies label, whose tenants include representatives of a very broad array of conventional academic disciplines, from anthropology to applied economics and from literature to social psychology, and whose interdisciplinary nature invites cross-fertilisation across the imagined boundaries between any or all of them.

As courses begin to proliferate, using tourism history to contribute to a broader picture as well as taking it as the central theme, the time is ripe for the production of accessible collections of scholarly essays on tourism history, which can also be used as readers on (especially) comparative courses. This book is intended as a contribution towards meeting that emergent need. It offers international coverage, with case studies drawn from Austria, Germany, Spain, Japan and the Roman Empire as well as the United Kingdom and the British Empire. It also offers, appropriately, an interdisciplinary approach to the study of tourisms past, with borrowings drawn especially from cultural studies, literature, sociology and cultural geography. Among the concepts that help to define approaches, structure arguments and generate sceptical commentary in the chapters that follow are several familiar but still stimulating staples of tourism studies, themselves originating from several external sources as well as from within the discourses of contributions to tourism studies itself, including the tourist gaze, staged authenticity, the construction of identities across a broad front (national, cultural, class, gender etc.), liminality, orientalism, post-colonial studies and the resort product cycle (Baranowski & Furlough, 2001; Blunt, 1994; MacCannell, 1989; MacKenzie, 1995; Sheller, 2003; Shields, 1991; Urbain, 1991; Urry, 1990, 1995). Just as tourism studies, as a set of programmes drawn together under an academic subject label which may sometimes owe more to course marketing than to internal coherence (although something similar might be said of geography or even history), is escaping from an early dependence on basic economic concepts and an obsession with the mechanical analysis of questionnaires and with similar attempts to convert the intangible into the apparently quantifiable, so historians working on tourism are striving to endow their findings with meanings wider than can be derived from studying the past for its own sake, to put them in wider thematic contexts and to make appropriate borrowings from contingent disciplines in pursuit of broader and deeper understanding. This increasing openness, from both points of departure, should help to bring the disciplines together.

It is particularly important that tourism studies should begin to pay serious attention to the relevance of historical research and writing to its concerns. Despite the growing interest in issues of heritage, authenticity and historical representation in the provision of tourist experiences and the analysis of consumer expectations and responses to them, which entails assessment of the ways in which tourism uses 'history' and, occasionally, the ways in which 'history' might use (or even be regarded as) tourism, the attention paid to the serious examination of the past in much tourism studies literature retains a tendency towards the derivative and perfunctory, especially in the introductory texts that so often set the tone for the student experience. It would almost be better not to bother to mention tourism's past than to provide the tired, limp parade of inaccurate clichés that constitutes the token obeisance to history in some such texts on tourism, with the material often passed on almost unchanged from one text to another without being contaminated by the slightest exposure to any developments in historical writing on the subject. It is as if the authors think that history, as the past, is unchanging and graven on stone tablets, and historians have the simple task of passing on received wisdom. Life would be much easier, and less interesting, if that were so. It is perhaps worth repeating here the commonplaces that each succeeding generation rewrites history in response to the dominant issues and changing agenda of the time; that historical sources are not a static, unchanging 'given' but can be pursued and created in negotiation with others (most obviously through oral history); that the processes of archiving and archival retrieval involve choices and priorities about what to preserve and how to order and communicate it that reflect power structures and themselves have a history; that historical interpretation is ultimately fluid, contested and always open to challenge (especially since the rise of post-modernism); and that (especially in an emergent field like the history of tourism) new studies of particular aspects, angles, cultures, places and institutions are always changing the picture, not least by adding new dimensions and perspectives (Evans, 1997, and debates in the journal *Rethinking History*). Recent historical initiatives have, indeed, drawn attention to the important linkages between tourism and the most traditional of historical concerns, the world of international diplomacy, pointing up the need to pay heed to the 'consumer diplomacy' of tourism in making unofficial contacts between nations and cultures and to the efforts of official diplomacy to influence this process, especially in the years after the Second World War (Buades, 2004; Endy, 2004; Pells, 1997; Tissot, 2003). Less unexpected, but still very important, is the developing relationship between ideas about tourism and discourses of national and regional identity which has become such an important theme at the meeting point between political and cultural history in recent years (Matless, 1998; Moreno, 2004; Russell, 2004; Shaffer, 2001). But such initiatives, and the broader history of tourism project, have yet to gain full admission to the core of tourism studies, too many of whose introductory texts tend to provide little more than a paragraph on the Grand Tour, another on Thomas Cook and a third on the post-war rise of 'mass tourism', interpreted in terms of the Mediterranean package holiday and its successors, with no critical analysis of terms, processes or debates and no attention to the growing literature on the history of tourism in the context of consumption, consumerism and globalisation.

As regards these preoccupations, it should be emphasised that there is now an extensive (but too often ignored) historiography of the Grand Tour and related themes (Black, 1992; Chard, 1999; Ousby, 1991), while the iconic role assigned to Thomas Cook (not least through the unique richness of the firm's archive) is coming under challenge as myths of origin and primacy are deconstructed and the obscured importance of competitors (not least American Express) is given due weight (Brendon, 1991; Green, 2004; Grossman, 1987; Withey, 1997). Meanwhile, the loose use of the term 'mass tourism', which is sometimes applied with an apparent lack of discrimination to any or all several categories, especially the first 'Cook's tourists' of the mid-19th century, the extension of excursion activity and holiday-making among sectors of the lower middle and working classes in Britain in the late 19th century and the new developments of the inter-war years in popular tourism, as well as the more usual formula that is based on the rise of the 'package holiday' after the Second World War, cries out for deconstruction, especially in the light of the value-laden and question-begging assumptions about uniformity of culture, manipulation of experience and sheep-like passivity of consumers that are usually associated with the phrase. But these assumptions, too, are beginning to be questioned (Wright, 2002). There are significant exceptions to the general neglect of historical work within tourism studies, beginning with the work of John Towner on the Grand Tour and on the historical geography of tourism more generally in the 1990s, which probably constituted the first sustained effort to build bridges between the disciplines, and has been followed by the inclusion of historical chapters in other works dealing primarily with contemporary tourism (Barke *et al.*, 1996; Hind & Mitchell, 2004; Shaw & Williams, 1997; Towner, 1996). These initiatives run parallel with the first efforts, during the mid-1990s, by historians to draw attention to the importance of tourism history (Engerman, 1994; Walton, 1997). This agenda has been extended recently by the efforts of Conrad Lashley (especially) to persuade academics in the closely related subject area of hospitality to take seriously the insights on offer from the humanities in general and historical studies in particular (Lashley & Morrison, 2000; Walton, 2003b). But there is much to be done.

Those readers of this book who come from a tourism studies orientation will probably already be broadly sympathetic to these arguments, although the evangelical tone sometimes adopted here is coloured by years of frustration at the unwillingness of some of their colleagues to see the relevance of history's contribution, not least in providing rich comparative case-studies for their students to work on. This book presents a themed collection of chapters dealing with important aspects of the history of tourism in its own right, as something worth understanding for its own sake in terms of process and impact (not least on tourist destinations, which are eminently worthy of comparative study in their own right) (Aron, 1999; Battilani, 2001; Gottdiener *et al.*, 1999; Johnson, 2002; Levenstein, 1998; Meller, 2001; Pastoriza, 2002; Rauch, 1996; Schwartz, 1997; Walton, 2000a) which also adds depth and comparative grasp to our understanding of the present and its potentialities and discontents, without falling into the trap of present-mindedness or forgetting the need to try to understand past societies on their own terms. This concern to recover understandings of the past as such distinguishes the history of tourism from the extensive literature on the relationships between history, 'heritage' and museum studies, with their interesting debates on authenticity and how to stage it, on the nature and plausibility of professional historians' claims to tell truer and more satisfying stories than other interpreters and users of the past, and on the relationships between historical remains, historical re-creations, the educational process, the provision of entertainment and the market (Berghoff *et al.*, 2002; Cross & Walton, 2005; Dicks, 2003; Herbert, 1995; Hewison, 1987; Mandler, 1997; Samuel, 1995, 1998).

This is a lively and important field, and the one in which history and tourism studies have made closest contact, often mediated through other disciplines. But it is our argument that the history of tourism is essential in its own right. At a basic level, it is important to enrich our understanding by making comparisons over time as well as between places and contemporary cultures: after all, the past is indeed a foreign country. But it is also of the utmost importance to understand processes in all their complexity. A problem in tourism studies has been a prevailing present-mindedness and superficiality, refusing deep, grounded or sustained historical analysis even when dealing with essentially historical processes like the resort product cycle, which is about change over time but usually treated schematically and without reference to how the product has developed, under what circumstances, constraints and cultural conditions and how that might affect its present prospects. Recent work within this paradigm has shown increasing awareness of these issues without developing the historical depth of field that is necessary to an understanding of the complexity of historical processes over periods longer than a generation or so (Agarwal, 2002; Priestley & Mundet, 1998). By the same token, for example, the immensely fruitful concept of the 'tourist gaze' (fruitful not least in terms of the controversy it is now engendering) would benefit enormously from a much more serious and sustained understanding across time than it has so far received (Urry, 1990, 1995); but its own progenitor, John Urry, is much more at home with the development of stimulating transferable ideas on a broad compass than with locating the timing, nature and springs of action governing their working out in particular cultures and settings (Urry, 1988, 1997). The title of the recently established *Journal of Tourism and Cultural Change* implies a commitment to the understanding of historical processes, however contemporary, as change necessarily occurs over time; but here again a commitment to critical engagement with historical processes operating over more than a generation will itself take time to work through, not least in the nature of the papers that are offered. Recent indications that established tourism studies journals are opening their doors more readily to contributions from historians provide welcome hints of change (Mazierska, 2002; Worthington, 2003). Historians, in turn, have been slow to supply what is needed, in this and other contexts.

Part of the problem here has been a prevailing concern among historians with what most tourism studies practitioners might regard as a more distant past, whose relevance to understanding the background to current concerns decays with distance from them. Until the last few years, there has been a great deal more historical research on the 18th and 19th centuries than on the 20th, an imbalance that is now being rectified as historians have woken up, first (and, over the last two decades, dramatically) to the richness of the 20th century, and then, more recently and especially since the fall of the Soviet Union and its allies, to the opportunity to get a purchase on the decades following the Second World War. A particular feature of the present book is its predominant focus on conflicts and developments in the 20th century and especially since the First World War, which have been given much less emphasis than the 18th century and the Victorian and Edwardian years in most previous publications, although new angles on 19th-century tourisms are also opened out and a new synthesis of tourist activities in classical antiquity is presented, providing a salutary reminder of the apparent 'modernity' of many of the prevailing tourist practices of the Roman Empire in its heyday.

The recurrent theme that dominates the book is the reciprocal relationship between tourism and the construction of imagined collective identities, both in terms of pulling together shared characteristics that might mark out a serviceable collective cultural or political identity for the representation and advancement of common interests, and of identifying 'other' collectivities that may be imagined and represented as exotic, challenging, different, dangerous and (in crucial senses) inferior, thereby rendering them attractive for tourism purposes (providing that perceptions of danger and less compelling fears of the 'other' do not override the attractions of interest and potential profit), and reinforcing and validating the values and practices ascribed to one's own imagined community. Analyses of the politics and cultural expression of such identities constitute a very important strand in current historical discourse, perhaps especially in the British context in response to debates on devolution and the 'nations without a state' in the British Isles but also in relation to the decline of the British Empire and the changing relationships between its constituent parts and the 'mother country', especially regarding the consequences of migration flows and settlement both out of and into the 'mother country' (Caunce *et al.*, 2004; Hansen, 1996; Kirk, 2000; MacKenzie, 1995; Matless, 1998; Morley & Robins, 2001; Royle, 1998; Shaffer, 2001; Sheller, 2003; Spode, 2004; Walton, 2000c). Tourism both participates in the construction and consolidation of such identities, and affects the nature of what is constructed from the perspective both of hosts and guests, compromising the pristine 'innocence' of established scenes, artifacts and practices by bringing them into the market place, promoting hybridization between the 'global' (or a regional sub-set of that category) and the 'local', and placing authenticity on a pedestal which is also a stage, changing its nature from within. Such developments are productive of conflict in several dimensions. They arise within the host community, as members decide how to react to tourist presences, generating processes of conflict and negotiation which become more complex as the resort product cycle moves on, from reactions to early incursions, threats and opportunities to the involvement of residential commuter and retirement interests who have themselves been tourists in the past, as indeed will many practitioners in the hospitality and entertainment industries. As tourist practices and destinations change over time, usually in the direction of democratisation of access and provision, conflicts develop within the tourist industries (also involving the residential interests) as to which markets to promote, how to allocate potentially conflicting visitor cultures to different districts or to different times of year, week or day and how to manage those valued spaces that all or most of the visitors want to share. These, in turn, are, responses, in part, to antagonisms between different groups within the visiting public, whether based on nationality, region, class, age, ethnicity, sexual orientation or other factors that may generate damaging conflict in an environment where commercial success is based on the provision of relaxed enjoyment and security of property and the person, and where the nature and intrusiveness of the maintenance of order and agreed standards of public behaviour also becomes an issue. Tourism therefore both promotes and reinforces collective identities, and generates and exacerbates conflict, while at the same time playing its own part in the construction and content of those identities. It provides an excellent laboratory for the examination of a spectrum of social tensions on a very public stage, where interests, hopes and fears are articulated with unusual openness. And these processes can be studied at all levels, from the local as microcosm to the global as macrocosm. This book brings together 13 such studies, from the fine-grained local (Chase on the beach-huts of Frinton and Pussard on the detailed spatial and temporal organization of Belle Vue and the Crystal Palace) to the imperial and effectively the global (Lomine on the Roman Empire, MacKenzie on guide-books as representations of the British Empire). This is, perhaps, the key unifying theme of what follows (Baranowski & Furlough, 2001; Furlough, 1998; Gunn & Morris, 2001; Matless, 1998; Parry, 2002; Pastoriza, 2002; Shields, 1991).

We begin with three chapters on the representation of tourist journeys and destinations for advertising and advisory purposes, looking at how the 'gaze' of the intending tourist was directed and at the ways in which different kinds of journey and destination might be presented to a variety of potential markets. John MacKenzie's chapter takes a global perspective, examining guide-books to the British Empire, comparing output and priorities over time and between areas and taking in a variety of projected travel experiences alongside those of the tourist *per se*, who is particularly difficult to detach from 'the traveller' in this context. This builds on and feeds into lively current debates among cultural and political historians on the reciprocal relationships between 'metropole' and Empire, and on orientalism, to which MacKenzie himself has been a distinguished contributor (MacKenzie, 1995; Said, 1978). Jill Steward paints on a similarly broad canvas in looking at the development of the 'travel press' over the transitional half-century before the First World War, making a novel contribution to an important aspect of media history as well as that of tourism, while John Beckerson and John Walton occupy related territory by examining the literature on a neglected aspect of the representation and promotion of health-based tourism in Britain, the ascription of therapeutic properties to the air of places that were promoted as health resorts, whether mainly on the strength of such qualities (in a few cases) or as part of wider discourses about therapeutic environments (Ward, 1998).

The following six chapters move on from the issues introduced in the first three, to focus on the relationships between tourism promotion, tourist practices and the construction and representation of national and imperial identities, as foreshadowed especially by MacKenzie's chapter (see also Poutet, 1995). Lomine's chapter reminds us (not for the first time but pulling together a novel array of sources with verve and humour, and relating his material to concepts used in tourism studies) that the Roman Empire of the Augustan period anticipated many developments in tourism that it is too easy to label as simply 'modern'; and that these were bound up with a shared sense of what it was to be a citizen of the Roman Empire. Larrinaga examines the development of a sophisticated and distinctive tourist industry over the century before the First World War in that 'nation without a state', the Basque Country in northern Spain, drawing on a neglected model advanced for south-western France by Michel Chadefaud to provide the first systematic account in English of this important phenomenon, which effectively pioneered the development of a recognisable modern tourist industry in Spain (Chadefaud, 1987). Hashimoto's attractive chapter opens out themes involving orientalism, imperial stereotypes, 'race', gender and the tourist gaze, analysing the representations of Japan from a tourism perspective that emerged in a popular and very successful musical comedy on the London stage in the 1890s, and offering transferable perspectives of relevance to debates on later periods and other parts of the world. There then follows a cluster of three strongly interrelated chapters, which examine tourism and national identities in what became the Third Reich. Baranowski and Semmens take complementary approaches to the role of tourism in Nazi Germany, the former looking at the limitations to and contradictions involved in the state's promotion of popular tourism for propaganda purposes through the 'Strength through Joy' movement, while the latter examines the role of the state in tourism promotion and its influences on the representations generated by tourist offices and guide-books. Peniston-Bird provides further insights into relationships between tourism and the construction and representation of national identity, complementing Baranowski and Semmens in another way by examining developments in post-imperial Austria as it struggled to articulate a marketable tourist identity over the generation before it was absorbed into Hitler's Germany in 1938.

The last four chapters pursue questions of space, identity and conflict in smaller but highly evocative and emblematic settings, with a more direct focus on the internal dynamics of tourist destinations. We begin with Walton's analysis of the development of Mallorca as a 'paradise island' for tourists and expatriates during the second quarter of the 20th century, exploring the contradictions and changes entailed in the contested paradigm of 'paradise' and the imagery associated with it, with special reference to changing representations of the contested space of El Terreno, to the west of Palma de Mallorca, as economic and cultural changes shifted it from being associated with nature, tranquillity and a version of the simple life towards an alternative version of 'paradise' founded on hedonism and self-indulgence. Pussard's chapter returns us to Britain, looking comparatively at complex popular pleasure destinations with multiple attractions, markets and meanings, and emphasising the kaleidoscopic and changing variety of messages and experiences to be encountered at the commercially-run Belle Vue entertainment centre at Manchester as compared with the less commercial and more overtly educative 'rational recreation' ethos of the Crystal Palace complex at Sydenham in the south-west London suburbs. An important theme of both chapters is the deconstruction of simplistic notions of 'mass tourism'. As discussed earlier, this is a term whose uncritical, contradictory and value-laden use, emerging from and extending the snobberies of the 'traveller/tourist' distinction (Buzard, 1993), continues to bedevil much of the literature; and Pussard's work also raises questions about the relationships between theme parks, exhibitions and museums, between the thrilling, the hedonistic, the recreational and the educational in commercial tourist destinations, which resonate with several current debates (Cross & Walton, 2005). Finally, the chapters by O'Neill and Chase focus on the contested meanings given to valued spaces in English tourist settings in the inter-war years. At this point, the English Lake District, a literary landscape where tensions between seekers after contemplative quiet and visitors who wanted to use the challenging environment as a playground had already been emerging strongly in the late 19th century (with earlier antecedents), was experiencing new pressures from the internal combustion engine (middle-class motorists, motorboat users and 'trippers' in 'charabancs') (Hind & Mitchell, 2004), while the Essex coast resorts, where a desirable environment was constructed in terms of sea-bathing and 'social tone', tried to cope with conflicts over new fashions in bathing and beachwear, which were reflected in the allocation and use of private and public space on beaches and foreshores in contrasting ways at exclusive Frinton and plebeian Clacton (see also Booth, 2001; Daley, 2003; Huntsman, 2001).

A further important theme of this book concerns the need to continue to develop the use of methodologies and sources involving media and visual representations. The critical and constructive use of guide-books, travel writing, architecture, planning documents and the content and reported nature of stage performances, alongside more conventional historical archives and newspapers, as deployed in the present book, needs to be extended to embrace the systematic use of photographic, film, television and other media sources, to say nothing of oral history (Mazierska, 2002; Urry, 1995; Walton, 2004b; Wright, 2002). Representations of landscape in relation to tourism and the construction and reconstruction of identity are crucial here (Matless, 1998). Such approaches take the historian on to territory colonised hitherto mainly by exponents of cultural, literary, visual and media studies, but with a growing cultural history presence. A further set of issues that requires attention involves analysis of the origins of the immense environmental footprints that tourist industries leave across the globe, requiring tourism historians to engage more directly than hitherto with developments in environmental history (O'Neill, 2001). Such engagement will provide new dimensions to the well-established association between histories of tourism, travel and means of transport (Lyth, 2003).

This book thus contributes in distinctive ways to an expanding historical literature, which is not the exclusive 'property' of historians (nor is it written exclusively by them), and of which many researchers in tourism studies need to become more aware. The only 'text-book' covering the field is John Towner's *An Historical Geography of Recreation and Tourism in the Western World* (1996), a comprehensive and painstaking review of the literature (allied to the author's own research on the Grand Tour and 19th-century Spain), which lacked a distinctive voice of its own and never got into paperback. The pick of a varied crop of recent surveys is Orvar Löfgren, *On Holiday: A History of Vacationing* (1999), whose anthropological perspective and central focus on comparisons between Sweden and the USA make for a distinctive viewpoint that complements the present volume (Löfgren, 1999; see also Goldstone, 2001; Turner & Ash, 1975). The best work in literary and cultural studies concentrates more on the 18th and 19th centuries than the 20th, as in the work of James Buzard and Chloe Chard, although Paul Fussell's problematic work has also been influential for a later period (Buzard, 1993; Chard, 1999; Fussell, 1982). John Pemble's classic piece of cultural history *The Mediterranean Passion* also has a predominantly 19th-century focus, while Lynne Withey's *From Grand Tours to Cook's Tours* is a well-written, well-documented story with limited bibliographical, critical or conceptual range (Pemble, 1987; Withey, 1997). The seductive title of Fred Inglis's *The Delicious History of the Holiday* (Inglis, 2000), which was reviewed with enthusiasm in some circles within tourism studies, is particularly misleading. This book has some interesting transferable ideas but it is not a history, as the author himself acknowledges; and such speculative claims as the one that Thomas Cook made a significant contribution to the growth of Blackpool, for which no evidence is offered because there is none (Walton, 1998), take post-modern relativism further than most of us would want to go. The book illustrates the limited extent of current exchanges between historians and many tourism studies practitioners by ignoring, for example, the extensive literature on the urban, economic, political and cultural history of resort destinations in Britain, which is now developing counterparts elsewhere in the world.

Overlapping with these developments, a growing literature on the cultural history of beach tourism should be emphasised. It is of variable quality but takes much of its inspiration from Alain Corbin's stimulating treatment of the cultural revolution that gave rise to the possibility of the sea becoming a favoured tourist destination, *The Lure of the Sea*, a book whose innovative and almost incantatory power transcends the francophone and francocentric limitations of its geographical coverage (Corbin, 1994; and see also Urbain, 1994). Other general histories of the beach, more extensive in their temporal and geographical coverage if less sharply focused on particular theoretical interpretations, also have insights to offer (Lencek & Bosker, 1998); and explorations of national and other identities in relation to the beach and related phenomena in the anglophone southern hemisphere have recently extended the agenda (Booth, 2001; Daley, 2003; Fiske, 1989: chap. 3; Huntsman, 2001). Similar developments with regard to mountains and the outdoors, also associated with both the Enlightenment and the Romantic movement, are also developing a historiography (Andrews, 1989; Bernard, 1978; Hansen, 1995, 1999; Ring, 2000;

Taylor, 1997; Tissot, 2000). And historical studies relating tourism to environmental issues are beginning to appear, opening out profitable links between perceptions of preferred environments, development, policy, conflict and resolution, and building bridges to the new historical studies of tourism and morality (gambling, alcohol, drugs and sex as well as environmental issues) that are now emerging (Anderson & Tabb, 2002; Hassan, 2000; Lencek & Bosker, 1998). Alongside the single-issue monographs and articles, the field is being enriched by collections of essays, often arising from symposia like the recent ones at Tübingen and Sion (Switzerland), the latter of which led into the first session on the history of tourism to be held at the International Economic History Association conference, at Buenos Aires in 2002 (Berghoff *et al.*, 2002; Tissot, 2003). This was preceded by the pioneer international conference on tourism history, at the University of Central Lancashire in 2001, which was followed two years later at the same venue by the first such conference to take place under the auspices of the recently-founded International Commission. Meanwhile, the next step is the session on Tourism and Empires at the International Commission for the Historical Sciences conference at Sydney in 2005, which will bring tourism historians from the southern hemisphere (especially Australia and New Zealand, where highly interesting developments are becoming visible) into firmer and more productive contact with those in northern Europe and North America, just as the Buenos Aires conference brought together historians from northern Europe and Latin America, especially the cluster of historians at Montevideo and Mar del Plata who are studying the seaside resorts of the River Plate estuary (Da Cunha, 2003; Pastoriza, 2002). Interested parties in tourism studies and contributory disciplines need to be aware of this extensive array of developments and to welcome their contribution to an expanded understanding of tourism through time as well as across spaces and cultures.

As part of the developing process of cultural exchange within academe, the history of tourism needs to continue to articulate its relationships with more established historical concerns, providing new contexts for them and new angles of vision while at the same time facilitating richer and deeper understandings of the phenomena of tourism in themselves. The history of tourism needs to be incorporated into a holistic vision of cultural and social, economic and political changes (and continuities) over time, rather than developing as just another sub-discipline defending its frontiers against interlopers and competing with them for attention and resources. This is an interdisciplinary enterprise or it is nothing. The themes explored in this book demonstrate the capacity for tourism history to link up with and illuminate (for example) contested cultural histories of local, national and imperial identity; media representations of the experience of journeys, destinations and contested spaces; debates over the content and consequences of leisure and related ideas about respectability and transgression; changing attitudes to the body and sexuality and to physical recreation and display; the important and neglected historical dimensions to ideas about orientalism, globalisation and McDonaldisation; and the relationships between tourism, politics (local, national and international) and cultural diplomacy that are now gaining ground in the historical literature. These are all, of course, interrelated issues; and the history of tourism also leads directly into considerations of travel, trade, transport, cultural dissemination and interaction; class conflict, emulation and negotiation (including the relationships between tourism and labour history, which have hardly been pursued at all) (Schumacher, 2003; Walton & Smith, 1994); and, most obviously, the history of leisure, consumption and consumerism, although it has been surprisingly omitted from an otherwise excellent recent monograph on this theme covering 20th-century Britain (Hill, 2002; Hilton, 2003). Tourists also move on into other states of existence, of course: they may stay or return as tourist industry workers, owners of businesses, expatriates or retirement migrants, and all these aspects of the extension and adaptation of tourism are of interest in their own right, not least in terms of their impact on host communities (King *et al.*, 2000; O'Reilly, 2000). In pursuing these and related themes, it will be important not to become bogged down in issues of definition and the division of categories (traveller / tourist / expatriate / retirement migrant) while at the same time retaining awareness of the importance of such distinctions in the development of arguments.

All this underlines the enduring need for histories of tourism to recognise the necessity, in this field even more than in many others, for comparative cross-cultural research that reaches across national and cultural boundaries as well as disciplinary ones, just as tourism itself is supposed to do. Such efforts have been, and are being, made but their quality and academic depth has been variable and the journalistic has sometimes prevailed over the scholarly in their presentation and content. To engage with such contested concepts and questions as globalisation and McDonaldisation, rigorous history with a holistic approach and an awareness of the problems of systematic cross-cultural comparison needs to be generated. A global phenomenon needs global histories and it is hoped that collections of case studies such as those on offer in the present book will contribute to the making of such grounded syntheses in the future. Here, alongside utility for teaching and in the advancement of new themes, lies another justification for this book (Engerman, 1994; Goldstone, 2001; Lofgren, 1999; Turner & Ash, 1975; Walton, 2000b, 2003a, 2004a).

References

Agarwal, S. (2002) Restructuring seaside tourism: The resort cycle. *Annals of Tourism Research* 29, 25–55.

Andrews, M. (1989) *The Search for the Picturesque*. Stanford, CA: Stanford University Press.

Anderson, S.C. and Tabb, B.H. (eds) (2002) *Water, Leisure and Culture*. Oxford: Berg.

Aron, C. (1999) *Working at Play: A History of Vacations in the United States*. New York: Oxford University Press.

Baranowski, S. and Furlough, E. (eds) (2001) *Being Elsewhere: Tourism, Consumer Culture and Identity in Modern Europe and North America*. Ann Arbor: University of Michigan Press.

Barke, M., Towner, J. and Newton, M.T. (eds) (1996) *Tourism in Spain: Critical Issues*. Wallingford: CAB International.

Battilani, P. (2001) *Vacanze di Pochi, Vacanze di Tutti*. Bologna.

Berghoff, H., Korte, B., Schneider, R. and Harvie, C. (eds) (2002) *The Making of Modern Tourism: the Cultural History of the British Experience*. London: Palgrave.

Bernard, P. (1978) *The Rush to the Alps: the Evolution of Vacationing in Switzerland*. New York: Columbia University Press.

Black, J. (1992) *The British and the Grand Tour*. London: Alan Sutton.

Blunt, A. (1994) *Travel, Gender and Imperialism*. London: Guilford.

Booth, D. (2001) *Australian Beach Cultures: The History of Sun, Sand and Surf*. London: Frank Cass.

Brendon, P. (1991) *Thomas Cook*. London: Secker and Warburg.

Buades, J. (2004) *On Brilla el Sol: Turisme a Balears abans del Boom*. Eivissa: Res Publica Edicions.

Buzard, J. (1993) *The Beaten Track: European Tourism, Literature and the Ways to Culture*. Oxford: Clarendon Press.

Chadefaud, M. (1987) *Aux Origines du Tourisme dans les Pays de l'Adour*. Pau: Université de Pau.

Caunce, S., Mazierska, E., Sydney-Smith, S. and Walton, J.K. (eds) (2004) *Relocating Britishness*. Manchester: Manchester University Press.

Chard, C. (1999) *Pleasure and Guilt on the Grand Tour*. Manchester: Manchester University Press.

Corbin, A. (1994) *The Lure of the Sea*. London: Verso.

Cross, G. and Walton, J.K. (2005) *The Playful Crowd*. New York: Columbia University Press.

Da Cunha, N. (2003) La construction touristique de la côte uruguayenne. In L. Tissot (ed.) *Development of a Tourist Industry in the Nineteenth and Twentieth Centuries* (pp. 245–59). Neuchatel: Editions Alphil.

Daley, C. (2003) *Leisure and Pleasure: Reshaping the New Zealand Body 1900–1960*. Auckland, NZ: Auckland University Press.

Dicks, B. (2003) *Culture on Display: the Production of Contemporary Visitability*. Maidenhead: Open University Press.

Endy, C. (2004) *Cold War Holidays: American Tourism in France*. Raleigh: University of North Carolina Press.

Engerman, D. (1994) A research agenda for the history of tourism: Towards an international social history. *American Studies International* 32, 3–31.

Evans, R. (1997) *In Defence of History*. London: Granta.

Fiske, J. (1989) *Reading the Popular*. London: Routledge.

Furlough, E. (1998) Making mass vacations: Tourism and consumer culture in France, 1930s–1970s. *Comparative Studies in Society and History* 40, 247–86.

Fussell, P. (1982) *Abroad: British Literary Travellers between the Wars*. Oxford: Oxford University Press.

Goldstone, P. (2001) *Making the World Safe for Tourism*. New Haven, CT: Yale University Press.

Gottdiener, M., Collins, C.C. and Dickens, D.R. (1999) *Las Vegas: The Social Production of an All-American City*. Oxford: Blackwell.

Green, M.S. (2004) Thomas Cook and tourism history: A critical analysis. MA dissertation, University of Central Lancashire.

Grossman, P.Z. (1987) *American Express: The Unofficial History of the People who Built the Great Financial Empire*. New York: Crown Publishers.

Gunn, S.A.L. and Morris, R.J. (eds) (2001) *Identities in Space*. Aldershot: Ashgate.

Hansen, P.H. (1995) Albert Smith, the Alpine Club and the invention of mountaineering in mid-Victorian Britain. *Journal of British Studies* 34, 300–24.

Hansen, P.H. (1996) Vertical boundaries, national identities: Victorian mountaineering on the frontiers of Europe and Empire. *Journal of Imperial and Commonwealth History* 24, 48–71.

Hansen, P.H. (1999) Partners: Guides and sherpas in the Alps and the Himalayas, 1850s–1950s. In J. Elsner and J-P. Rubiés (eds) *Voyages and Visions*. London: Reaktion.

Hassan, J. (2000) *The Seaside, Health and the Environment in England and Wales since 1800*. Aldershot: Ashgate.

Herbert, D.T. (ed.) (1995) *Heritage, Tourism and Society*. London: Mansell.

Hewison, R. (1987) *The Heritage Industry*. London: Methuen.

Hill, J. (2002) *Sport, Leisure and Culture in Twentieth-century Britain*. London: Palgrave.

Hilton, M. (2003) *Consumerism in 20th-century Britain*. Cambridge: Cambridge University Press.

Hind, D.W.G. and Mitchell, J.P. (eds) (2004) *Sustainable Tourism in the English Lake District*. Sunderland: Business Education.

Historia Contemporánea (2002) *Turismo y Nueva Sociedad* 25 (2). Universidad del País Vasco.

Huntsman, L. (2001) *Sand in Our Souls: The Beach in Australian History*. Melbourne: Melbourne University Press.

Inglis, F. (2000) *The Delicious History of the Holiday*. London: Routledge.

Johnson, N. (2002) *Boardwalk Empire: The Birth, High Times and Corruption of Atlantic City*. Medford, NJ: Plexus.

King, R., Warnes, T. and Williams, A. (2000) *Sunset Lives*. Oxford: Berg.

Kirk, N. (ed.) (2000) *Northern Identities*. Aldershot: Scolar Press.

Lashley, C. and Morrison, A. (eds) (2000) *In Search of Hospitality*. London: Butterworth Heinemann.

Lencek, L. and Bosker, G. (1998) *The Beach: The History of Paradise on Earth*. London: Secker and Warburg.

Levenstein, H. (1998) *Seductive Journey: American Tourists in France from Jefferson to the Jazz Age*. Chicago: University of Chicago Press.

Löfgren, O. (1999) *On Holiday*. Stanford: Stanford University Press.

Lyth, P. (2003) 'Gimme a ticket on an airplane…': The jet engine and the revolution in leisure travel. In L. Tissot (ed.) *Development of a Tourist Industry* (pp. 111–22). Neuchatel: Editions Alphil.

MacCannell, D. (1989) *The Tourist: A New Theory of the Leisure Class*. New York: Schocken Books.
MacKenzie, J.M. (1995) *Orientalism, History, Theory and the Arts*. Manchester: Manchester University Press.
Mandler, P. (1997) *The Fall and Rise of the Stately Home*. New Haven, CT: Yale University Press.
Matless, D. (1998) *Landscape and Englishness*. London: Reaktion.
Mazierska, E. (2002) Road to authenticity and stability. *Tourist Studies* 2, 223–46.
Meller, H. (2001) *European Cities 1890–1930s*. Chichester: John Wiley and Sons.
Moreno Garrido, A. (2004) Turismo y nación: la definición de la identidad nacional a través de los símbolos turísticos (Espana 1908–1929). Doctoral thesis, Universidad Complutense, Madrid.
Morley, D. and Robins, K. (eds) (2001) *British Cultural Studies: Geography, Nationality and Identity*. Oxford: Oxford University Press.
O'Neill, C. (2001) Visions of Lakeland: Tourism, preservation and the development of the Lake District. PhD thesis, Lancaster University.
Ousby, I. (1990) *The Englishman's England: Travel, Taste and the Rise of Tourism*. Cambridge: Cambridge University Press.
Pastoriza, E. (2002) *Las Puertas al Mar*. Mar del Plata: Biblus.
Pells, R.H. (1997) *Not Like Us: How Europeans have Loved, Hated and Transformed American Culture since World War II*. New York: Basic Books.
Pemble, J. (1987) *The Mediterranean Passion*. Oxford: Clarendon Press.
Poutet, H. (1995) *Images Touristiques de l'Espagne. De la Propagande Politique à la Promotion Touristique*. Paris: L'Harmattan.
Priestley, G. and Mundet, L. (1998) The post-stagnation phase of the resort cycle. *Annals of Tourism Research* 25, 125–48.
Rauch, A. (1996) *Vacances en France de 1830 à Nos Jours*. Paris: Hachette.
Ring, J. (2000) *How the English Made the Alps*. London: John Murray.
Royle, E. (ed.) (1998) *Issues of Regional Identity*. Manchester: Manchester University Press.
Russell, D. (2004) *Looking North: The North in the National Imagination*. Manchester: Manchester University Press.
Said, E. (1978) *Orientalism*. London: Routledge and Kegan Paul.
Samuel, R. (1995, 1998) *Theatres of Memory* (2 Vols). London: Verso.
Schumacher, B. (2003) Popularizing vacationing and trade union politics. The Railway Men's Holiday Home: A Swiss case study 1890–1930. In L. Tissot (ed.), *Development of a Tourist Industry* (pp. 293–305). Neuchatel: Editions Alphil.
Schwartz, R. (1997) *Pleasure Island: Tourism and Temptation in Cuba*. Lincoln: University of Nebraska Press.
Shaffer, M. (2001) *See America First: Tourism and National Identity, 1880–1940*. Washington: Smithsonian Institution Press.
Shaw, G. and Williams, A. (eds) (1997) *The Rise and Fall of British Coastal Resorts: Cultural and Economic Perspectives*. London: Mansell.
Sheller, M. (2003) *Consuming the Caribbean*. London: Routledge.
Shields, R. (1991) *Places on the Margin: Alternative Geographies of Modernity*. London: Routledge.
Spode, H. (2004) Fordism, mass tourism and the Third Reich: The 'Strength through Joy' seaside resort as an index fossil. *Journal of Social History* 39.
Storia del Turismo (2002–) Napoli: FrancoAngeli, for the Istituto per la Storia del Risorgimento Italiano, Comitato di Napoli.

Taylor, H. (1997) *A Claim on the Countryside. A History of the British Outdoor Movement*. Edinburgh: Keele University Press.

Tissot, L. (2000) *Naissance d'une Industrie Touristique: les Anglais et la Suisse au XIX siècle*. Lausanne: Payot Lausanne.

Tissot, L. (ed.) (2003) *Development of a Tourist Industry in the Nineteenth and Twentieth Centuries. International Perspectives*. Neuchatel: Editions Alphil.

Towner, J. (1996) *An Historical Geography of Recreation and Tourism in the Western World, 1540–1940*. Chichester: John Wiley.

Turner, L. and Ash, J. (1975) *The Golden Hordes: International Tourism and the Pleasure Periphery*. London: Constable.

Urbain, J.-D. (1991) *L'Idiot du Voyage*. Paris: Plon.

Urbain, J.-D. (1994) *Sur la Plage: Moeurs et Coutumes Balnéaires*. Paris: Payot.

Urry, J. (1988) Cultural change and contemporary holiday-making. *Theory, Culture and Society* 5, 35–55.

Urry, J. (1990) *The Tourist Gaze*. London: Sage.

Urry, J. (1995) *Consuming Places*. London: Routledge.

Urry, J. (1997) Cultural change and the seaside resort. In G. Shaw and A. Williams (eds) *The Rise and Fall of British Coastal Resorts* (pp. 102–13). London: Mansell.

Walton, J.K. (1997) Taking the history of tourism seriously. *European History Quarterly* 27, 573–81.

Walton, J.K. (1998) *Blackpool*. Edinburgh: Keele Edinburgh University Press.

Walton, J.K. (2000a) *The British Seaside: Holidays and Resorts in the Twentieth Century*. Manchester: Manchester University Press.

Walton, J.K. (2000b) Seaside tourism in the 19th and 20th centuries: Some transatlantic comparisons. In W. Kaufman and H.S. Macpherson (eds) *Transatlantic Studies* (pp. 143–58). Lanham, MD: University Press of America.

Walton, J.K. (2000c) Tradition and tourism: Representing Basque identities in Guipúzcoa and San Sebastián, 1848–1936. In N. Kirk (ed.) *Northern Identities* (pp. 87–108). Aldershot: Scolar Press.

Walton, J.K. (2003a) Tourism, war and politics in elite beach resorts: San Sebastián and Ostend, *c*. 1830–1939. In L. Tissot (ed.) *Development of a Tourist Industry* (pp. 307–21). Neuchatel: Editions Alphil.

Walton, J.K. (2003b) Hospitality and history. *The Hospitality Review* 5, 40–4.

Walton, J.K. (2004a) The transatlantic seaside: Blackpool and Coney Island. In N. Campbell, J. Davies and G. McKay (eds) *Issues in Americanisation and Culture* (pp. 111–25). Edinburgh: Edinburgh University Press.

Walton, J.K. (2004b) The seaside and the holiday crowd. In V. Toulmin, P. Russell and S. Popple (eds) *The Lost World of Mitchell and Kenyon: Edwardian People on Film* (pp. 158–68). London: *bfi* Publishing.

Walton, J.K. and Smith, J. (1994) The rhetoric of community and the business of pleasure: The San Sebastián waiters' strike of 1920. *International Review of Social History* 39, 1–30.

Ward, S.V. (1998) *Selling Places: The Marketing and Promotion of Towns and Cities 1850–2000*. London: Spon.

Withey, L. (1997) *Grand Tours and Cook's Tours*. London: Aurum Press.

Worthington, B. (2003) Change in an Estonian resort: Contrasting development contexts. *Annals of Tourism Research* 30, 369–85.

Wright, S. (2002) Sun, sea, sand and self-expression: Mass tourism as an individual experience. In H. Berghoff, B. Korte, R. Schneider and C. Harvie (eds) *The Making of Modern Tourism* (pp. 181–202). London: Palgrave.

Chapter 1

Empires of Travel: British Guide Books and Cultural Imperialism in the 19th and 20th Centuries[1]

JOHN M. MACKENZIE

When the Castle Line shipping company first published its Guide to South Africa in the 1890s, it declared that it was for the use of 'Tourists, Sportsmen, Invalids and Settlers'. It is an intriguing group of middle-class travellers which reflects the manner in which 19th-century imperialism and its associated shipping lines sought to capture an essentially bourgeois market. Indeed the very existence of the guides reflected the existence and expansion of just that market. The Castle Line Guides were but one example of a whole range of imperial guides produced in the 19th century to satisfy the demands of a wide spectrum of middle-class readers beyond the four acknowledged by the Castle Line – administrators, members of all manner of technical and professional services, missionaries and teachers, businessmen and the ubiquitous officers from the army and the largest navy the world had seen. Some of these people travelled with servants, who may also have had access to the guide-books. Moreover, not all settlers were driven to travel by poverty and displacement. Many had capital and sought social and economic advancement in new geographical contexts. Women, of course, featured among several of these categories as settlers, missionaries, teachers, servants, wives, wealthy travellers and, from the late 19th century, as professionals too.

Indeed we often miss the fact that the British and other empires were not only empires of war, of economic exploitation, of settlement and of cultural diffusion. They were also increasingly empires of travel. They were playgrounds for the rich or the merely comfortable. They were places where various forms of cultural heritage could be explored. As well as locations for the spread of Christianity, the supposed working out of a divine and evangelical purpose, they offered the best evidence of progress, that defining bourgeois philosophy of the age. They neatly demonstrated the onward march of modernism, as particularly expressed in the spread of the technology of steam, the telegraph, sanitation, urbanism and western science and medicine. In the European empires, travellers pursued an essentially schizophrenic purpose. On the one hand, they appeared to seek other cultures, of both past and present, other climes, other landscapes, other flora and fauna, sometimes other morals; on the other hand, they also charted the comforting extension of what they saw as their own achievements and their own mores. For the British, being imperial was being modern and that was the fundamental value to which all other values referred.

Among these empires, the British inevitably saw themselves as supreme. Almost more than any other, they indulged in the obsessive collection of data which Thomas Richards has characterised as the imperial archive (Richards, 1993). The empire was a vast laboratory offering opportunities for the complete taxonomising of the globe. There can be no better insight into the ideology of modern empire than the notion that such an ambition was achievable at all. Through empire the world could be engrossed and enumerated, identified and indexed. Mapping was, of course, seen as a vital part of this embracing and exposing of the globe: the imperial project was, in many respects, a cartographic one. The East India Company began the great surveys of India in the 18th century. The more technically advanced great trigonometrical survey began at the beginning of the 19th century and was developed from the 1820s (Edney, 1997).

Major cartographic projects were similarly developed in South and North America, in Australasia and, by the end of the century, in Africa (Stone, 1995). Capitalists and settlers, administrators and soldiers, anthropologists and foresters all required maps. And this fascination with the morphology of the land was, of course, matched by the careful surveys of coastlines and oceans which followed the era of oceanographic exploration in the 18th century. The British Admiralty commissioned major surveys like those of Captains Matthew Flinders on the coasts of Australia or William Owen on the East Coast of Africa (Admiralty Hydrographic Department, 1966, 1967). The 'Pilots' are coastal guide-books, which retained their essentially imperial nature long after decolonisation. Their work fed into the series of published 'pilots' through which the coasts of empire were captured, analysed and laid bare for the use of mariners feeling their way along them. The globe could thus be reduced, compressed within the covers of a few books and atlases, encapsulated within a single room.

The development of the travellers' handbook or guide can be seen as a central aspect of this process of marking and miniaturisation. Yet they have never received the attention they deserve. It is perhaps tempting to see them as merely the ephemeral help-mates of the jaded and arrogant imperial traveller. In fact, they unveil a complete mindset. Their compilers and publishers sought to offer the first complete descriptions of the territories and regions to which they were devoted. Often they were inexorable in their gazetteering gaze, few places being so insignificant as to be left out. But as we shall see they were also obsessed, among other things, with historicisation, with progress, with economic development, with architecture, and with the development of modern urban forms. The contrasts, or in some cases similarities, between them and the modern Lonely Planet and Rough Guides are intriguing and reflect the dramatic changes, and also continuities, that are characteristic of the final decades of the 20th century.

The guide-books also illuminate and modify at least three of the central aspects of the oft-quoted work of Benedict Anderson (Anderson, 1983). On the one hand, their existence, their form and their repeated editions reflect the enormous growth of 'print capitalism' in the 19th and 20th centuries, as well as the technical advances and the cheapening of unit cost which made these guides readily available to all. Moreover, many of their guides strengthened their connections with imperial enterprise, both in its large- and small-scale guises, by publishing advertisements for all manner of enterprises, shipping lines, mines, hotels, shops and railway companies, among others. Second, they tell us something about an 'imagined community' which extended far beyond Anderson's efforts to explain the emergence of the nation. Anderson's imperial examples are generally drawn from the Spanish empire where he makes a severe distinction between the metropolitan Hispanic and the Creole as a device to explain his contentious idea that nationalism is invented in the New World. But the British Empire was not like that. People born in the Dominions served elsewhere in the British 'dependent empire', even up to the rank of governor. Analysis of the guides indicates that they were directed at a white imperial 'imagined community' which was global in its extent. Implicit in their pages is the notion, assiduously propagated by such figures as John Buchan and J.A. Cramb, that imperialism constituted an antidote to nationalism. In 1900, Cramb, writing propaganda about the Boer War, even wrote of 'the dying principle of Nationality' (Mackenzie, 1999). Indeed, the central myth of these guides is that there was an anglophone supra-nationality which embraced the world through travel and the traveller's gazetteer. Finally, when Anderson included an additional chapter on 'Census, Map, Museum' in his new edition in 1991, he could have included the Guide-book for, in a very real sense, these guides engrossed the other three in popular form (Anderson, 1983: chap. 10).

The new style of travellers' handbook and guide has its origins in the 1830s. The German publisher, Karl Baedeker, was of course one of its most famous exponents and he eventually produced guides to imperial territories like Egypt (which effectively became part of the British Empire in 1882), Canada and India. Baedeker issued a guide to Lower Egypt, in English, in 1877 and to Upper Egypt in 1891. They had, of course, appeared in German much earlier. German Egyptologists supplied the technical historical and archaeological information. Baedeker published in Leipzig and was published in London by T. Fisher Unwin and in New York by Charles Scribner. Some aspects of 'print capitalism' were highly international (information from the British Library catalogue and US Library of Congress National Union Catalogue). But the emphasis in this chapter is going to be on those published in Britain, primarily for the anglophone world. When these works are surveyed and carefully analysed, it becomes apparent that the British Empire was built not only on the sword and the gun, the Bible and the flag, Christianity and commerce but also the guide and the map. This was as true of informal empire as it was of the formal. What follows is an examination of some typical, even classic, guides. It is not an exhaustive survey but it is certainly representative.

The most notable British supplier of handbooks was the publisher John Murray. A significant aspect of Murray's reputation was the successful publication of the works of explorers. For example, Murray published David Livingstone's *Missionary Travels and Researches in Southern Africa* in 1857, one of the great best-sellers of the 19th century. Murray began to issue travellers' handbooks in the 1830s and it was a project which continued to occupy the publishing house until at least the middle of the 20th century. Among the earliest guides was a *Handbook for Travellers on the Continent* [of Europe], which was first published in 1836 and sold 10,000 copies within five years. It was soon being broken down into the individual countries. This was followed by guides to the English counties, London and Ireland. Switzerland appeared in 1838, North Germany in 1841, North Italy in 1842 and Central Italy in 1843. As well as Egypt and India, Murray had reached out to Algeria in 1873 and Japan in 1884, as the firm very swiftly went beyond Britain and Europe in a symbolic reaching outwards which both followed and reinforced the tentacles of imperialism.

The importance of Egypt in European tourism is well represented by the manner in which guide-books were issued by both Baedeker and Murray fairly early in their global expansion (John Murray, 1847; Wilkinson, 1847; Wilson, 1895). Murray issued his first guide to India, embracing mainly the presidencies of Bombay and Madras, in 1859, a mere two years after the great revolt of 1857, and a year after the abolition of the East India Company and the imposition of direct Crown rule in the Indian sub-continent. Print capitalism thus seemed intent on acknowledging the shift from company to state. But the scale of the operation was such that some years elapsed before the entire Indian Empire was covered. A series of separate volumes were issued from the late 1870s, by which time Queen Victoria had been proclaimed Empress and one of the major railway networks of the world was in the process of construction. Four volumes covering Madras, Bombay, Bengal, Punjab and the North West appeared between 1879 and 1883. But in 1891 something interesting happens. Whereas Murray had divided up his European guide into separate nation states (sometimes preceding political unification), the Indian guides were now combined into one volume. It is intriguing that this fits into the imperial propaganda of the time: that the British had created a great empire out of a congeries of states, that they were forging an astonishing union out of a South Asian Balkans. If Europe offered the nation as the organising principle of the guide, India reflected the assimilative supra-nationality of empire. This single-volume handbook, which initially threw the net even wider by including sections on Burma and Ceylon, continued to be issued in much the same format until the 1960s. Indeed, for much of this period, the handbooks received a semi-official stamp of approval since the prefaces and the entries on Ceylon and Burma were written by imperial officials (John Murray, 1906 [10th edn, 1919; 20th edn, 1965]). Murray was proud that the first edition of the *Handbook* had appeared before the *Imperial Gazetteer of India*, edited by Sir W.W. Hunter. Officials involved with Murray included Captain E.B. Eastwick, MP, Sir George Forest, Sir Arthur Gordon, Charles Buckland and, later, Sir John Cumming and Sir Evan Cotton. In such ways were these handbooks given almost an official imperial imprimatur. By the 1960s, the editing of the *Handbook* had passed to the academic Professor Rushbrook Williams, who based his work on the 18th edition edited by Sir Arthur Lothian.

Murray's followed Baedeker in organising their handbooks with a large quantity of preliminary information, often the most interesting material of all for the historian, the pages numbered in Roman numerals, before moving on to the tours and gazetteer numbered in Arabic. The 1906 edition, the fifth in the single-volume format, contained no fewer than cxv (115) general pages and 524 of the guide. By the 10th edition of 1919 (the frequency of new editions had been stepped up), this had risen to clxxv (175) and 726. Although the *Handbook* was sold on the basis of the 'glorious field which in India is opened up for the enjoyment of travel and sport' (John Murray, 1906: vi), it was effectively a major text-book of considerable value to all who worked there. That work, and British rule in general, were clearly sanctified by the history of the British in the sub-continent, particularly the history of their martyrdoms in the Mutiny or revolt of 1857. Indeed, in the third edition of 1898, a lengthy section on the history of the Mutiny was added. There were also major sections on the rulers of India before the British (emphasising, of course, the tradition of foreign rule), on the British administrative and communications systems, on population (based on the most recent British census in India), on irrigation, famine, plague and on 'sport', which generally meant opportunities for shooting game, both large and small. It may well be debated whether these extensions represented the growing self-confidence of empire, the 'illusion of permanence' or whether they represented a developing *fin de siècle* apprehension. The text explicitly emphasises the former over the latter.

In the traditional guide-book manner, advice was also offered on clothing, health, the engaging of servants, accommodation, useful functionaries and the like. Further emphasis was placed upon the antiquities, the architecture and arts of India and the efforts of the British to preserve these through the Archaeological Survey and the schools of art founded by the British. Interestingly, the figure most frequently quoted was the 19th-century British authority on Indian architecture and sculpture, James Fergusson, who was himself obsessed with notions of 'golden ages' and cultural decline (Fergusson, 1866, 1876; Mackenzie, 1995: 95–6; Mitter, 1977). The *Handbook* also contained a description of the voyage to India, a very specialist genre of its own to which I shall return later.

The gazetteer was organised in the form of railway tours. This had the effect of emphasising a network which was quintessentially British and which embraced and consolidated the whole of the sub-continent, from the coastal ports to almost every part of the interior, to the princely states and even into the foothills of the Himalayas and the mountains of the North-West frontier. India was to be unlocked and known through the traveller's exploitation of the new modernist technology. The very form of the *Handbook* imposed a web, a grid which neatly represented the linearity of modernism, a version of the coordinates of the map. Side excursions to antiquities or caves were to be made from railway stations and, in the larger centres, their attendant hotels. Distant regions for the more adventurous would likewise be accessed from a convenient railhead.

A number of powerful themes emerge in these tour descriptions. One is a fascination with the growth of towns and cities, with the development of their westernised architecture and transportation systems, with statuary and memorials devoted to Queen Victoria, notable administrators and heroes of the 19th century and with public and botanical gardens. The description of each distinctively British urban centre or cantonment was invariably juxtaposed with advice on excursions into the native town. Thus, the modern and the exotic are not located on separate continents but in adjacent space. The European traveller can live within his or her own culture, with only the climate and the colour of the servants as a reminder of location, and make comfortably brief forays into the neighbouring oriental territory. In a sense, metropole and periphery are juxtaposed. Thus, the traveller is enjoined to be careful to alight at the cantonment and not the town station at many places (John Murray, 1906: xxii). To get off at the town would cause serious disorientation between the railway technology and the traditional sights and sounds of India, as well as being simply inconvenient for the havens of hotels and clubs. Thus, there was a severe distinction between exotic space, the indigenous environment, and modernist place, the site of European order.

The second major emphasis is upon history. Each place is historicised in one way or another. Sometimes, this relates to the Hindu, Buddhist, Muslim or Sikh past, to the arrival of conquerors, notably the Mughals, their battles and the establishment of their rule. But by far the greatest portion of this historicisation relates to the British themselves. Inevitably, there are some references to the battles and events of the 18th century, such as the Black Hole of Calcutta of 1756. There are references too to the battlegrounds of the Mysore, Maratha, Pindari and Sikh wars. But the relentless historical allusiveness of the *Handbook* particularly concentrates on the 1857 Mutiny. Almost every place in northern and central India seems to have a story to tell. In the major centres of the Mutiny, like Delhi or Lucknow or Cawnpore (now Kanpur), many pages are devoted to the events of 1857. The Lucknow residency was described as 'the spot which all Englishmen will wish to visit first', while the chief interest of Cawnpore lay in the 'sad events' and 'cowardly massacre' of June 1857 (John Murray, 1906: 285, 301). Each place was full of inscriptions, tablets, statues, memorials and sculptures. It was as though the British were seeking to overlay the historical and artistic exuberance of India with their own more solemn patina. Martyrdom offered legitimacy. And the traveller along the web of railway lines stopped off to view these imperial sites of memory, the architecture and sculpture of public history which seemed to proliferate everywhere, offering that legitimating reassurance.

There were other forms of reassurance too, above all the command which the British had established over the Indian environment. As we have seen, railway and telegraph lines, towns and cities, modernising architectural forms all contributed to this. But there were additional important signifiers. Engineering achievements produced the loops, tunnels, reversing and run-off lines of the railways over the *ghats* (or western hills), into the Himalayas or the North-West. Above all, the bridges which spanned the great rivers of India were seen as one of the noblest expressions of imperial power. Similar sensations were promoted through the British reconstruction and extension of the canals, the great irrigation systems of India; the creation of extensive botanic gardens; and the protection of vast forest areas. The Indian environment provided opportunities for Europeans to enjoy *shikar*, hunting and shooting across the Indian landscape in a form of symbolic domination of the natural world that struck resonances with ancient cultures, with medieval European kingship and, above all, with the Mughals themselves. Thus, the guides became passports to 'the empire of nature', the classic control of the environment afforded to the upper-class traveller by 'field sports' and the gun (Mackenzie, 1988). In an intriguing paradox, forests and hunting grounds were wild, beyond the pale of civilisation but thereby attractive and fascinating. Indeed, forest reservation and the cultural overlay of the hunt served to throw the imperial net upon them. In all these ways, the *Handbook* was more than a guide to travel. It was a relentless textualisation of dominion and control, expressed through the places and incidents and forms of both past and present through which that imperial power was supremely expressed.

Two other important sources for the publication of imperial guides were travel firms and shipping companies. The celebrated agency Thomas Cook and Son, so often credited with inventing the concept of the package tour, also issued guides. The first of these may well date from 1845 and covered a journey no more exotic than to the North-West of England. From 1875, these handbooks became a more prominent part of Cook's business selling as many as 10,000 copies per year (at five shillings or, in modern terms, 25 pence each), and covering many locations in the wider world, including North Africa. They were regarded by the company as a 'useful sideline' which paid their way while 'providing a permanent means of propaganda' (Brendon, 1991: 272, see also 36–7, 46, 157). Booksellers were consequently suspicious of them but as their quality improved they became very similar in format to the guides issued by Murray or by another celebrated publisher that became active in the field, Macmillan. As the market clearly expanded, Macmillan issued the *Guide to Egypt and the Sudan Including a Description of the Route through Uganda and Mombasa* in 1901. It reached its fifth edition in 1908. Stanford also issued maps (handily within boards) for travellers, e.g. 'Map of the Nile from the Equatorial Lakes to the Mediterranean embracing the Egyptian Sudan and Abyssinia' was issued in July 1889 (well before the British re-conquest of the Sudan in 1898) and about the same time a 'Map of Ceylon'. Cook concentrated on North Africa and the Middle East, important locations of their tours but a crowded market given the interests of Baedeker, Murray and Macmillan in the same region. But, presumably spotting a gap in the market, Cook's also issued a guide to Burma.

The shipping lines, whose foundation and success were inseparably bound up with the development of the British Empire, were inevitably eager to promote the concept of travel as a pleasurable and healthy, as well as a profitable and culturally enlightened activity. As the speed of ships was enhanced by their triple expansion, and later turbine, engines, so their size and the range of their amenities grew. It became important for the shipping companies to emphasise the ease and comfort with which travellers could access imperial territories, as settlers or businessmen, tourists or invalids, administrators or missionaries. A number of companies began to issue guides and their content also helps to illuminate many aspects of cultural and other forms of imperialism.

The *Orient Line Guide* was first published for the Orient and Pacific Steam Navigation companies (which later amalgamated) by another important travel publisher, Edward Stanford, in 1882. It was sub-titled 'chapters for travellers by sea and by land' and was written by a prolific author, W.J. Loftie, an Irishman by birth who also held the office of assistant chaplain to the Chapel Royal (Loftie, various editions). Subsequent editions of this guide were issued in 1885, 1888, 1890, 1894 and 1901 and intriguing changes in emphasis occurred through these dates. The guides themselves celebrated the advances that were taking place in ship size and technology as the Orient Line introduced new and larger steamers which were described as 'vast floating hotels'. Indeed the guide, which was published in an impressive hard-back, illustrated form for a mere half crown (or 12½ pence), concentrated a great deal on western science and engineering. As well as the inevitable illustrations of ships and plans of their accommodation, there were chapters on astronomy, seamanship, navigation, meteorology and surprisingly complex technical details were offered on the production of electricity at sea and on refrigeration. In addition to all the usual tips on clothing, hygiene and medical aspects of the voyage, table after table of thermometer readings were offered to illustrate the equable temperatures and healthy air of the sea, emphasised by the 'tonic value of ozone' and the absence of fumes or any oxygen loss as a result of lighting by electricity.

Murray's *Handbooks* to India contained a section on the sea journey to India, which particularly emphasised the historic naval battles which had occurred on the route (John Murray, 1906: xxx–xxxvii). The *Orient Guide* took this idea further, even commissioning a specific author to contribute the naval material (Loftie, 1889: chap. 4). Battles of the Dutch wars of the 17th century, the 18th-century wars against France and, of course, the Napoleonic period were all described, developing into a nautical litany of Gravesend, Cap La Hogue, Cape St Vincent, Trafalgar and the Nile. If the events of 1857 somehow sanctified British rule in India, these battles justified British global power. Indeed, the sense of possession was particularly emphasised in the *Orient Guide*. The British acquisition of Gibraltar, Malta, Cyprus, Egypt, Aden, even such obscure islands as Perim and Socotra, were all described. If the sea lanes of the world were dominated by the British Royal Navy, so was the commerce of the globe. The oft-quoted statistic that nine out of ten ships passing through the Suez Canal were British matched the notion that it was possible to sail to Australia calling at, or observing, a string of British possessions on the way, ranging from the celebrated and important Ceylon to the little-known Diego Garcia (Loftie, 1889: 160, 182–91).

The *Orient Guide* considered that the amazing rise of Australia offered a solace for the loss of the American colonies. It constituted a new home for the British race, a genuinely New World which had been acquired 'without the sword', without the need for any conquest. Since it had been wrested from 'barbarism and desolation', there was 'no ancient civilisation to reproach us with its extinction' (Loftie, 1889: 304, 335). Aborigines were thus dismissed with barely a mention. The traveller could be comforted by what seemed to the Reverend W.J. Loftie to be racial, demographic and cultural truisms. The final section of the guide evaluated the economic, social and political potential of the Australasian and Pacific colonies. Descriptions of the landscape and resources of each colony tended to give way rapidly to an enthusiastic description of the extent of western civilisation demonstrated through the development and appearance of cities. This mirrored the predilections of the settlers themselves who tended to be town- rather than rural-dwellers. The cities were, of course, emblematic of modernism and Englishness and this quality of coherence with the parent culture was found to be particularly evident in New Zealand, the England of the South Seas. There the Maori wars had promoted the decline of the indigenous people and the race problem had been solved by 'the decrease in the number of natives' (Loftie, 1889: 347). There was thus nothing to impede New Zealand's essential Britishness.

By 1901, the *Orient Guide* had cut down on some of the complex material it had offered on the sea journey and naval battles. Instead, it expanded its sections on the wonders of Egypt and, in particular, on the

Australasian colonies. Greater use was made of official statistics and more was made of economic potential, the growth of trade and revenues. An entire chapter was now devoted to the cities of the antipodes, filled with architectural splendours and all created in Victoria's reign. The traveller or settler was reassured that 'if the rich colouring and barbarian picturesqueness of Asian and south-eastern Europe are absent, their smells and nameless abominations are absent too' (Loftie, 1901: chap. XVII, 231). It was perhaps also reassuring that absolutely no mention whatsoever was made of penal colonies and the origins of many settlers in the transportation of alleged convicts. However, by 1901, it was impossible to be as dismissive about the Maori as the earlier editions had been.

Loftie was born in 1839 and died in 1911. There can be little doubt that the Orient guides bore the stamp of this rather elderly, old-fashioned and conservative clergyman. The *Union–Castle Guides to South Africa* conveyed a slightly different tone, although they too were inevitably deeply steeped in the imperial world view. The Union and Castle lines, the latter inseparably associated with Sir Donald Currie, had been trading to the Cape for several decades. They amalgamated in 1900, by which time the *Guide* was well established. Currie had first issued a *Handbook and Emigrants' Guide to South Africa* in 1888 but, in 1893, he heard of a new publication, *Brown's Guide to South Africa,* a private venture produced by two brothers. This guide was designed to encourage the British to emigrate to or invest in the South African goldfields which by then were beginning to boom. It was even sold from hawkers' barrows outside the Stock Exchange in London and, within a few weeks, the entire first edition of 2000 had been sold. Currie bought out the two editors and it became the *Castle Line Guide to South Africa,* issued annually until the 1960s. The Brown brothers continued to edit the *Guide* for over 45 years and were succeeded by a son of one of them (Murray, 1953: 311–12). The *Guide* added East Africa to its area of interest in 1910 and ultimately became so bulky that it was divided into two volumes in 1950. To give some impression of this inflation in size, the 1899–1900 issue, published during the Boer War, was 420 pages in length. It reached nearly 500 pages in 1911–12, 914 in 1930, 1163 in 1948 with the two volumes combined weighing in at almost 1300 pages in 1957 (Brown & Brown, 1899–1900 and subsequent editions to 1957). In later years, it added an atlas running to more than 60 maps. All guides went through this process of elephantiasis, an inflation which neatly represented the continuing cultural significance of imperialism.

The earliest editions offered information on how to book seats on coaches for the goldfields but as railway lines spread throughout southern Africa, the *Guide* was able to adopt the railway tours approach. Like the

Orient Guide, it was eager to boost the virtues of the ships and the health-giving properties of an ocean voyage. Indeed, a great deal of attention was devoted to the climate and healthy characteristics of southern Africa, with extensive testimonies from medical men and quotations from medical works. The obsession with health and climate, which John Pemble identified in his book *The Mediterranean Passion*, was transferred to Africa (Pemble, 1987). Sulphur and hot springs were described in various places at the Cape and putative health resorts with hotels and sanatoria were identified in the mountains and in the drier areas of the region. There was considerable detail on pulmonary ailments and other diseases which benefited from a stay in Africa (Castle Line, 1911–12: vii–viii and passim).

The prime focus, however, was unquestionably on economic matters. The mineral and other resources were examined in infinite detail as were the fortunes of the various mining companies and concessions. A good deal of information was also offered on prospects for the purchase of land and for agricultural development. The range of potential crops and stock and the characteristics of each area were described in some detail, together with marketing opportunities. The prospects for the production of fruit and for its successful transportation by Castle ships to Britain were analysed. But, as always, there was a powerful emphasis on modernity, on cities, their architecture, facilities and transport as well as on the railway networks. Advice was offered on wages, on black labour, and on the cost of living.

One implicit theme is to be found running through all the early editions and that is the backwardness of both the Portuguese and the Boers. The Portuguese are seen as having largely failed to develop their colonies and, as late as the 1911–12 edition, Mozambique is described as being 'not entirely under control' (which was probably a not inaccurate assessment) (Castle Line, 1911–12: 117A). The Boers are depicted as being resistant to progress, the enemies of the modernising efforts of the British. They are described, for example, as having a 'prejudice against the iron horse', marking them out as enemies of modernism and, therefore, of imperialism (Castle Line, 1911–12: 25). The rural areas of the Orange Free State and the Transvaal were inevitably contrasted with the equivalents and the forward-looking towns of the Cape and Natal. After the Boer War, the tours of the country are specifically designed to take in the sites of the sieges and battles of the Boer War and the Boers continue to be described as the enemy even after 1910 when the creation of the Union of South Africa had ensured their political supremacy (for imperial pilgrimage to the metropole, see Lloyd, 1998). The Zulu and Boer Wars assume the role of the Mutiny in India, illustrating the early origins of battlefield tourism.

Monuments, statues and buildings were described in some detail, including often the costs of construction. Like India, southern Africa was full of sites of memory, together with the European historicisation of the landscape which offered legitimacy to white rule in general and British rule in particular.

The South African guides seem to be largely free of the overt social Darwinian racism which characterised Loftie's approach to Australia and New Zealand. This may have been because the prospect of extinction, which Loftie so confidently predicted in the Australasian case, was transparently impossible in southern Africa. Africans, however, are largely distinguished by their absence. Considering the size and extent of black populations in the region, the *Guide* succeeds in largely leaving them out of account. African customs are described as 'most interesting'. Some of the contemporary conventions about African culture are certainly repeated. The communal system of agriculture was described as ensuring that wealth was impossible but that poverty was unknown, an interesting balance that, for once, offered an implied critique of the extremes of wealth and poverty of capitalism. Fertile land, plenty of game and a favourable climate ensured that Africans were unwilling to work in the European economy. But the favourite African rulers of the whites were duly complimented. Moshesh of the Sotho was described as brave and talented, while Khama of the Ngwato was considered to have been a 'remarkable man', an 'ardent Christian' who had built a 'handsome Gothic church'. However, the separatist Ethiopian church was seen as a 'menace' which helped to give Africans 'an inflated idea of their importance and their abilities' (Castle Line, 1911–12: 4, 129, 268A, 279, 341). The tourist mapping of South Africa could not fail to allude to some of the central political and racial issues of the day.

Guide-book authors allowed themselves moments of both irritation and eccentricity. The Browns' guide inveighed against tourists who helped to destroy some of the cave formations and paintings of South Africa, for example at the celebrated Cango Caves. In dealing with ostriches, they announced that the worst an attacking cock ostrich could do was sit on its victim. However, they wryly observed, science had not yet established how long an ostrich would continue to sit upon a man before releasing him (Castle Line, 1911–12: 359, 176). This is the only joke to be found in the Guide!

Perhaps the most eccentric and opinionated of the guides was that produced by Sir Algernon Aspinall (1871–1952) for the West Indies. This was first published in 1907, shortly after the Jamaica earthquake, and it seemed to provide Aspinall, a London barrister, with a reputation as a

West Indies expert that led him to sit on various colonial committees such as the West Indies Shipping Committee, the Cotton-growing and Cocoa Associations, the West Indies Currency and Air Transportation Committees, and the governing body of the Imperial College of Tropical Agriculture. He was also the honorary commissioner of the West Indies exhibits at the British Empire Exhibition at Wembley in 1924–25. His guide-book certainly had a strongly economic slant, infused with imperial sentiment.

In common with the other guides, he was anxious to portray the comforts of the modern sea voyage, together with the striking range of shipping companies that served the West Indies. He was also eager to point up the key historical moments in the imperial history of the British in the Caribbean. His frontispiece was an engraving in which De Grasse delivered his sword to Rodney on the Glorious First of April 1782, 'which secured to us our West Indian colonies' (Aspinall, 1907). The associations with other celebrated British admirals were highlighted, including Nelson's marriage on Anguilla in 1787 and his connection with Antigua, where he refitted in 1805. However, the history of slavery and of revolt in the West Indies was largely ignored. But while Aspinall clearly pursued the places and incidents which most interested him, he made it clear that his primary purpose was economic. His entry on each colony started with the history of white settlement and went on to detail products, the extent of trade and of revenues. [He spread out beyond the British territories, including entries on Danish, Dutch, French and American possessions.] In this first edition, most of the illustrations were from photographs taken by himself.

Like so many other guides, it was clearly a considerable success. By 1931, it had reached six editions. It had been taken over by another publisher, included territories previously omitted, and had begun to look much like the other imperial guides with detailed entries on transportation and facilities in each colony. Much material remained the same, although the tables of imports and exports, revenue and expenditure tended to disappear (Aspinall, 1931). It grew in size and, after Aspinall's death in 1952, continued to be revised by Professor J. Sydney Dash (Aspinall, 1960). Indeed, it is interesting that academics often take over the revision of guides in the more modern period.

The economic emphasis was also a prominent aspect of the *South American Handbook*, a major compilation of information. This was based upon works by W.H. Koebel (1872–1923), a journalist and writer who specialised in South America. He published a number of handbooks to individual countries before the First World War and was involved in a special mission to the region for the British Government in 1919. His single-volume handbook was continued on an annual basis after his death (Davies, 1930). This work was designed primarily for businessmen, tourists and the framers of government policy. It specifically warned off speculative English-speaking settlers, although it described the very considerable opportunities for business and for people with capital. To make the political position quite clear, it actually included the complete text of Monroe's statement of his famous doctrine in December 1823 (Davies, 1930: 14, 17).

But, in many ways, it was a paean of praise to informal imperialism and the opportunities for British trade and investment. There were, therefore, both similarities and differences between guides to formal and informal empire. The former certainly gave a greater sense of 'possession' and were aimed at a wider constituency. The latter emphasised investment, trade and business generally. They combined tourism with business analysis.

The entries on each territory detailed the extent of British capital invested, the degree of British involvement in railway construction and operation and their activities in trade and shipping. The size of British communities, their clubs, sports, Masonic Lodges, churches and schools were enumerated in detail. Resources, opportunities for growth and the 'rules of engagement' under which trade was conducted, together with the impositions placed upon 'commercial travellers' were carefully laid out. As late as the 1930 edition, it was frequently pointed out that British investment was higher than that of the USA. But, in addition to all of this, the tourist information offered was very much akin to that laid out in the handbooks designed for formal imperial territories. While tourists were warned that they would find many 'primitive touches' in South America, they were also wonderfully reassured that afternoon tea, 'made as it ought to be made', was available in all the principal cities (Davies, 1930: 9–10). What more could the British tourist want?

There was perhaps a lot more. While the South American environment clearly offered distinctive experiences for the traveller, there were the usual constant reassurances about modernism. Hotels were comfortable and sanitation good. Buenos Aires, the sixth city of the world, was described as being 'of a renowned magnificence' (Davies, 1930: 47). Railways were generally efficient and often run by Britons. The British would find their own sports reassuringly disseminated in many countries of the region. There were also reassuring remarks about race. The 1930 edition suggested that 'to remove misconception...members of the Negro races in Argentina are insignificant in number', while a mere 350,000 of the population were described as being of 'mixed or inferior blood' (Davies,

1930: 101). Other reassuring comparisons were made. The size of each territory was often linked to that of one better known to the British, while the scenery of the Argentine southern lakes was likened to the Scottish Highlands, a very common world-wide comparison that never wholly makes sense (Davies, 1930: 104). In British Honduras, British Guiana and the Falklands or Malvinas, the British could be further reassured that they would enjoy formally administered British territories. In the case of Georgetown, British Guiana, they could find the 'finest cricket ground in the tropics' (Davies, 1930: 199). The handbook also included lengthy separate sections on shooting, angling and sport, shipping services, products, banking and insurance and railways, as well as a considerable number of classified advertisements. Although there are differences in emphasis, the handbook bears as many similar marks of the imperial world view as those for the territories directly administered by the British. And it is a world view which continues well into the post-Second World War era.

Travellers' handbooks and guide-books are an extremely rewarding source. They represent a significant element in the imperial taxonomy, a listing of place within a wider pre-modernist and sometimes threatening space. Such places abound with historical, modernising and economic significance, while the regions around offer both an ethnographic and a zoological nature to be penetrated in brief forays. Their objective is clearly the charting of progress, the development of the processes of imperial modernisation. Often they seem more concerned to emphasise the similarities with the imperial metropole rather than the exotic differences, though the latter could be penetrated by the more adventurous. In the period when imperial ideology, and the entire developmental philosophy, is reaching its apogee at the end of the 19th and the beginning of the 20th centuries, they acted as significant sites of propaganda. They often contained large numbers of advertisements, which clearly helped to keep their sale price down and increase their circulation but, inevitably, they also represented the interests and objectives of the companies who helped to finance them. They also give the impression of activity, the pursuit of business or sport, settlement or even health. It is interesting that the *'Arandora Star' Cruise Guide*, issued by the Blue Star Line, 2nd edition, 1937, begins to offer a more modern sense of leisure and relaxation as the attributes of the voyage. This is an active, masculinist empire. Written by men, their concerns are essentially those of males, a bias perhaps reflected in the imperial project itself. As we become increasingly aware of the complexities of the involvement of women in empire, it would be intriguing to know how extensive their female readership was and what their women readers made of them.

Tourists, invalids and settlers were just as likely to be women and sometimes they even participated in the violent sports of empire.

But it is clear that the guide-books are entirely innocent of the spirit of apprehension and fear of coming degeneration which strikes the late Victorians. Anxieties about the so-called yellow peril, about the racial and cultural degeneration of the West, about the threats posed by other peoples, by microbes and by scientific laws of thermodynamics that were perceived to be inexorable are entirely absent from their concerns. So is any sense that the British Empire was in comparative decline in the face of the rapid industrialisation of the USA and of Germany. Although the elite may have communicated such anxieties to each other, popular materials steered well clear of them. And all the evidence points to the very considerable popularity of these handbooks and guides. They were often issued almost annually or ran through many editions. Publishers and shipping lines were eager to be involved in them. Apart from school texts and popular journals, they must have been a prime means whereby the imperial world view was transmitted to bourgeois travellers and, in some cases, settlers from other sections of the social spectrum. If they were seldom read in their entirety, they must have been extensively dipped into.

Moreover, it is a world view in which a modernist economic plenitude as well as cultural creativity are inexorably celebrated. In them, Europe reigned supreme, a hyper-real global entity. Non-Europeans seldom aspired to a coeval sharing in this modernist cargo, though, in some cases, an imperial conversion was possible, if at some distant time. The voice of the Other scarcely intrudes at all. In this, as in other matters, the guides are replete with structural silences. Indeed, implicit throughout these handbooks was the suggestion that they would only be used by dominant and not subordinate peoples, although it is hard to imagine that they did not reach the eyes of educated elites in India and the West Indies. Above all, they underscored writing and the text as the prerequisite of modernity, a popular expression of the enterprise of knowledge. Here was print capitalism devoted to an embryonic globalisation, a hierarchisation of modernism placed in contiguous and severely contrasting relations with a pre-modern exotic. These hierarchies could also be divided up on a regional basis. The Latin American countries were graded according to levels of investment, urban growth, infrastructural provision, in other words stage of modernisation. Thus the guides offered a geographical exhibitionary complex on a world-wide scale, embracing informal as well as formal empire.

Moreover, they absolutely confirm the view which I expressed 20 years ago, that the imperial ethos, far from being killed in the First World War as so many historians used to argue, continues alive and well until at least the 1950s (Mackenzie, 1984). The genre of 19th-century imperial guide-book remains intact until the 1950s and 1960s. The format is the same. Sometimes the entries are almost identical over a period of more than 60 years. *The Union–Castle Guide to South and East Africa,* Murray's *Handbook of India,* Aspinall's *Guide to the West Indies* and the *South American Handbook* all sail on serenely into the 1960s and beyond. Some of the imperial sentiments are toned down but the approach is essentially the same. It is hard to escape the implication that the imperial world view, at least to a certain extent, survived decolonisation. The cultural mapping of the globe remained a prerogative of the wealthier West, at least until the tiger economies of the Pacific rim extended the pool of tourists. Yet, even then, it may be that the Lonely Planet and Rough Guides represent not so much a revolution but a neo-colonial continuity. It is certainly arguable that they continue to exhibit the cultural imperialism of the rich and advanced world, but there are also striking differences. They are generally no longer interested in statistics and in business opportunities, which have migrated into the work of specialist analysts. But their critical spirit, their concern with pleasure-seeking and their advice for minority groups like gays and lesbians do represent a striking break with the guides of the past. Their form of cultural imperialism would require another chapter. But there can certainly be little doubt that the imperial guides surveyed in this one were a major tool of imperialism. Large numbers of those involved in the imperial project in all its diversity must have mapped their way across both the cultures and the modernising tendencies of the Mediterranean world, the Middle East, India, Australasia, South and East Africa, the Caribbean and South America with the help of those amazingly detailed gazetteers, filled as they were with so many of the perceptions and prejudices of their age.

Acknowledgement

The author expresses his gratitude to Professor Ricardo Salvatore for helpful comments.

Note

1. An earlier version of this paper was delivered at a conference at the Universidad de Torcuato de Tella, Buenos Aires, in August 2000.

References

Admiralty Hydrographic Department (1966) *Bay of Bengal Pilot* (9th edn). London: Admiralty Hydrographic Department.

Admiralty Hydrographic Department (1967) *Africa Pilot,* Volume III. *Comprising the Southern and Eastern Coasts of Africa from Cape Hangklip to Ras Hafun* (12th edn). London: Admiralty Hydrographic Department.

Anderson, B. (1983) *Imagined Communities: Reflections on the Origin and Spread of Nationalism*. London: Verso.

Aspinall, A.E. (1907, 1931, 1960) *The Pocket Guide to the West Indies*. London: Edward Stanford.

Blue Star Line (1937) *'Arandora Star' Cruise Guide* (2nd edn). London: Blue Star Line.

Brendon, P. (1991) *Thomas Cook: 150 Years of Popular Tourism*. London: Secker and Warburg.

Brown, A.S. and G.G. (eds) (1899–1900) *The Guide to South Africa, for the Use of Tourists, Invalids and Settlers with Coloured Maps, Plans, and Diagrams* (7th edn). London: Castle Packets Co.

Castle Line (1911–1912) *Guide to South and East Africa* (18th edn). London: Castle Line.

Davies, H. (ed.) (1930) *The South American Handbook* (7th annual edn). London: Trade and Travel Publications.

Edney, M.H. (1997) *Mapping an Empire: The Geographical Constitution of British India*. Chicago: University of Chicago Press.

Fergusson, J. (1866) *On the Study of Indian Architecture*. London.

Fergusson, J. (1876) *The History of Indian and Eastern Architecture* (2 Vols). London, reprinted New Delhi, 1976.

Guide to Egypt and the Sudan including a Description of the Route through Uganda and Mombasa (1901, 5th edn 1908). London: Macmillan.

John Murray (1847) *Handbook for Travellers in Turkey, including Constantinople*. London: John Murray.

John Murray (1906) *Handbook for Travellers in India, Burma and Ceylon* (5th edn). London: John Murray. Also Calcutta: Thacker, Spink and Co.

John Murray (1965) *Handbook for Travellers in India, etc*. London: John Murray.

Lloyd, D.W. (1998) *Battlefield Tourism: Pilgrimage and the Commemoration of the Great War in Britain, Australia and Canada*. Oxford: Berg.

Loftie, W.J. (ed.) (1882, 1888, 1889, 1890, 1894, 1901) *Orient Line Guide: Chapters for Travellers by Sea and by Land*. London: Sampson Low and Edward Stanford.

MacKenzie, J.M. (1984) *Propaganda and Empire: The Manipulation of British Public Opinion, 1880–1960*. Manchester: Manchester University Press.

MacKenzie, J.M. (1988) *The Empire of Nature: Hunting, Conservation and British Imperialism*. Manchester: Manchester University Press.

MacKenzie, J.M. (1995) *Orientalism, History, Theory and the Arts*. Manchester: Manchester University Press.

MacKenzie, J.M. (1999) Review article: Books relating to the Ottoman Empire. *European History Quarterly* 29 (2), 305–310.

Martens, O. and Karstedt, O. (1932) *The African Handbook and Travellers' Guide*. London: Allen and Unwin.

Mitter, P. (1977) *Much Maligned Monsters: A History of European Reactions to Indian Art*. Oxford: Oxford University Press.

Murray, Marischal (1953) *Union-Castle Chronicle, 1853–1953*. London: Longmans.
Pemble, J. (1987) *The Mediterranean Passion. Victorians and Edwardians in the South* Oxford: Clarendon.
Richards, T. (1993) *The Imperial Archive: Knowledge and the Fantasy of Empire*. London: Verso.
Stone, J.C. (1995) *A Short History of the Cartography of Africa*. Lewiston: Edwin Mellen Press.
Wilkinson, Sir G. (ed.) (1847) *Handbook for Travellers to Egypt*. London: John Murray.
Wilson, Sir C. (1895) *Asia Minor, Transcaucasia, Persia*. London: John Murray.

Chapter 2

'How and Where To Go': The Role of Travel Journalism in Britain and the Evolution of Foreign Tourism, 1840–1914

JILL STEWARD

At the beginning of the 21st century, whole sections of the weekend papers and slots of prime-time television are given over to travel journalists who earn a living by telling us 'where and how to go' and the bookshops are full of travel books that often originated as essays in the printed media. Many are written by household names who use their writing to finance their travels (Holland & Huggan, 1998). New aspirants to the genre participate in the relentless competition for public attention. This chapter examines earlier incarnations of this theme, exploring the nature and function of early forms of travel journalism in Britain and its role in the creation of a 'culture of travel' in which popular tourism to foreign destinations began to expand and flourish.

Foreign travel has become something we take for granted. Historians of travel and travel writing are so busy uncovering the many forgotten travellers of the past, particularly women, that they are inclined to forget the novelty attached to foreign travel in the early days of modern tourism and what the experience meant for the many for whom 'abroad' was still uncharted territory. And yet, it was then that the idea of foreign holidays as a normal and desirable part of life first seeped into general consciousness. Tourism in the second half of the 19th century began to serve as a vehicle for the expression of distinctive personal and social identities in ways that laid the foundations for the further development of tourism in the following century. An example of the extent to which a 'culture of travel' had become part of popular consciousness is the late 19th-century phenomenon of the fugue, a form of flight from the everyday that enjoyed an ephemeral status as a form of mental disorder, which Ian Hacking argues was formed by popular tourism, on the one hand, and vagrancy, on the other (Hacking, 2000). Press coverage reveals a growing complexity in the image of the tourist at the same time as the commercial promotion of tourism anticipated the strategies of modern marketing and its preoccupation with the identification of tourist types differentiated by tastes, preferences and motivations. As magazines and journals began to target reading communities increasingly distinguished by social class and gender, attitudes to tourism as exemplified in the choice of travel destination, type of holiday and tourist practices became important elements in the patterns of consumption and lifestyles of different social groups.

The various genres constituting the body of travel literature are distinguished from each other not so much by their constituent features as through the functions they perform (Todorov, 1998: 287–94). This is certainly true of 19th-century travel literature where the boundaries between the genres replicated the fluidity of boundaries dividing journalism from literature. In this context, not enough credit has been given to the role of the press as a promoter of tourism. Arguably, it was the coverage of foreign travel in the press that helped to make the activity seem normal and routine and a 'taken-for-granted' feature of middle-class life. While it is undoubtedly true that the emergence of new forms of visual culture, allied to popular entertainments in the form of dioramas and panoramas, played an major part in familiarising the public with faraway places and making them attractive and fashionable, so too did the circulation of illustrated printed materials using the new reproductive technologies.

The role played by tourist literature in the formation and maintenance of cultural identity was evident in the practices associated with the aristocratic Grand Tour of the previous two centuries (Towner, 2002), not least of which was the recording of the experience by its participants. As James Douglas (1907) put it: 'Many a man in the epistolary age could not face the terrors of the Grand Tour, for he knew that he would be obliged to spend most of his time describing what he saw or ought to have seen' (cited in Staff, 1978: 79). Published memoirs of particular tours were extremely popular while discussions of the Tour's value featured prominently in the 18th-century press (Towner, 2002: 228). As the aristocratic Grand Tour gave way to its middle-class successor, published accounts of tourist experiences continued to play a role in the formation and codification of the cultural practices through which different social groups defined themselves and others. The new middle-class tourists belonged to a culture in which the time and the expense incurred by foreign travel required justification, so that the task of framing and articulating impressions of what had been seen, expressed in the appropriate way, was an intrinsic part of the experience of travelling. Sometimes travellers would attempt to impress a wider public than just family and friends with their respectability and cultivation by reworking their diaries, journals and letters home into publishable form.

The expansion in the volume of published travel literature indicated both the persistent desire of tourists to see themselves in print and the belief of editors and publishers in the commercial benefits of matching the vanity of authors with the widespread interest in travel. From the 1830s and 1840s onwards, the widespread circulation of articles in newspapers and periodicals through libraries like Mudie's (opened 1842) encouraged their readers' urge to travel. At the same time, the press provided an arena in which different kinds of tourists were able to defend and promote the particular tastes and preferences of the social circles they represented. The removal of newspaper taxes in 1855 initiated a rapid growth in the number of periodical and daily titles enabling many would-be professional writers to make the bulk of their living by writing for the weekly and daily papers. Many took advantage of the fluidity of the boundaries between literature and journalism making it easy to move between them.

The Swedish anthropologist Orvar Löfgren has written of the early pioneers of tourism that their 'aspirations to describe, represent, evaluate and compare also produced an urge to communicate; to show off, to write, to force others into comparison. Competition requires social exchanges – you cannot remain silent' (Löfgren, 1999: 26). Early tourism, he says, is therefore very much about the struggle with new modes of experience – how to select, judge and represent it and the norms and genres of representation to which the struggle gave rise. While much of this concerned the aesthetic dimensions of the tourist experience, there was a related social dimension to this phenomenon, as newly emerging professional groups fought for social space and cultural recognition. Nowhere were the competitive exchanges which marked this struggle pursued as energetically or as publicly as in the periodical press, the expansion of which created a space and a context that allowed the tourists from different social and cultural milieus, afflicted with the 'urge to communicate', to give voice to their experiences.

The different contexts in which communication took place provided readers of these 'exchanges' not just with the materials for what Löfgren calls 'mind-travelling' but with different models of how to be a tourist and the particular codes of civility they represented. Nineteenth-century travel literature took a number of forms ranging from the well-established formats of the conventional travelogue, diaries and letters and articles in the periodical press and the daily papers, to the memoirs of 'special' or 'foreign correspondents' (Matthews, 1986: 23–4) who often wrote about their travels. In addition, there were more specialised works such as handbooks and spa guides, reviews of new travel books and, from the 1880s onwards, self-conscious literary essays and directive articles of the 'where and how to go' variety. Editors began to find travel features were useful not just as 'fillers' but as a means of articulating and representing the interests, experiences and aspirations of their particular readers.

Professional journalists were particularly eager to share their experiences. George Augustus Sala, for example, began his career as a travel writer with his account of a journey to Russia, which led to a misunderstanding with his editor Charles Dickens; he was then sent abroad as a special correspondent in America for *The Daily Telegraph*. Like his colleagues, Sala regarded himself as a commentator on the social scene, treating changes in the social profile of Britons travelling abroad as symptomatic of social change at home. These journalists extended to tourists and their habits the same kind of curious interest that they bestowed on the indigenous life and customs of the places they visited. Many of the professional writers, artists and illustrators associated with London's 'Bohemia' found themselves occupying social positions that were sufficiently fragile to make them particularly sensitive to the social significance of the behaviour and cultural habits of their fellow citizens (Fox, 1988: 255–6). Not surprisingly therefore, tourists were often the targets of satirical treatment by the artists and writers of humorous magazines like *Punch, Fun* and the *Man in the Moon* who were preoccupied with the behaviours of the new social types appearing on British streets.

The press were particularly quick to pick up on the growing popularity of short trips abroad among the new suburban types as they ventured to the Channel ports, Paris or down the Rhine, their new geographical mobility hinting at their growing social mobility. Journalists often mocked the new tourists for their xenophobia and fear of foreign ways. The journalist Albert Smith, whose interest in travel took him to Constantinople in 1850 (Smith, 1850) and encouraged his diatribe against the British hotel trade (Smith, 1855), made the 'Gent' the subject of one of his *Natural Histories*, in which he mocked this character's visit to Boulogne (Smith, 1847). Drawing heavily on the stereotypical images of national characteristics circulating in the British press, he made fun of the 'Gent's' attachment to '"good John Bull joint, and no French kickshaws"... John Bull being generally represented as a vulgar top-booted man verging on apoplexy, with evidently, few ideas of refinement, obstinate, hard-natured; but the Gent conceiveth that on occasions it is ennobling to form an attachment to him' (Smith, 1847: 86–7). A few years later, Richard

Doyle's popular sketch-book narrative the *Foreign Tour of Messrs. Brown, Jones and Robinson* depicted the misfortunes suffered by characters originally created for the *Cornhill Magazine* and *Punch* as they pursued a 'middle class tour' abroad (Doyle, 1854). Their experiences seemed to illustrate William Makepeace Thackeray's observation:

> It is amongst the great and often-noticed faults of the Englishman in a foreign land (and particularly of the class we allude to) that he seems to think everyman's hand is against him, and that he assimilates himself with difficulty to the habits of the people amongst whom he resides. His self-created troubles commence on landing and follow him like a spectre on the road.

Cited in 1859 by John Murray in the introduction to his *Handbook to the Continent*, this passage served as a reprimand to those who adopted a negative attitude to travel (Murray, 1859: iii).

An article entitled 'Off for the Holidays' in the *Cornhill Magazine* (Clayden, 1867: 315–22) indicated the appearance of a more relaxed attitude to leisure and growing recognition of the restorative value of a foreign holiday among the cultivated and professional classes. The latter preferred to represent themselves as relatively sophisticated travellers as they enthused over the Alps and took the 'cure' in continental watering places. Accounts of sojourns in foreign resorts (often written by the editorial staff), of Easter in Rome, summer in the Alps and winter on the Riviera appeared in family magazines like *Blackwood's Magazine* and the *Cornhill* at the upper end of the market, encouraging readers to think of continental travel as normal, desirable and relatively straightforward. However, it was these readers who most inclined to dissociate themselves from tourists from outside their own particular social circles, who were invading their favourite resorts and turning the Alps into 'the playground of Europe', according to Leslie Stephen, editor of the *Cornhill*, in 1871.

Most of the *Cornhill's* contributors came from the same background as its audience. As a family magazine, it consciously made an effort to address itself to women by including not only novels but articles by women (Harris, 1986: 382–92). Elizabeth Tuckett's descriptions of informal family holidays in the less-well-known areas of the Alps (Francis Tuckett, her brother, was a prominent member of the Alpine Club) were calculated to appeal to the tastes of her audience and reveal the active involvement of women in new forms of active tourism: her illustrations depicted the ladies tobogganing, for example (Tuckett, 1865a, 1865b: 572–85; 1866, passim). Tuckett's sketches of family holidays in alpine resorts illustrate the routines of sightseeing, social events and communal meals and the formal and informal rules of conduct structuring life in such places (Tuckett, 1867), and her publisher expressed the hope that the work 'may prove useful to some inexperienced travellers who wish to explore parts of the Tyrol that are readily accessible and well-adapted to ladies' (Tuckett, 1866: 312).

Mountain climbing became a vehicle through which members of the professional classes articulated the codes of conduct which defined masculinity and gentility (Hansen, 1995: 300–24). Members of the British Alpine Club often wrote about their activities in the press, which took a close interest in activities which were often described in a kind of rhetorical language that was closely allied to that of imperialism (Hansen, 1995: 319–20). The journalist Albert Smith was thrilled by his ascent of Mont Blanc and he recreated the event so successfully on the London stage 'that Piccadilly and Mont Blanc became allied, as it were, in the public mind' (Hansen, 1995: 308). Sala did not help matters when he told readers of *The Daily Telegraph* that 'the beauties of Swiss scenery can be appreciated by travellers of a very low intellectual calibre…delights girls and children as well as matrons and old men, and, to all save idiots, is cheap' (Sala, 1869: 42). Press attention to the conduct of British visitors abroad distressed 'respectable' tourists like the Rev. Harry Jones, who were anxious that their compatriots' apparent ignorance of the codes of civility should not reflect badly on their 'betters'. In his *Regular Swiss Round: in Three Trips* (1868), the Rev. Jones instructed readers on how to view the Alps in the proper manner so that they would not be mistaken for members of the company of 'idlers and the gamblers, who travel for luxurious pleasure or evil gain' (Jones, 1868: 222).

Not all middle-class tourists were experienced travellers. Advice for such people was to be found in *Queen: the Ladies' Magazine*, founded in 1860 by the publisher Samuel Beeton for a readership comprising a cross-section of middle-class women. Beeton was one of the first editors to grasp that informative features on tourism could help to sell magazines. For three decades, the anonymous editor of *Queen* was Helen Rowe, who had travelled as an 'unprotected female' in Norway (Lowe, 1857) and Sicily (Lowe, 1859) in the company of her mother. She continued to write in this vein for her journal (Watkins, 1985: 185–200). *Queen* made a feature of its travel column '*The Tourist*', which was among the first and most professional of its kind. It set out to meet the concerns of its readers, particularly their anxieties about foreign travel, by offering them highly practical advice on 'where and how to go' and detailed suggestions on accommodation, travel arrangements, etiquette, general behaviour and dress. The question and answer section and postal information service created a form of direct interaction with readers, many of whom still regarded foreign travel as an unknown quantity. *Queen*'s columns encouraged women to regard tourism as a liberating and invigorating experience, teaching them to negotiate the perils of life in foreign resorts and encounters with strangers. A number of published queries came from women travelling alone or with female companions, a group for whom the services of Thomas Cook's 'personally conducted' tours were particularly valuable.

Cook's activities were viewed with considerable resentment by certain sections of the public, especially those who resented the invasion of their favourite haunts by their 'social inferiors'. They provided the press with plenty of material for a rancorous debate which threw into relief middle-class assumptions about the relationship between social class and tourist practices. One of the best known diatribes against Cook's 'escorted parties' was written by Cornelius O' Dowd, alias Charles Lever, who regaled readers of the conservative *Blackwood's Magazine* with a particularly virulent piece disparaging the dress, manners and deportment of Mr Cook's customers (Lever, 1865: 230–3). *Punch* frequently ridiculed the social ineptitude of the inexperienced traveller, appealing to its readers' sense of social superiority, and offering jocular advice to the inexperienced (*Punch*, 12 September 1863: 107).

> Always *shout* your English sentences at foreigners. They are all deaf...
> Take it for granted that everyone is trying to cheat and impose upon you.
> Dispute every item in every bill separately.
> To ensure civility and respect, see that all your portmanteaus, bags, and hat boxes be labelled MURRAY in the largest capitals. (Anon, 1863)

The up-market London papers like the *Belgravia*, the *Westminster Gazette* and the *Pall Mall Gazette* were all energetic critics of Cook's 'Cockney hordes'. Favourite lines of attack focused on the vulgarity of Cook's clients, whom they regarded as social upstarts, and their inability to benefit from their travels. Adopting an aggressive attitude to his critics, Cook denounced the insolence of the 'hirelings and witlings of a very small section of the London press' in his monthly magazine the *Excursionist and Tourist Advertiser* (Brendon, 1991: 95). Using these attacks for publicity purposes, he addressed an angry retort in a pamphlet supported by testimonials from customers who were much aggrieved by public attacks on their respectability. In an interview with Edmund Yates, 'My excursion agent' for the journal *All the Year Round* (1864), he defended the respectability of his parties, pointing out that while the social profile of his Swiss parties varied according to the season and therefore included 'the cockney element …[who] carry London everywhere about them in dress, habits, and conversation, and rush back, convinced that they are great travellers', at other times they were composed of 'the ushers and governesses, practical people from the provinces, and representatives of the better style of the London mercantile community… all travel as if impressed with the notion that they are engaged in fulfilling the wishes of a lifetime, in a pleasant duty never to be repeated' (Wilson, 1951: 311–12). In his own publicity magazine the *Traveller's Gazette and Excursionist* (subsequently the *Excursionist and International Tourist Adviser*), Cook briskly joined issue in 1872 with the *Athenaeum*'s criticism of his proposed 'Archaeological Tour to Rome' pointing out that he was actively attempting 'to awaken in the mind of the multitude that thirst for intellectual knowledge, the absence or deficiency of which the *Athenaeum* has so often deplored' (Cook, 1872).

Cook was not without friends in the press. Albert Smith's (n.d.) *The Adventures of Christopher Tadpole* gave a sympathetic account of a young man and his aunt enjoying Italy with Mr Cook, while the approach of Arthur Sketchley (a pseudonym of George Rose) to the 'Cookists', as Sala labelled them, took the form of cockney monologues describing the adventures of the loquacious Mrs Brown, her husband and friends, as they travelled in the care of the 'sainted Mr Cook' (Sketchley, 1870). *Out for a Holiday with Cooks* (1870) drew on Rose's own first-hand experience (at Cook's invitation). Usually read as condescending middle-class commentaries on Cook's clientele, these pieces could also be taken as glowing testimonials to the efficiency of the organisation and the satisfaction of its customers. By the end of the decade, as George Augustus Sala (always a supporter) was able to point out, 'Mr Cook can afford to smile at his detractors' (Sala, 1879: 1, 157).

Agency magazines like the *Excursionist* were particularly important vehicles for the promotion of tourist opportunities. Cook's monthly magazine remained the best known and Cook initially wrote much of it himself. In 1864, the *Excursionist* had circulation figures of just over 2000. Three years later, this had risen to about 58,000. By 1873, as a sign of Cook's growing respectability, it was taken by London clubs and an American edition began. By 1892, it had a global circulation of 120,000 with French, Austrian, American, Indian, Australian and German editions. At the end of the century, it was published in several different languages in London, Hamburg, Vienna, Paris and New York, each edition adapted to a particular clientele (Brendon, 1991: 326, n. 17). The Paris edition was the most old-fashioned in its layout and typography and reflected the relative conservatism of the French market, while the Hamburg edition became increasingly nationalistic in its tone. Shifts in contents and growing sensitivity to potential markets can be seen as indices of social change, as for example, in an anonymous short story about a pair of young American women (Anon., 1906), published in the Hamburg edition (an important entry point for American visitors to Europe), suggesting an awareness of the potential market among young women.

Underlying the expansion of tourism and publishing was a developing consumer culture with a strong visual component. The production of popular, illustrated travel literature aimed at a wider and less affluent market drew on the same reproductive technologies that placed advertising at the heart of the new visual culture, and linked changes in society to new forms of consumer culture. Stereoscopes, travel posters, postcards and the early cinema at first supplemented and then replaced the dioramas and panoramas of earlier days and gave visual expression to the stereotypical descriptions of people and places constantly reiterated by the travel press. Images of pretty girls were used to sell a range of products including magazines, while advertisements for travel and travel goods positioned readers as potential travellers. The growth of the travel press was bound up with the expansion of the tourist industry where internal competition encouraged the development of new forms of health and recreational tourism. A number of writers began to specialise in the production of travel literature, anticipating the appearance of the modern travel journalist as they helped readers to choose from the many new foreign resorts and spas by identifying the kind of society they attracted, their principal attractions and the range of health and sports facilities they offered.

Press coverage of elite tourism was indicative of the way that the upper classes were fragmenting into discrete circles as their members began to define themselves in terms of wealth, lifestyle, tastes and disposable wealth rather than their social origins (Davidoff, 1973). Choice of recreational activities became an element in the mechanisms by which particular social circles created and maintained the distinctions between themselves and others. The press contributed to this process as it chronicled the presence and habits of the celebrities of British high society and their 'sets' at play in their favourite foreign resorts, and made tourist travel into yet another form of conspicuous consumption through which the socially ambitious sought to improve their position.

Newspapers and journals responded to growing competition by targeting different reading communities and catering for their particular tastes and interests (Jackson, 2001: 30, 272–4). The *Pall Mall Gazette* for example, like *Belgravia,* included travel pieces by urbane professionals such as Grant Allen (Steward, 2005) in an attempt to accommodate both its more sophisticated readers and those with life-style aspirations (Onslow, 2002: 160–77). Allen expressed himself in typically acerbic mode as he reflected on the wealthy London types to be found in the casino at Monte Carlo (Allen, 1893: 4). *Queen*'s coverage continued to be pre-eminent although the magazine's circulation declined from 23,500 in 1890 to 16,000 in 1900. The magazine adopted a format that brought it closer to the newer artistic and literary magazines like the *Idler,* the *Author, To-Day* and the *Sketch* as it became more focused on the leisure activities of the 'upper 10,000' as it termed them, many of whom were to be found in the newly fashionable resorts of the Caribbean and the spa resorts of North Africa. *Queen*'s preoccupation with fashionable health treatments, such as the air and sun cures at Veldes (1900), was very much in tune with prevalent upper-class concerns about 'degeneration' expressed in medical diagnoses of 'brain-fag', hysteria and neurasthenia (Steward, 2002: 23–36). From 1894 onwards, the *Queen Book of Travel* began to issue its useful annual compendia of up-to-date travel information, including lists of all the principal resorts at home and abroad, both new and traditional (Cox, 1894). It placed particular emphasis on health resorts, indicating their appropriateness to the reader's social situation, pocket and the season and presenting a 'tourist geography' in which places were distinguished by their distinctive qualities of their sun, air, waters and snow, the nature of their health regimes and accommodation and their popularity or obscurity (Shields, 1991; Hughes, 1998).

The enthusiasm for health and exercise was noted by *Punch,* for whom F.C. Burnand dutifully sampled the 'cures' for modern life offered by continental spas and noted their debilitating effects (Burnand, 1884: 148–9). The vogue for active tourism among the aristocracy was extensively covered by *Queen*'s competitors such as the *Badminton Magazine of Sports and Pastimes.* George Newnes' *Wide World Magazine,* the editorial motto of which was 'truth is stranger than fiction', aimed at a more popular market and featured anecdotal articles by men and women engaged in active sports such as cycling, tobogganing and shooting, many of whom were anxious to see themselves in print, often accompanied by photographs (Jackson, 2001). The Pennells, a husband and wife team, were particularly active in this respect. Their journey from 'Berlin to Budapest on a Bicycle' (1892), complete with Joseph Pennell's illustrations, was serialised in the *Illustrated London News.* At the turn of the century, motoring became a fashionable new diversion. New specialist magazines also appeared. The *Picture Postcard: a Magazine of Travel, Philately and Art* offered something of everything. The short-lived *New Traveller's Magazine* was published by one of the many women's clubs springing up in the West End of London (Rappaport, 2000). Its editor, H. Ellen Browning, had previously published a travel book describing her Hungarian adventures (Browning, 1896).

Henry Lunn had begun began his career as a travel agent selling Switzerland to the clergy and he continued to seek out various kinds of niche markets not covered by Cook, which he publicised through his magazine *Travel* (Lunn, 1940). He now took advantage of the fashion for active sports, founding the Public Schools Alpine Association, as well as putting on Mediterranean cruises which, complete with educational lectures, eventually became the Swan Hellenic tours. Lunn encouraged his clients to put their experiences into print via the pages of *Travel.* Taking advantage of the publicity accruing to cycling feats, he serialised John Foster Fraser's account of his trip round the world in the company of a younger Lunn although the itineraries of the company's own cycle tours were rather less adventurous (Foster Fraser, 1897–8).

Lunn's Co-operative parties targeted a new generation of cultural tourists, often young teachers of the kind who were graduating from organisations like Canon Barnett's Toynbee Hall and the Regent Street Polytechnic, both of which were introducing their students to the educational benefits of foreign travel (Bailey, 1978). Always alert for new customers, Lunn commissioned L.T. Meade, an established writer for young people, to write a short story for his promotional magazine *Travel,* for which he adopted the format of an ordinary magazine. Meade's story combined the image of the 'modern' young working woman with that of tourist as the 'lady-like' young heroine, exemplifying the new type of independent 'working girl', finds herself out of work and takes a trip to Rome with a Co-operative tour party. Competence as a tourist brings romance and a job as a professional travel writer (Meade, 1898–9: 571–7).

As this story suggests, from the 1890s onwards a number of authors were able to make a living as professional travel writers. One of *Queen*'s leading contributors for the period was the travel writer Douglas Sladen, Honorary Secretary of the Authors' Club, whom *Queen*'s new editor Percy Cox commissioned to write a series of articles on Canada reflecting the upper-class fashion for travel in the dominions (Watkins, 1985: 198). Sladen's young assistant Norma Lorimer went on to become a travel writer in her own right. Journalism was now a fashionable career for young women wishing to enter the labour market (Onslow, 2001). For these young people, Mrs Alex Tweedie must have seemed something of a role model. Making her name with *A Girl's Ride in Iceland* (1889), she went on to earn a reasonable living as a travel writer, working for a number of different periodicals including *The New York Times, Badminton* and *Queen.*

Writers with literary ambitions and pecuniary needs found that travel writing could be more highly regarded than 'popular fiction' and appeared to be less affected by the exclusive and hierarchical distinctions structuring the market for novels (Frawley, 1994). Even so, in a competitive and over-subscribed market, it was often difficult for would-be writers to find ways of selling themselves and their travels or positioning themselves at the more prestigious end of the literary market place. Here, the location was less significant than the treatment of the subject. 'Sensitivity' and high cultural content frequently reflected the cultural capital of their authors, many of whom remained anxious to distance themselves from the 'common herd' and the commercial taint of 'Grub street'. A good strategy was to be first to a place; but that honour, once bestowed, was gone forever. A more realistic strategy was to seek places off the 'beaten track' or beyond the well-established boundaries of the main tourist regions. It became ever harder to find peasants who had never posed for a camera or new examples of the disappearing peasant cultures feted in the pages of the arts and crafts magazine, *Studio.* The latter's Austrian correspondent Amelia S. Levetus had begun her own career as the Viennese correspondent of *The Daily Graphic* when she had turned in a number of articles on Austrian resorts, before becoming an art critic.

The European borderlands of Russian Poland, the Balkans or the Adriatic all made good copy. 'Adventures' in these regions were made considerably easier and more comfortable by the extension of the railway networks and the appearance of tourist associations in remote areas like the Carpathians. The relative unfamiliarity of such places gave them a novelty value of the kind appreciated by editors and that testified to the authenticity of their experiences and the originality of the author's performance as intrepid tourist. The travel press contributed to changing perceptions of Europe by helping to redefine the relationship between the centre and the periphery, clothing the more backward and alien areas in the language of tourism and making them seem less remote and intimidating, although Emily Gerard's account of the superstitious Romanian peasants in *Land Beyond the Forest* (1888) (first published as a series of articles) caught the imagination of Bram Stoker, author of *Dracula* (1897).

The domestication of these areas was assisted by the activities of a handful of young women to whom the press accorded celebrity status. The scourge of the 1890s New Woman, Mrs Lynn Linton, declared in the *Nineteenth Century* (1891: 602–3): 'We are becoming a little surfeited with

Wild Women as globetrotters and travellers... for the sake of a subsequent book of travels, and the *kudo*s with the pence accruing'. She was possibly referring to Muriel Menie Dowie, whose articles on her Carpathian experiences in the *Fortnightly Review* (1890) describing her costume (knickerbockers and leggings), shooting practice (in case of attack by bears and wolves) and sleeping in the open, caused a minor sensation (Dowie, 1890: 520–30). Dowie's personal attractiveness, eye-catching outfits and interest in publicity allowed her to infiltrate the world of journalism by making her into a subject of considerable media interest, reinforced by her book about cross-dressing women adventurers and New Woman novel *Gallia* (1895) (Furniss, 1923).

James Clifford and others have recently reminded us that the feelings evoked by particular sights, places and modes of journeying are constituted by the distinctions recognised in the forms of the language in which they are embedded (Clifford, 1997). The authors of the new tourist literature, like many aspiring professionals in Victorian society, were sensitive to their right to social and cultural space and to the implications of the distinction between 'art' and 'commodity' that mapped on to the divisions between 'travellers' and 'tourists' (Buzard, 1993), 'gentlemen' and 'players', 'writers' and 'journalists', 'amateurs' and 'professionals' and the distinctions of feeling, sentiment and moral worth associated with them. The figure of the authentic 'writer' as a form of 'pilgrim', for whom both travel and writing constituted part of an inner journey, could only be given definition by contrast with the 'literary hacks' of 'Grub Street', who, like the generalised figure of the stereotypical 'tourist' for whom they catered, became a metaphor for the commercialised production of literature and the inferior form of cultural experience it engendered.

But '[H]onour the tourist: he walks in a halo of romance', declared Vernon Lee in an essay on 'modern travelling' in *Macmillan's Magazine*, thinking of the schoolteacher, clerk or typist for whom tourist travel was a transformative experience (Lee, 1894: 310–11). The sociologist Zygmunt Bauman, who, like others, has taken the tourist as a kind of allegorical figure for a way of existing that is expressive of our times, commented in 1995 that

> one thinks of identity whenever one is not sure where one belongs; that is, one is not sure of how to place oneself among the evident variety of behavioural styles and patterns, and how to make sure both sides would know how to go on in each other's presence. (Bauman, 1995: 81–2, 96)

If, as Bauman argues, tourism has now become a central element in contemporary negotiations of identity, I suggest that the travel press played a part in the early stages of this process. For it was in the competitive arena of the periodical press that the world was presented as something to be consumed and it was here that the search for novelty, authenticity and difference was at its most frenetic. The new breed of travel journalists not only constructed their images of their own social and cultural identities but also contributed to the formation of those available to others. By presenting readers with the world as a set of potential experiences to be chosen and consumed, by constantly asking 'Where will you go next?', they presented their readers with a set of choices through which they could express their individual tastes and preferences, and thereby their desires and fantasies, if not in reality, at least in their dreams.

References

Allen, G. (1893) On the casino terrace. *Westminster Gazette* 1 (1 March), 4.

Anon. (1863) How, when and where? Or, the modern tourists' guide to the Continent. *Punch or the London Charivari* (12 September), 107.

Anon. (1906) Ein pyramidaler antrag: eine Liebesgeschichte auf einer Cooks Mittelmeer-Vernugungsfahrt. *Welt-Reise Zeitung* Hamburg: Thomas Cook (11th edn, pp. 10–13; 12th edn, pp. 10–13).

Badminton Magazine of Sports and Pastimes (1895–1921) London: Longmans.

Bailey, P. (1978) *Leisure and Class in Victorian England: Rational Recreation and the Contest for Control, 1830–1865.* London: Routledge and Kegan Paul.

Bauman, Z. (1995) *Life in Fragments: Essays in Postmodern Morality.* Oxford: Blackwell.

Brendon, P. (1991) *Thomas Cook, 150 Years of Popular Tourism.* London: Secker and Warburg.

Browning, H.E. (1896) *A Girl's Wanderings in Hungary.* London: Longmans.

Burnand. F.C. Anon. (1884) Very much abroad: V. *Punch or the London Charivari* 27 (September), 148–9. (Reprinted as (1890) *Very Much Abroad.* London: Bradbury, Agnew.)

Buzard, J. (1993) *The Beaten Track: European Tourism, Literature and the Ways to 'Culture': 1800–1918.* Oxford: Clarendon Press

Clayden, P. (1867) Off for the holidays: The rationale of recreation. *Cornhill Magazine* 16: 315–22.

Clifford, J. (1997) *Routes: Travel and Translation in the Late Nineteenth Century.* Cambridge, MA. Harvard.

Cook, T. (1872) *Cook's Excursionist and International Tourist Advertiser* (21 September, p. 2). London: Thomas Cook.

Cox, H. (1894) *The Queen 'Newspaper' Book of Travel.* London: Horace Cox.

Davidoff, L. (1973) *Best Circles: Society, Etiquette and the Season.* London: Croom Helm.

Dowie, M.M. [neé Norman; Fitzgerald] (1890) In Ruthenia. *Fortnightly Review* (n.s) 48, 520–30.

Doyle, R. (1854) *The Foreign Tour of Messrs, Brown, Jones and Robinson in Belgium, Germany, Switzerland and Italy*. London: Bradbury and Evans.

Foster Fraser, J. (1897–9) *Round the World on a Wheel: Being the Narrative of a Bicycle Ride.* London: Methuen.

Fox, C. (1988) *Graphic Journalism in England during the 1830s and 1840s*. New York and London: Garland.

Frawley, M. (1994) *A Wider Range: Travel Writing by Women in Victorian England.* Rutherford, NJ: Fairleigh Dickinson.

Furniss, H. (1923) *Some Victorian Women: Good Bad and Indifferent.* Oxford: J. Lane, Bodley Head.

Gerard, E. (1888) *Land Beyond the Forest.* London; Blackwell.

Hacking, I. (2000) *Reflections on the Reality of Transient Mental Illnesses.* Charlottesville / London, University of Virginia.

Hansen, P. (1995) Albert Smith, the Alpine Club, and the invention of mountaineering in mid-Victorian Britain. *Journal of British Studies* 34 (July), 300–24.

Harris, J.H. (1986) Not suffering and not still: Women writers at the *Cornhill Magazine,* 1860–1900. *Modern Language Quarterly* 47 (4), 382–92.

Holland, P. and Huggan, G. (1998) *Tourists with Typewriters: Critical Reflections on Contemporary Travel Writing,* Ann Arbor, MI: University of Michigan Press.

Hughes, G. (1998) Tourism and the semiological representation of space. In G. Ringer (ed.) *Destinations: Cultural Landscapes of Tourism.* London / New York: Routledge.

Jackson, K. (2001) *George Newnes and the New Journalism in Britain 1880–1910: Culture and Profit.* Aldershot: Ashgate.

Jones, H. (1868) *Regular Swiss Round: In Three Trips* (p. 222). London.

Lee, V. [V. Paget] (1894) On modern travelling. *Macmillan's Magazine* 69, 306–11.

Lever, C. [C. O'Dowd] (1865) Continental excursionists. *Blackwood's Magazine* 97 (Feb.), 23–33.

Linton, E.L. (1891) The wild women as social insurgents. *Nineteenth Century* 30, 596–605.

Löfgren, Ovar (1999) *On Holiday: A History of Vacationing.* Berkeley, LA, London: University of California Press.

Lowe, E. (H.) (1857) *Unprotected Females in Norway and the Pleasantest Ways of Travelling There, Passing through Denmark and Sweden.* London: George Routledge.

Lowe, E. (H.) (1859) *Unprotected Females in Sicily, Calabria, and on the Top of Mount Aetna.* London: George Routledge.

Lunn, A. (1940) *Come What May.* London: Eyre and Spottiswood.

Matthews, J. (1986) The profession of war correspondence. *Journalism Quarterly* 33 (1), 23–4.

Meade, L.T. (1898–99) A lover of the beautiful. *Travel* 3, 571–7.

Murray, J. (1859) *A Handbook for Travellers on the Continent.* London: John Murray.

Onslow, B. (2002) Sensationalising science: Braddon's marketing of science. *'Belgravia'. Victorian Publications Review* 35 (2), 160–77.

Onslow, B. (2001) *Women of the Press in the Nineteenth Century.* Basingstoke: Macmillan.

Rappaport, E. (2000) *Shopping for Pleasure: Women in the Making of London's West End.* Princeton, NJ: Princeton University Press.

Sala, G.A. (1869) *Rome and Venice with Other Wanderings in Italy in 1866–67.* London: Tinsley Brothers.

Sala, G.A. (1879) *Paris Herself Again in 1878–79.* (2 Vols). London: Remington.

Shields, R. (1991) *Places on the Margin: Alternative Geographies of Modernity*. London/New York: Routledge.
Sketchley, A. (1870) *Out for a Holiday with Cook's Excursion, through Switzerland and Italy*. London: Cook.
Smith, A. (1847) *The Natural History of the Gent*. London: D. Bogue.
Smith, A. (1850) *A Month at Constantinople*. London : D. Bogue.
Smith, A. (1855) *The English Hotel Nuisance*. London: David Bryce.
Smith, A. (n.d.) *The Adventures of Christopher Tadpole*. London: King.
Staff, F. (1978) *The Picture Postcard and its History*. London: Lutterworth.
Stephen, L. (1871) *The Playground of Europe*. London: Longmans, Green.
Steward, J. (2002) The culture of the water cure: Civilisation and its discontents. In S.C. Anderson and B.H. Tabb (eds) *Water, Leisure and Culture, European Historical Perspectives* (pp. 23–36). Oxford/New York: Berg.
Steward, J. (forthcoming) Grant Allen and the business of travel. In W. Greenslade and T. Rodgers (eds) *Grant Allen and the Cultural Politics of the Fin-de-Siècle*. Aldershot: Ashgate.
The Picture Postcard: A Magazine of Travel, Philately, Art (1900–07)
Todorov, T. (1998) The journey and its narratives. In C. Chard and H. Langdon (eds) *Transports: Travel, Pleasure and Imaginative Geography 1600–1830* (pp. 287–94). New Haven/London: Yale.
Towner, J. (2002) Literature, tourism and the Grand Tour. In H-C. Andersen and M. Robinson (eds) *Literature and Tourism: Reading and Writing Tourism Texts* (pp. 226–38). London: Continuum.
Travel (1885–1905) London: Continental Travel Limited.
Traveller's Magazine (1902–04) then as the *New Traveller's Magazine* (organ of the New Travellers Club) (1904–06).
Tuckett, E. (1865a) Sketches from Pontresina. *Cornhill Magazine* 15 (January), 47–62.
Tuckett, E. (1865b), 'Sketches from Bertesgarten and the Zillerthal'. *Cornhill Magazine* (15 May), 572–85.
Tuckett, E. (1866) *Beaten Tracks: Or Pen and Pencil Sketches in Italy*. London: Longmans, Green.
Tuckett, E. (1867) *Pictures in the Tyrol and Elsewhere: From a Family Sketchbook*. London: Longmans, Green.
Tweedie, Mrs A. [as Ethel B. Harley] (1889) *A Girl's Ride in Iceland*. London: Griffith, Farran, Okeden and Welsh.
Watkins, C.C. (1985) Editing a 'class journal': Four decades of *Queen*. In Joel H. Wiener (ed.) *Innovators and Preachers: The Role of the Editor in Victorian England* (pp. 185–200). Westport, CT; London: Greenwood Press.
Wilson, M. (1951) Travel and holidays. In G.M. Young (ed.) *Early Victorian England, 1830–1865* (pp. 288–313). London: Oxford University Press.

Chapter 3

Selling Air: Marketing the Intangible at British Resorts

JOHN BECKERSON and JOHN K. WALTON

Much has been written about the history of resort visiting from both medical and cultural perspectives. From the mid-18th century onwards (but with earlier origins), it became an accepted leisure activity for the aristocracy and gentry and increasingly for the expanding middle ranks, the 'polite and commercial' but competitive and status-conscious people of an increasingly consumer-oriented society. It was always linked to health and the concept of healthy air was part of the range of attractions associated with resort visiting from an early stage, both in positive terms (the air at the destination having desirable and salubrious characteristics) and in negative ones (escape from the coal smoke and miasmatic effluvia of the growing towns). The selling of air built on existing medical discourses about the environment and the health of different places (Mosley, 2001). It was not the same as the marketing of a health-giving climate, which dealt in the statistics of sunlight, rainfall, humidity and prevailing winds: this was a qualitative issue, dealing with the perceived characteristics of the air (as opposed to the atmosphere) of particular places and its alleged capacity to invigorate, rejuvenate or sustain those who breathed in copious doses of it. A literature on the healthiness of the seaside atmosphere was in existence by the late 18th century and, by the early 19th century, such positive statements about the qualities and capacities of (especially) seaside air were commonplace.

Seaside visiting began as 'an adjunct to the spa season' (Walton, 1983: 9), but, by the late 18th century, it had a life of its own. Desires for health, self-improvement and fashionable recognition were all conveniently satisfied by a trip to the seaside. The pursuit of health, in particular, provided a perfect 'moral legitimation of seaside pleasure' in other forms, especially as the seaside became a fashionable destination in its own right (Funnell, 1983).

Access to resorts grew steadily, boosted by the development of the railway system, until by the 1880s, where this chapter truly begins, most middle-class families could afford a seaside vacation of at least a week. As leisure time grew, more commonly separated from work, it was commodified, and competed for. The leisure of growing urban crowds had a cash value and businesses began to cater for health and pleasure seekers. 'The crowd', notes Benjamin, 'had become a customer' (Richards, 1990: 235). Thus, the search for health and pleasure at the seaside supported a significant service sector of the economy by the later 19th century. This, of course, contributed to noticeable urban growth (Walton, 1983).

The fastest growing popular resorts of the late 19th century drew on the increasingly working-class markets of the industrial north-west of England, especially the Lancashire 'cotton towns', where smoke was viewed as an unavoidable sign of industrial virility and prosperity, and the domestic hearth was romanticised as a symbol of familial cosiness (Mosley, 2001). Resort publicity did not challenge these assumptions but it emphasised the restorative value of a week of clean, fresh air to palliate the ill effects of this way of life, blow away the cobwebs (a favourite metaphor) and revitalise workers for another year of productive labour.

We think of sea-bathing as central to the Victorian resort experience but it was already declining in importance by the late 19th century for working- and upper-class visitors, though middle-class families remained firmly wedded to the idea. At Brighton, the upper classes 'promenaded endlessly to and fro', according to Richard Jeffries in 1885, but ignored the beach altogether. As sea bathing lost its aura of physic, it became more recreational and less medically regulated:

> The health giving properties of the seaside resolved themselves into sea air, sunshine and climate generally. (Walton, 1983: 42)

Some simple facts may have contributed. Compared to sea bathing, especially from an uncomfortable bathing-machine which imposed a charge for access to the water, sea air was accessible, free and pleasant (if sometimes cold and assertive). Unlike access to the sea under the restrictive conditions of Victorian bathing regimes, which effectively privatised bathing by channelling it through the bathing-machine proprietor, sea air could not be directly commodified, although this contrast is blurred somewhat by evidence that the bathing regulations, even at their mid-Victorian height, were readily avoidable in practice at many resorts. Sewage pollution of the sea, which sometimes extended into bathing waters, might taint the air as well, but only locally and temporarily, and the reputation for the health of sea breezes survived intact, while in most places those that came off the land had no industrial smoke in places where such activities were firmly discouraged (Travis, 1993: 23–30).

These attributes made sea air, as a common good identified with particular locations, a particularly easy thing to publicise, especially as the qualitative assertions favoured by the publicists were impossible to disprove. However, this publicity could not have been generated so easily without drawing upon and strengthening a rhetoric that emphasised the connections between seaside air and health. Guide-books (published for profit but also for civic boosting) by doctors, journalists and municipalities stressed the health-restoring qualities not only of sea, situation and climate but specifically those attributable to the local *air*. Over time, the publicity literature paid less attention to the tonic effect of sea bathing and more to assertions about air quality in general terms. It was not long before people with business interests in resorts saw the profits to be made from 'selling air'. Conveniently, they could readily derive support from public health campaigners, and the therapeutic and prophylactic value of sea air soon became a matter of common sense to its votaries.

The selling of British resorts using the distinctive characteristics and quality of their air was most prevalent from the late 19th to mid 20th century and was largely confined to the domestic market in Britain. National publicity organisations which sought to attract international visitors from the 1920s tended to steer clear of all aspects of the British climate, preferring to emphasise landscape and heritage; their emphasis was always on the capital, historic towns and buildings and scenery rather than seaside resorts (Beckerson, 2003).

The two key terms used by publicists, whether medical or lay, in connection with seaside air are *ozone* and *bracing*, although *tonic* (an overlapping usage) also had its devotees. Although some parts of the coastline traded on the mild and relaxing nature of their atmosphere, especially in winter, most British resorts, right through to the 1960s and even beyond, preferred to emphasise the strength, briskness and invigorating qualities of their air, a ploy that made them particularly vulnerable to changing fashions in the age of the Mediterranean suntan. Ozone was certainly identified with fresh, invigorating breezes, sometimes in combination or competition with bromine or iodine, whose virtues were already being touted as valuable constituents of seaside atmosphere in the 1830s and 1840s (Hassan, 2003: 76; Pooley, 1862). After the identification and naming of the gas in the latter decade, it soon passed into the armoury of medical commentators. Dr Spencer Thomson, writing in 1860, identified seaside and mountain locations as prolific in ozone, which would promote vigour and positive health, though he was (like many subsequent writers) unclear about exactly what it was or how it worked (Hassan, 2003: 7). Ironically, in view of subsequent discoveries about the health hazards posed by concentrations of the gas in the lower atmosphere, ozone became positively associated with coastal regions after early experiments found that seaside air was heavily impregnated with it. It was thought to transfer the curative properties of the ocean to the air in 'ozone laden winds' and was a central marketing point for sea air from at least the 1860s to the 1930s. Dr Oliver of Redcar maintained in 1869 that the sea air at this exposed point on the Cleveland coast 'constantly contains *a large quantity of ozone*, which stimulates all the vital functions' (emphasis in the original). It was particularly in evidence 'near the track of the tide breaking and dispersing on the beach... it is largely charged with ozone, iodine, particles of saline matter, and a fine spray of sea water from broken waves... it is also highly electric'. This is a reminder that from a medical perspective ozone, important though it might be, was part of a wider array of interacting curative functions of seaside air (Gordon, 1869: 41–2). In 1873, Dr Cornelius Fox of Scarborough undertook a careful study of what was already an ample literature on ozone and, whilst remaining ultimately doubtful about its benefit to health, still remarked that

> [O]n the mountain, at the seaside – in one word, at the bright and beautiful country which God made – where pure and invigorating air largely supplied with ozone abounds ... men are cheerful, and living things present for the most part a healthy appearance. (Fox, 1873)

The assumed positive association between ozone and countryside as well as seaside is noticeable here and helped to promote the development of rural resorts as well as coastal ones, although the strongest popular associations were always with the coastline.

The proposed or assumed positive relationship between ozone and health was already being seriously called into question in some scientific circles in the 1870s. Von Pettenkofer's critique, published in 1877, found no demonstrable relationship between ozone and disease statistics, although he, like subsequent critics, was unwilling to dismiss it altogether (Hassan, 2003: 78). Even as positive ideas about ozone and health were challenged in scientific medicine, however, they had broken free from it to enter the popular imagination and to find an enduring place in resort promotional literature. We find accounts of holidaymakers talking about the benefits of ozone from the 1870s and of turn of the century tourists urging each other to 'begin the day with a dose of ozone' and throwing open windows at every opportunity (Bennett, 1902: chap. 10). In 1902, for example, a locally-produced guide to Grange-over-Sands, a small resort on Morecambe Bay, assured intending summer visitors that,

> The idea that Grange is only a winter resort, and that in summer it is extremely hot and enervating, is very erroneous, as in the warmest weather there is always a refreshing breeze blowing gently in from the open expanse of the estuary, and its ozonic properties are far from relaxing. (*Mason's Pocket Guide*, *c.* 1902: 3)

In 1913, the south-east Devon resorts were described as 'soberly gay' (i.e. not in the boisterous way that Douglas or Blackpool were gay) and 'thronged with thousands of visitors drinking in the ozone-laden air' (Ward Lock, 1913–14: xv). Blackpool itself was promoting itself as 'the zone of ozone' at this time. The term retained its currency in popular parlance through the inter-war years and beyond, despite a particularly damaging attack by Dr Leonard Hill in 1924, and its use extended to medical commentators whose specialisms lay elsewhere, as when Sir Laurence Chubb extolled the health-giving qualities of ozone in 1938 (Hassan, 2003: 78). It had passed into a realm of popular 'common sense' that made it resistant to scientific challenge.

The promotion of resorts as bracing was even longer lived and more successful than the ozone motif. It was already being deployed at the beginning of Victoria's reign and remained in common use for more than a generation after the Second World War. In 1841, for example, the air of Gravesend was represented as 'dry, pure, bracing and extremely healthy' (Stafford & Yates, 1985: 34). Bracing air was a particularly useful device for the northern resorts, which suffered a worse climate than their southern counterparts, especially those in the north-west that were open to the prevailing south-westerly winds and those on the east coast that were afflicted by cold air from the North Sea. East coast resorts laid claim consistently to the health-giving qualities of 'bracing' air in the most general of terms. Great Yarmouth in 1916 had 'an air without a rival for its invigorating qualities... this health-giving, bracing air'. Bridlington in 1912 disarmingly made 'no claim... that the climate... possesses specific qualities for the cure of any particular disease [but], it is a matter of common observation that the bracing and invigorating character of the air proves highly beneficial to convalescents' (Ward Lock, 1916–17: ix, 1912–13: 7). As with ozone, the label 'bracing' could be presented as part of a broader and quite sophisticated-looking medical analysis of the properties of air in different local microclimates, as in Dr G. Oliver's presentation of the north-eastern resort of Saltburn in 1869:

> A considerable variety of atmosphere is presented... a dense energising sea air on the beach... a lighter sea air tempered by a mountain quality on the cliffs and high grounds; a warm soothing atmosphere in the glen; and a fine bracing mountain air inland. (Gordon, 1869: 28)

But south coast resorts could be 'bracing' too: Seaton in Devon had 'a fine bracing climate, tempered by a soft mildness', while as late as the early 1960s Bognor Regis could be described as 'moderately bracing and cool in summer', the latter attribute being still a virtue (Ward Lock, 1913–14: xiv, *c.* 1963: 7). Bracing air was dry air, whether inland or at the seaside. Harrogate in 1908 was 'dry and bracing as a rule'; and, in 1910, 'North Cornwall is distinctly more bracing than the south coast. The speciality is the dryness of the air' (Breare, 1908: 183; Ward Lock, 1910: 6). But the fact that the same label could be used to entice visitors and residents to places as contrasting as Seaton and Saltburn, Rhyl and the emergent Greater London outer suburb of Berkhamsted (Hertfordshire), suggests that by the early 20th century 'bracing' had lost what limited analytical specificity it had ever enjoyed, and become an attractive label emptied of real descriptive pretensions (*Bracing Berkhamsted*, 1927; Polkinghorne, 1905).

Bracing as a category overlapped with 'tonic', which was also in extensive use from an early stage, also in conjunction with ozone. Dr Oliver in 1869 added it to his list of quasi-medical adjectives in support of Redcar, this time as a resort for children: 'the strong tonic properties of the sea air on the East Coast, which stimulate so powerfully the nutrition and growth of children, exist to perfection at Redcar' (Gordon, 1869: 42). In the mid-1920s, the British Spa Federation asserted: 'The British spas are perhaps the most tonic in the world', explaining that, '[T]he tonic quality of a spa depends chiefly on the temperature and other qualities of the air' (British Spa Federation, *c.* 1923: ix). 'Tonic' seems to have connotations of lifting the spirits and stimulating the appetite, without the overtones of boisterous breezes and challenging temperatures that were associated with 'bracing'; but the use of these words in and beyond the medical discourse of resort promoters and commentators would merit further investigation.

The geographer Stephen Ward suggests that the importance of bracing air to the British was linked to theories of climatic determinism, widely accepted in the heyday of Empire (Ward, 1998). In this system of belief, it was suggested that the creativity, enterprise and drive that sustained British innovation, trade, wealth and empire owed its origins to a stimulating climate, which encouraged energetic activity. To holiday at a bracing resort, therefore, was to share in this ideology and hope to derive the corresponding benefits. A bracing British holiday was not only especially suited for refreshing the tired worker for new labours: it was patriotic and conducive to economic success. Holiday publicity aimed at the healthy found 'bracing' to be a most convenient term, especially for the accessible popular resorts on exposed north-western and eastern shores: one which suggested improved health and vigour while making a virtue of necessity as regards the climate, and without implying that a resort was a place for the sickly. Celebrations of the sportive or boisterous wind, especially at the seaside, or of the threatening but contained sublimity of the great waves that might be whipped up by a gale to provide an exciting and attractive spectacle, often contributed to resort publicity in various forms (Walton, 1998).

Interestingly, the positive desire for a 'bracing' experience was distinctive to Britain, although early Spanish seaside resorts on the Bay of Biscay emphasised their refreshing climate by contrast with the heat of Madrid, as well as the healthy virtues of big waves and cold northern seas (Walton & Smith, 1996). The Americans tended to stress relief from urban heat and humidity (Immerso, 2002). French resorts used images of sensuality, sweetness, warmth and languor when publicising their airs. In Britain, even the warmest of UK resorts on the south coast carefully shunned the idea that they might actually enjoy hot summers, although the imagery of the Riviera became popular in the early decades of the 20th century and the idea of a warm, comfortable summer climate was promoted especially assiduously in parts of the south-west (Morgan, 1992).

Ozone and bracing or tonic air fitted in well alongside the long-lived rhetoric of rational recreation which encouraged holidaymakers to enjoy finding out about the natural world as part of an 'improving' holiday experience, finding specimens to collect, classify, preserve and display. The origins of this can be seen in guide-books from the late 18th century but lists of local flora and wildlife were still commonplace in inter-war guide-books and other publicity, especially for smaller and more rural resorts, and these activities fitted in well with the inter-war cult of the outdoors and of rambling. These investigations into the distinctive aspects of local natural history were activities undertaken in the fresh air and could be presented as integral to the health-giving, relaxing but mentally as well as physically improving aspects of (especially but not exclusively) a middle-class family holiday (Allen, 2001; Taylor, 1997). This version of the enjoyment of Nature was important to a particular middle-class idea of what a resort should offer. It was a sign that the resort was a place where the city and its threats to health and vitality could be escaped. However, the enjoyment of nature at the seaside did not fundamentally question the urban experience in any way. It provided a foil to it; and an alternative middle-class holiday philosophy of hedonism, consumerism and display found plenty of outlets in large, urban, fashionable resorts like Brighton. The metropolis was consistently preferred to the seaside in the pages of *Punch*, where the rustic delights of Cornwall might be compared with the fleshpots of the metropolis to the great advantage of the latter. One contributor adapted the language of 'bracing' to the social rather than the natural environment, parodying seaside medical propaganda in the process, to make a point about the boredom of the seaside holiday in a small resort: he professed himself eager to exchange 'the awful perfume of rotten seaweed for the bracing atmosphere of glorious London' (*Mr Punch c.* 1900: 87; Walton, 2001).

British resorts wishing to improve their advertising often looked to the USA for inspiration. Just as in Britain, the depiction of the seaside as a healthy and natural refuge from 'the debilitating city' gave rise to much valuable publicity. The resort of Atlantic City sold itself in the 1880s in verse:

> The panting city cried to the sea,
> I am faint with heat, O, breathe on me!
> So, to the city, hot with flame,
>
> Of the pitiless sun, the east wind came.
> It came from the heaving breast of the deep,
> Silent as dreams, and sudden sleep.
> (Funnell, 1983: 135)

Such 'gifts of nature' as cooling winds and pine trees allegedly breathing ozone were all part of a successful marketing mix (Budden, 1912). Here again, air was especially useful. Many of the most successful British seaside resorts became increasingly commercialised and urbanised in the late 19th century at the same time as their publicity became more sophisticated. The idea of healthy air blowing in from the sea and, therefore, uncontaminated by urban expansion on the shore gave a link to ideas of nature and health without any cost to leisure providers or municipalities.

How did resorts publicise their bracing, ozone-laden, tonic air? Throughout our period, publicity flowed out from railway companies, leisure providers, hoteliers and municipal organisations. The overall output was so huge that we will concentrate on municipal work in this chapter. Such efforts were a useful gauge of how towns chose to collectively present themselves and reveal which groups had the power to form and sell images of place.

In early days, in the mid-19th century, a common technique was to form a resort publicity committee of the great and good. From an early date, resort publicity committees sought to give an image of their towns as healthy. The Isle of Man Advertising Committee of 1852 reprinted an article from *The Liverpool Standard,* which praised the Island's 'health restoring influence'. Unfortunately for them, the 'glowing accounts of Douglas' were revealed to be misleading. They failed to 'tell the truth' and glossed over the 'dirty and insanitary condition of the town'. Concerned residents argued that 'when the town is teeming with filth, how can the air be pure?' (Beckerson, 2003). Such responses, which made use of the resort's need for good publicity to promote a sanitary reform agenda within the town, were common in the aftermath of the 1848 cholera epidemic and on the occasion of Board of Health inspections in the early 1850s; and dissenting voices were ever-present in the local newspapers of al resorts, although muffled by a general desire not to rock the boat on this sensitive issue (Walton, 1983).

By the early 1870s, resort publicists had worked out a tidy position on health. An influential Manx journalist, guidebook producer and founder of the Douglas Advertising Committee put it as follows:

> Our visitors get value for money for what they spend; they give us their gold, we give them the health which enables them to go back to their hives of industry reinvigorated. (*Isle of Man Times*, 27 May 1871)

Not for nothing was the seaside town lobby group called the Association of Health and Pleasure Resorts. The association of health with pleasure, even as the latter came to dominate the image of many of the larger popular resorts, was a successful and enduring strategy used at all levels of the holiday industry. When John Hassall produced his famous 1908 poster of the fisherman on the beach, with the legend 'Skegness is *so* bracing' (emphasis in original), for the resort's Advancement Association, he knew nothing about the town except that the open shoreline was notorious for chilly easterly winds even in the height of summer. Yet he brilliantly combined a sense of energetic fun with a figure suggesting tradition, rejuvenation and a healthy zest for life (for the poster, www.postershop.com/Hassall-John-p.html).

Bracing breezes were difficult to measure and compare competitively but were only one aspect of competitive resort propaganda about weather and climate. A veritable climatic war was waged over many decades with rainfall and sunlight statistics, which could be recorded and presented with some claim to objectivity. Ozone levels were also part of the story. The Isle of Man paid for its weather to be reported in several London newspapers, so convinced was the Board of Advertising that this was an essential part of its advertising strategy. 'Resorts in the south-east had the most evidence to back up their claims, so those further north tried to emphasise their fresh air and healthy atmosphere' (Yates, 1988: 25).

Although ozone, bracing and tonic were key terms, we can find other attributes of air in Victorian publicity. Fresh air was sometimes portrayed as social lubricant and a symbol of conviviality and freedom. A resort guide of 1898 noted:

> There is a recognised system of lounging, reclining, and assembling for chatting on the steps outside the boarding establishments and hotels [where] the commingling of sea and mountain air [is] both bracing and soothing, and as life is passed chiefly in the open air – the visitors' desire being to get as much of it as possible – perfect liberty is afforded to holiday makers, but license is a thing unknown; though an air of freedom is exhibited on every hand it is seldom taken advantage … (*Black's Guide to the Isle of Man*, 1898)

Most publicity courted the healthy, for these represented the majority of potential resort customers. However, a specific subsection of resort publicity targeted medical men, the sick and the worried well. An early guide to the Isle of Man noted that (Anon., 1824)

> Douglas [offers] comfortable accommodation for genteel families disposed to take up their summer residence … the salubrity of the air and the cleanness and strength of the waters are very powerful inducements for invalids to visit this place.

Such inducements were common in guide-books and were taken up by local government when it became involved in resort publicity. Soon after the Isle of Man's Official Board of Advertising was formed in 1893, it initiated a policy of sending thousands of guidebooks to 'medical men' every year, in the hope that they would recommend the Island as a health resort to patients (Manx Museum, Board Minutes, 13 March 1900). Across the country, municipal Medical Officers of Health were pressed into service to boost ideas of healthiness, as were other local government luminaries. Assertions about the distinctive qualities of local air played their part in the propaganda, as Medical Officers lent their scientific aura to the vaguest of claims. At Ilfracombe in North Devon in about 1890, for example, the air in summer (according to Dr E.J. Slade-King) 'is remarkable for frequent agitation, generally bracing without being keen, and fresh without pungency' (Twiss & Sons, *c.* 1890: 3).

Over many decades, resorts and businesses continued to make claims about their power to restore as well as reinforce health and to put them to the medical profession and the sickly. The enduring presence of pulmonary disease until the 1930s was convenient and, although no resort was keen to attract the sick, most were delighted to welcome non-infectious and profitable convalescents. For such purposes, commercial and municipal interests contributed to publications that expounded the merits of all aspects of resorts, including water supply and subsoil, for the health of visitors and (increasingly) residents. From this perspective, of course, the claims about air were part of a much wider set of discourses.

The claims the resorts made about their health-giving properties did sometimes arouse concerns. In 1920, it was argued in the House of Commons that doctors should investigate the 'dangerous' claims of the resorts, which 'may not be health resorts at all'. However, this was more of a tactical objection to the prospect of health resorts using the term to advertise on the rates (*Hansard*, 1920: *c.* 833).

Of course, only part of the publicity drive was directed at the medical profession. Much more time and effort was spent to sell the seaside directly to the general public, without benefit of medical intermediary, and this gathered pace between the wars. Resort publicists had long used Victorian theories about miasma and ozone with a good deal of success. But attitudes to health and efficiency, which developed in the 1920s and 1930s, were more problematic for traditional seaside businesses. As hiking, cycling and outdoor recreations grew, getting into the open air became not just a sign of health but also of personal freedom. The standard boarding house holiday came to be seen as 'stuffy' and dull and the inter-war years saw the continued and accelerating rise of the informal, self-built 'plotland' holiday settlement and the holiday camp, first tented, then with chalets on the model that was to be developed on an industrial scale by Butlin and his imitators after the Second World War (Hardy & Ward, 1984; Ward & Hardy, 1986). The open-air holiday movement caused a lot of worry to traditional resorts. Their trade was not heavily threatened, because of the growth in access to holidays and the coming of holidays with pay. But they worried about the loss of important groups, especially the young and the better-off, who were increasingly able to travel to the continent.

They fought back with new attractions, embracing their own version of the cult of the outdoors with new promenades, parks and outdoor bathing pools, all of which derived important aspects of their claims to health promotion from the presumed qualities of the sea air to which their users were exposed (Walton, 2000: chap. 5). New publicity became more important than ever. Far from dying, the promotion of air as a tourist asset proved remarkably durable. It was a classless selling point, which could be widely applied without fear of alienating existing clientele; and it was infinitely malleable, because the criteria for assessing the claims made for air quality were so wonderfully elastic and untestable.

As idea about healthiness developed, the old 'health resorts and watering places' re-branded themselves as 'health and pleasure resorts' which no longer spoke of curing illnesses but of vitality and superb well-being. So health was no longer taken so seriously, but its pursuit remained as a catch-all excuse for having some fun. The 'toning' qualities of air were ideal and had the advantage – in an age still haunted by the spectre of widespread pulmonary complaints – of offering a dream of fitness which would fit conveniently with contemporary fashions. Indeed, claimed one commentator who represented a resort, 'it is not necessary in order to go to a health resort that it should have anything to do with water'. The promotion of Church Stretton, in the Shropshire hills below the Long Mynd, as a health resort specialising in pure air, is an excellent illustration of this point (*Church Stretton*, 1922; *Hansard*, 1920: *c.* 839).

The skies had certainly never been bluer in 'ad-land'. This was a period when resort publicity flourished as new powers were conferred on towns and seized to the full. The Health and Watering Places Act of 1921 allowed all resorts to apply the proceeds of a penny in the pound tax on assessed property (a 'penny rate') to advertising, after which advertising departments within local government began to flourish, especially in the larger resorts (Yates, 1988). Claims about air quality remained an integral part of advertising discourse into the late 20th century.

Eventually, the emphasis on bracing air was reduced and the cult of the sun advanced correspondingly. The celebration of sunshine, already gathering momentum in the inter-war years, eventually overtook the imagined properties of sea air at the top of the advertising bill. But the preoccupation with sea air lingered on through the post-war generation. The Ward Lock Red Guide to the Yorkshire coast in the late 1960s, for example, still began by emphasising the 'bracing air' that characterised the whole coastline, along with 'wonderful scenery' (Ward Lock, *c.* 1966: 7). What is particularly interesting here is the evidence that so many guide-book writers and resort promoters, over such a long period, continued to believe that British holidaymakers wanted to be 'braced' by the air, as part of a holiday experience that continued to combine the restoration or reinforcement of good health with the manifold other enjoyments of a seaside or, indeed, a country holiday.

References

Allen, D.E. (2001) *Naturalists and Society*. Aldershot: Ashgate.

Anon. (1824) *A Guide to the Isle of Man*. London.

Beckerson, J.G. (2003) Marketing British tourism 1914–1950. PhD thesis, University of East Anglia.

Bennett, A. (1902) *Anna of the Five Towns*. London.

Black's Guide to the Isle of Man (1898) London: A. and C. Black.

Bracing Berkhamsted: Official Guide, etc. (1927) Cheltenham: E.J. Burrow and Co.

British Spa Federation (n.d. after 1923) *The Spas of Britain: The Official Handbook of the British Spa Federation*. Bath: British Spa Federation.

Breare, W.H. (1908) *Thorpe's Illustrated Guide to Harrogate*. Harrogate: R. Ackrill.

Budden, H. (1912) *The City of the Pines, or, Beautiful Bournemouth*. London: Ivor Novello.

Church Stretton (Shropshire): A Brief Guide (1922) Church Stretton: Stretton Press.

Fox, C. (1873) *Ozone and Antozone*. London.

Funnell, C. (1983) *By the Beautiful Sea*. New Brunswick, NJ: Rutgers University Press.

Gordon, S. (1869) *The Watering Places of Cleveland* (2nd edn). Guiseley: M.T. Rigg, 1972.

Hansard, 130 HC Deb., 5 ser. (1920) cols 833, 839.

Hardy, D. and Ward, C. (1984) *Arcadia for All*. London: Mansell.

Hassan, J. (2003) *The Seaside, Health and the Environment in England and Wales since 1800*. Aldershot: Ashgate.

Immerso, M. (2002) *Coney Island: The People's Playground*. Piscataway, NJ: Rutgers University Press.

Isle of Man Times, 27 May 1871.

Manx Museum, Board Minutes, 13 March 1900.

Mason's Pocket Guide to Grange-over-Sands (1902) Grange-over-Sands: H.T. Mason.

Mr Punch Goes on Holiday (n.d. *c.* 1900) London.

Morgan, N. (1992) Perceptions, patterns and policies of tourism. PhD thesis, University of Exeter.

Mosley, S. (2001) *The Chimney of the World*. Cambridge: White Horse Press.

Polkinghorne, J.D. (1905) *Bracing Rhyl*. Bournemouth: Mate's Illustrated Guides.

Pooley, C. (1862) *Ozone, not Iodine, The Cause of the Salubrity of Weston-super-Mare*. London.

Richards, T. (1990) *The Commodity Culture of Victorian England*. London: Verso.

Stafford, F. and Yates, N. (1985) *The Later Kentish Seaside*. Gloucester: Alan Sutton for the Kent Archives Office.

Taylor, H. (1997) *A Claim on the Countryside*. Edinburgh: Keele University Press.

Travis, J. (1993) Continuity and change in English sea-bathing, 1730–1900. In S. Fisher (ed.) *Recreation and the Sea*. Exeter: University of Exeter Press.

Twiss and Sons' Illustrated Guide to Ilfracombe and North Devon (*c.* 1890) Ilfracombe: Twiss and Sons.

Walton, J.K. (1983) *The English Seaside Resort: A Social History 1750–1914*. Leicester: Leicester University Press.

Walton, J.K. (1998) *Blackpool*. Edinburgh: Edinburgh University Press.

Walton, J.K. (2000) *The British Seaside: Holidays and Resorts in the Twentieth Century*. Manchester: Manchester University Press.

Walton, J.K. (2001) Respectability takes a holiday. In M. Hewitt (ed.) *Unrespectable Victorians* (pp. 176–93). Leeds: Leeds Centre for Victorian Studies.

Walton, J.K. and Smith, J. (1996) The first century of beach tourism in northern Spain. In M. Barke, J. Touner and M. T. Newton (eds) *Tourism in Spain: Critical Perspectives* (pp. 35–61). Wallingford: CABI.

Ward, C. and Hardy, D. (1986) *Goodnight Campers*. London: Mansell.

Ward, S.V. (1998) *Selling Places*. London: Spon.

Ward Lock and Co. (1910) *Red Guide to Newquay and North Cornwall*. London: Ward Lock.

Ward Lock and Co. (1912–13) *Red Guide to Bridlington*. London: Ward Lock.

Ward Lock and Co. (1913–14) *Red Guide to Sidmouth and South-East Devon*. London: Ward Lock.

Ward Lock and Co. (1916–17) *Red Guide to Great Yarmouth*. London: Ward Lock.

Ward Lock and Co. (*c.* 1963) *Red Guide to Bognor Regis*. London: Ward Lock.

Ward Lock and Co. (*c.* 1966) *Red Guide to the Yorkshire Coast*. London: Ward Lock.

Yates, N. (1988) Selling the seaside. *History Today* 38, 20–7.

Chapter 4

Tourism in Augustan Society (44 BC–AD 69)

LOYKIE LOMINE

This chapter discusses the significance of tourism in classical antiquity. It focuses on Augustan Rome and its Empire between 44 BC and AD 69, the period between the assassination of Caesar and the end of the reign of Nero and of the Julio-Claudian dynasty. It shows that, contrary to common beliefs and assumptions, tourism existed long before the famous Grand Tour of Mediterranean Europe by English aristocrats. The sophisticated Augustan society offered everything that is commonly regarded as typically modern (not to say post-modern) in terms of tourism: museums, guide-books, seaside resorts with drunk and noisy holidaymakers at night, candle-lit dinner parties in fashionable restaurants, promiscuous hotels, unavoidable sightseeing places, spas, souvenir shops, postcards, over-talkative and boring guides, concert halls and much more besides.

Methodologically, this chapter is based upon three main types of primary sources: archaeological evidence, inscriptions and Latin literature. Most Latin authors mention facts related to travel and tourism. Their names are here given in their common English version (e.g. Virgil for Vergilius) and references are made in a conventional way, mentioning not the page or year of publication of a specific edition but the exact localisation of the text, e.g. Propertius 1, 11, 30: book 1, piece 11, line 30, making it possible to find the quoted passage in any version. Archaeological evidence concerns transport (e.g. the paved roads facilitating travel, such as the 'Queen of Roads', the Appian Way from Puteoli to Rome, by which Saint Paul came to Rome [*Acts* 28.13]) and accommodation, notably the inns discovered in the ashes of Pompeii and Herculaneum, whose plans are reminiscent of the European hostelries of the 16th century (Bosi, 1979: 237–56; Mau, 1899; Tucker, 1910: 22). Inscriptions too are important as they give evidence in a very human way: they were made by average Augustan travellers and not by erudite people or scholars. They prove that yesterday as today, travellers often wish to inscribe indelible marks of their passage on stone, like many graffiti found in Egypt. For example 'I, Gaius Numidius Eros, was here in year 28 of Caesar, returning from India, in the month Phamenoth' (Braund, 1985: 277) or 'I, Lysa, slave of Publius Annius Plocannus, came here in year 35 of Caesar' (Ehrenberg, 1976: 360). Two bodies of literature are innovatively put together: texts about ancient history (such as Casson, 1974; Frebaugh, 1923; Fredouille, 1992) and texts about tourism studies (such as Horne, 1984; MacCannell, 1976; Urry, 1990). Epistemologically, this analysis relocates the study of tourism in Augustan society in the framework of current discourse on travel and tourism, by applying the tools and concepts developed by tourism studies to a discipline that usually follows different methods: the study of ancient history.

Historians do refer to tourism as a common phenomenon in Ancient Rome but they rarely linger on the subject. The *Oxford Classical Dictionary* recognises that 'a regular tourist industry on quite a modern scale seems to have developed' at the end of the Republic (Hammond, 1970: 1090). However, specialists do not expand on the topic: for example Cary only dedicates a few lines to tourism, at the very end of the chapter entitled 'Social Life' (Cary, 1940: 161); Dudley (1975) has one chapter about 'travel' (Chapter 37), Treble one chapter about 'roads and travel' (Chapter 11) and Tucker one chapter about 'travel within the Empire' (Chapter 2) but they do not reflect on the very notions of travel and tourism because they are (pure) historians: tourism is not their preoccupation or area of particular interest. Tucker (1910: 22) indeed wrote: 'We must not dwell too long upon this topic. Suffice it to say that travel was frequent and extensive, whether for military and political business, for commerce or for pleasure'. Hopkins (1978: Preface) addresses this critique to classical historians: unlike modern historians and medievalists they have 'isolated themselves' by refusing to 'take advantage of developments in the social sciences' and 'the results are clear: ... a gap between modern concepts and ancient sources'. This is particularly true for two works dealing with travel and tourism in the Ancient World (Badger, 1920; Casson, 1974): they have a purely descriptive approach, telling many details and anecdotes but analysing nothing.

Lexicological Insight

Lexicology provides an emic view into Augustan tourism, around three key concepts (*peregrinatio, otium, hospitium*) and the semantic fields they open. In Latin, a person who travels around is a *peregrinator*. This substantive etymologically means a person who has gone through lands (*per* meaning through, *ager* meaning land), which suggests quite a long trip rather than a short, local, one-day excursion. *Peregrinator* (a masculine term, as befits a society in which most tourists were men, with the exception of a few rich widows or other independent women) comes from the verb *peregrinare*, which has an ambiguous meaning: it means 'to go abroad, to travel' (Cicero, *Brutus* 13, 51) as well as 'to be a stranger' (Cicero, *De Finibus* 3, 12, 40). The *Oxford Latin Dictionary* (1968: 1335) focuses on the notion of travelling ('to go, to travel abroad or away from home; to travel in thought or in imagination; to reside, stay or sojourn abroad') and gives the adjective *peregrinus* the connotation of foreignness ('of persons: foreign, alien; of other creatures: not native, exotic; belonging to foreigners, outlandish; of places: situated abroad; not Roman', p. 1335). In the language itself, travelling is thus associated with the idea of foreignness: the Augustan *peregrinator* is far from home (*domi*, the root of domicile, domestic, as opposed to *peregri*), in a foreign, and potentially hostile, environment. Augustan travellers were aware that they remained strangers wherever they were: this corresponds to the much discussed view of the tourist as 'the Other' and tourism as 'The Quest for the Other' (Van Den Berge, 1994).

Another important term shedding some cultural light on Augustan tourism is *otium*, a key concept in Latin civilisation. As opposed to *negotium* (the Latin root of negotiate, *négoce* in French meaning business, trade), *otium* is 'unoccupied or spare time, as needed for doing something, "the time", "the leisure"; freedom from business, especially as devoted to cultural pursuits; rest or relaxation from work, a holiday; the productions of one's leisure' (*Oxford Latin Dictionary*, 1968: 1277). The term production is important: if *otium* is linked to idleness, it is not a negative idleness but a productive one, the source of relaxation and well-being or even the fruit of leisure; indeed, Ovid calls his poems '*otia nostra*' (*Tristia* 2, 224). Highlighting the importance of *otium* is a way to exclude all forms of travel that would modernly be described as business tourism: tourism is here understood as entailing a focus on leisure pursuits. Consequently, neither a merchant with his slaves and his bales, nor a body of gladiators taken to fight in the amphitheatre of some provincial town, nor a horseman scouring along with a despatch of the emperor nor a troop of actors and tumblers could be regarded as tourists as *otium* was not the key of their trip (Tucker, 1910: 23).

The third important Latin concept related to Augustan tourism is *hospitium*, whose meaning is much stronger than hospitality as a kindness in welcoming guests or strangers. *Hospitium* refers to 'the permanent relationship existing between host and guest, the ties of hospitality' (*Oxford Latin Dictionary*, 1968: 807). If in the city he is about to visit, there lives a person with whom he happens to be linked by *hospitium* (e.g. because his father had once put up or helped their father), an Augustan traveller is bound to stay at their place, where he will be received with honour. He can stay there many weeks, he will be treated like a prince but if ever this person (or someone recommended by them) visits him, he will be obliged to offer the same services.

Daremberg and Saglio's well respected *Dictionnaire des Antiquités Grecques et Romaines* (1899) devoted six pages to the article *hospitium*, explicating it as a religious duty deeply committing people to each other. This religious dimension is notably attested by the adjective *hospitalis* referring to the gods protecting the ties of hospitality (such as Jovis Hospitalis) and by the mythological legend of Philemon and Baucis. The old peasant Philemon and his wife Baucis agreed one night to put up two unknown travellers whom everyone in the village had repelled. The travellers were actually Jupiter and Mercury: to thank Philemon and Baucis, the gods offered to realise their dearest wish. The old couple only wanted to finish their life together. Jupiter destroyed all other houses in the village and turned Philemon and Baucis into two trees growing together at the door of his temple: an oak and a lime-tree (the Augustan poet Ovid has used this legend in his *Metamorphoses*). Such messages had two major consequences for the expression and development of tourism in Augustan society. First, the existence of such networks of potential hosts strongly encouraged Romans to travel to cities and regions even if they had no business reasons to go there, only visiting places for *otium*'s sake: *hospitium* contributed to the development of tourism because people knew where they would be welcome and accommodated. Second, if *hospitium* facilitated tourism, it stunted the development of hotels. Few hotels were needed indeed, as travellers would understandably rather go where they would find a free, welcoming roof. Existing hotels had names such as Cock Inn, Eagle or Elephant (Tucker, 1910: 21), and were of poor quality, mainly catering for two kinds of guests: travellers from modest backgrounds, who did not have links of *hospitium* because they were freedmen (i.e. ex-slaves) or parvenus (Frebaugh, 1923), and travellers uninterested in comfort but attracted by the licentious, promiscuous atmosphere of the place: Casson indeed compares Augustan hotels with brothels and describes how waitresses were waiting for guests and tempting them (Casson, 1974: 263).

The Augustan Grand Tour

Many sources attest to the existence of a formalised tourist itinerary, a series of all-important sightseeing places, a sort of 'obligatory route'

(Horne, 1984: 10). Augustan tourists were neither attracted by the western Mediterranean area (from Spain to Carthage) nor by the rich areas of Syria and Palestine (Antioch, Jerusalem). Many historians describe the Augustan Grand Tour as a trip to Greece (via Sicily), then to Asia Minor via some islands on the Aegean Sea and to Egypt, then back to Rome (Caspari, 1940: 161; Dudley, 1975: chap. 37; Treble, 1930: 93). Most of the main Augustan sightseeing places (if not all) are currently popular again:

- In Italy: from Ostia (port of Rome) or Puteoli (port of Napoli), via the Straits of Messina (possibly calling into Sicily to visit the temples of Artemis and Athena in Syracuse and to see Mount Etna).
- In Greece: Delphi (for the oracle of Apollo); Athens (the Acropolis, the port town); Corinth (and its isthmus); Epidaurus; Olympia (especially Phidias' statue of Zeus); and Sparta. Popular Greek islands included Delos for the sanctuary of Apollo, Samothrace and Rhodes.
- In Asia Minor: Cnidus (the home of Praxiteles' famous statue of Aphrodite); Ephesus; Smyrna; Colophon and Didyma for the local oracles of Apollo and, most importantly, 'Homer's Country' as the site of the Trojan war. The Trojan site occupies a particular place in Augustan tourist geography, between politics and mythology. After the Trojan war (1193–84 BC according to the tradition), the city was left in ruins; a new town called Ilion was rebuilt about 700 BC by Greek settlers but it remained quite modest until Julius Caesar (Augustus' predecessor, his great-uncle and adopted father) realised that politically and mythologically Troy was important both for him and for Rome. An understanding of mythology is necessary here. Priam (King of Troy) had many children, among them Pâris (whose Judgement and love for Helen, wife of Menelas King of Sparta, provoked the Trojan war) and Kreousa, wife of Aeneas (the son of Venus–Aphrodite). After Troy was destroyed by the Acheans (Agamemnon, Menelaus, Ulysses etc.), Aeneas fled with his son Iule. After many adventures, they arrived in Northern Italy where they laid the foundations of many cities and were the ancestors of Romulus, the founder of Rome. Julius Caesar's family claimed to be descended from Iule (hence the name Julius) and, thus, from Aeneas and Venus. As a consequence, Julius Caesar felt deeply involved in the Trojan legend and viewed the site both as a national shrine and as the root of the divine origin of his family. He therefore gave

honours to the city, independence, grants and exemption from taxes. Troy soon became a thriving business centre as the official custodian of Homer's country. Professional guides would help visitors identify all places mentioned in Homer's *Iliad*, for example the plain where the battles had taken place or the cave where Paris gave his Judgement. Tourists to Troy were at the same time visiting the site of Homer's legends, celebrating the Trojan origin of Rome and worshipping an extraordinary lineage from Venus to Augustus via Aeneas, Iule, Romulus and Julius Caesar.

- Egypt as a whole was a tourist paradise offering Romans an exotic landscape, a different way of life, unusual monuments and relatively easy travel. Main tourist attractions in Egypt included: the Lighthouse, the tomb of Alexander, the temple of Serapis, the sanctuary of Pan and the Museum (i.e. the Great Library) in Alexandria; Heliopolis (which was already in ruins; Augustus in 10 BC took two of its obelisks, which are still in Rome); Memphis (for its temple of Ptah and because it was the starting point for visits to the Pyramids); Crocodilopolis; Abydos for its famous Memnonium, the temple of the Pharao Seti; the Valley of the Kings and Thebes (which came to the forefront of Egyptian tourism in 27 BC when the statue of Memnon allegedly started to talk every morning).

Just like their camera-carrying descendents, Augustan tourists were interested in keeping pictorial mementoes of what they saw. If they were talented for sketching, they could sit down with papyrus, pen and ink or wax tablets and stylus, like 19th-century painters carrying their watercolour boxes, or they could ask a professional, quick-working miniaturist to draw their portrait with Athens' Parthenon or Delphi's Temple of Apollo as a background. In terms of souvenirs, as found in excavations and now in many museums, the amateur art lover visiting Athens could get a replica in miniature of Phidias' illustrious statue of Athena or some artefacts, paintings, glass bottles, models of statuettes in silver or just terracotta and pottery (even obscene pottery, according to Lucian, *Amores* 11). In *Acts* (19: 24–41), Saint Paul narrates that when he arrived at Ephesus, he had trouble with Demetrius, a silversmith specialising in 'silver temples of Diana' who opposed Saint Paul whose Christianity was going to ruin his business. This small-scale commercialisation is interesting in three respects. First, it illustrates in antiquity what MacCannell conceptualises as 'the spurious' as 'composed out of the information, memories, images and other representations which become detached from genuine cultural elements' (MacCannell, 1976: 147), as opposed to genuine structures 'composed of the values and material culture manifest in the "true" sights' (MacCannell, 1976: 155). Second, it confirms the well-known cultural fact that the Augustans were good semioticians, or at least that they liked deciphering signs, which here corresponds to Urry's view that 'tourism involves the collection of signs' (Urry, 1990: 3). Third, it shows that souvenirs and similar memorabilia are not at all modern inventions or signs of modernity.

Augustan Monuments and Tourist Attractions

The list of the Seven Wonders of the World (which entered the Hellenistic tradition in the third century BC) exemplifies the Augustan preference for glorious monuments rather than natural wonders. It gives a good idea of what the Ancient regarded as noteworthy: the Pyramids of Giza, the Hanging Gardens of Babylon, Phidias' statue of Zeus at Olympia, the Temple of Artemis at Ephesus, the Mausoleum at Halicarnassus, the Colossus of Rhodes, the Lighthouse at Alexandria. All of them are human built, all of them recall a glorious past and are stopping-places on the Augustan Grand Tour (except the Colossus, which had collapsed during an earthquake around 224 BC, and the Gardens of Babylon which were probably too far in the East to attract visitors from Rome).

Greek and Roman temples were a favourite type of attraction: every city had several and they drew visitors from all origins and walks of life. Initially they were not places of worship where crowds could have gathered but only represented the abode of a god through the majestic statue standing in the centre. Worship occurred outside, in front of the temple, around an altar. Augustan travellers visiting places of devotion did not have access to the back area (the inside, reserved for high priests) but could attend ceremonies such as processions, prayers and sacrifices (McKeever, 1995: 118). In *The Tourist*, MacCannell built on Goffman's structural division of front and back regions and applied this pattern to tourist places. In his continuum from front to back, Roman temples would be at stage 4 as 'a back region that is open to outsiders' (MacCannell, 1976: 101). For example, Augustans entering the temple of Ptah in Memphis surely had mixed feelings: on one hand, they could recognise familiar signs (in Hellenistic times Ptah was assimilated to the Greek god Hephaistos, thus corresponding to the Roman god Vulcan) and could take part in the ceremony but, on the other hand, the ritual remained culturally Egyptian and this distance made visitors aware that they were only visitors, tolerated outsiders.

Besides, most temples started to fulfil another cultural role to become what is nowadays called a museum: they started to contain large collections of statues, paintings, stuffed animals, artefacts or relics such as Tantalus' bones in Argos and Julius Caesar's sword in the temple of Mars in Rome. These temples were not primarily conceived as museums but, as analysed by Horne, monuments often see their function changed by tourists: just as 'the Parthenon was not built as a ruin celebrating western civilisation, Hagia Sophia was not erected to commemorate Byzantine culture [and] the Winter Palace was not built to commemorate the baroque' (Horne, 1984: 30), the Hellenistic temples were not constructed for Augustan tourists interested in the religious syncretism that gradually associated Greek, Roman and Egyptian divinities whose popular worship involved various secret rites. Is it then still appropriate to refer to those temples as tourist settings? MacCannell lists four characteristics of tourist settings: the only reason for visiting them is to see them; they are physically adjacent to serious social activity; they contain objects that have specialised use in specific, often esoteric routines; and they are open, at least during specified times, to visitation from outsiders (MacCannell, 1976: 100). Are these criteria met in the case of Augustan tourists and temples? Visitors indeed went to see them because of their beauty, fame and of the treasures they contained, and not for religious purposes; they were generally located in cities or at least in places where flows of visitors had brought about the set up of specific tourist structures; they contained objects of worship and sacrifice as a consequence of the initially religious dimension of the place, and most of them were open to the public, especially because visitors had to pay some entrance fees, either money, food or objects (Hacquard, 1952). The four criteria are met, so temples in the Ancient World can definitely be regarded as tourist settings: for Augustan tourists, temples were very much tourist places, like cathedrals or churches for today's tourists.

Staged Authenticity

Another concept developed by MacCannell and now well established in tourism studies is staged authenticity and it too proves useful to analyse Augustan tourism. One text by Strabo gives a good example of staged authenticity, in the case of performances offered by locals for tourists at Syene (Aswan) on the First Cataract on the Nile. Local boatmen would put on a special act they had prepared for visitors: working their way upstream to a point beyond the cataract, they turned around, set their craft drifting downstream and then shot the rapids (Strabo's *Geography* XVII:

817). This setting (in a theatrical sense) is a 'pseudo-event' in Boorstin's meaning: inauthenticity was flagrant, the boatmen were not in danger, they just made spectators believe they were present at a real near-disaster (Boorstin, 1962). Were the spectators fooled? Did they even care at all? Strabo unfortunately did not comment on the issue of tourists' expectations and reactions in staged situations, yet another example by the same Strabo can help us to understand the Augustans' concern for authenticity.

The talking statue of Memnon at Thebes was well known in Antiquity, with a fame comparable today to Paris' Eiffel Tower or the Sydney Opera House. Most people would have heard of it, although only a minority had really seen it, or rather heard it (in that particular instance, it was less 'the tourist gaze' that mattered than 'the tourist ear'). Strabo, who went to Thebes in 1 BC, wrote: 'An hour after sunrise, I heard the sound – whether it came from the base of the statue or was deliberately made by one of the people standing around, I cannot say for sure' (Strabo's *Geography* 17: 816). At stake were the questions of authenticity and the audience's gullibility. Strabo was distrustful and did not believe that the god's statue was really talking. He did not take part in the *communitas* of the place with the other spectators but kept a critical distance or, put another way, he did not behave like a credulous tourist but tried to understand what could be behind the strange phenomenon he was facing. By suggesting that someone by the statue could be responsible for the sounds, Strabo is no more a passive tourist but becomes analytical – in a way he is what Boorstin calls an intellectual (Boorstin, 1962). Strabo's uncertainty towards the talking statue can be regarded as the Augustan birth of a tourist consciousness, the awareness that tourism can be based on trickery and artfulness.

Augustan Destinations: Seaside Tourism

The Augustan Grand Tour was very similar to the famous English Grand Tour: 'Well-to-do youths, like Caesar and Cicero, might be found making the "Grand Tour" of Greece and Asia Minor in the same way as wealthy Englishmen of the seventeenth *[sic]* century travelling in France and Italy to finish their education' (Treble, 1930: 93). Yet just as only a few Britons went on the Grand Tour of France and Italy, in socio-economic terms the Augustan Grand Tour was mainly the privilege of two types of people: young men from good families, sent to Greece to complete their education, and citizens from the highest ranks, such as senators and equestrians. To embark on the Grand Tour, one needed time and money, yet this does not mean that the majority of Augustans did not have access to tourism pleasures. In summer the exodus from Rome was very heavy, notably because of the nerve-racking and oppressive heat there. Except in times of crisis, the senate suspended its sessions in August and households used to leave Rome for the cooler air of the seaside or the countryside.

The shoreline from Rome to Naples was comparable to the contemporary French Riviera. The most famous resorts were in the Bay of Naples, from Cumae and Cape Misenum on the west, to Sorrento peninsula just past Mount Vesuvius on the east. There, beautiful villas 'were so close to each other that the fish were feeling cramped' wrote the poet Horace humorously (*Carmen Saeculare* 3.1: 33–7). In the first century BC, the owners of these villas were the potentates of the Republic: Caesar, Lucullus, Pompey, Mark Antony (D'Arms, 1970). 'By the end of the republican era the habit of *villegiatura* had become firmly established among the wealthier Italian households' (Caspari, 1940: 160). These people spent a good part of their time visiting each other, organising sophisticated dinner parties. Riding along the shores in litters and going on excursions in oar-propelled yachts were two popular activities (Casson, 1974: 142). Less wealthy holidaymakers went to the same resorts and could enjoy themselves with other activities, some of them related to the specificities of the place (renting a boat to go fishing, shopping for souvenirs), most of them being replicas of recreation forms in Rome: baths (thanks to the hot springs along the shoreline), cultural or sporting events (Puteoli had two amphitheatres offering gladiators' fights as well as theatre plays, concerts with dancers, acrobats and jugglers), dining in restaurants, shopping or strolling at night in the illuminated streets. In Pompeii, excavation revealed that one main avenue some 500 yards long had 45 shops on either side; since each kept at least one lamp burning, there was a light every 10 yards or so (Mau, 1899). These seaside resorts reproduced the life and society of Rome in terms of social status and cultural habits: it was Rome away from Rome. Augustan tourists did not want to find themselves in a foreign, unusual, strange environment. The best example is probably Baiae. Located 10 miles west from Naples, Baiae is described by the historian Caspari as 'the queen of Italian holiday resorts' for 'fashionable society' (Caspari, 1940: 160), not only the richest Augustans but all those willing to enjoy themselves, often in a disorganised way that could only arouse moralists' wrath: 'Why must I look at drunks staggering along the shore or noisy boating parties … Who wants to listen to the squabbles of nocturnal serenaders?' complained Seneca (*Epistulae Morales* 51: 4–16). Baiae was popular for its night life where 'unmarried girls are common property, old men act like young boys and lots of young boys like young girls', wrote Varro (quoted in Nonius, *De Compendiosa Doctrina*: 153–4).

This promiscuity gave the resort its reputation of depravity, which is why the Augustan poet Propertius urged his beloved Cynthia to leave Baiae and its corruption: 'A pereant Baiae crimen amoris aquae! Perish, waters of Baiae, crime against love!' (Book 1, 11: 30).

Augustan Destinations: Green Tourism

The Augustans did not like mountain landscapes: the Alps were for them mere protuberances and obstructions to traffic, a view common until the 19th century. The only exception was Mount Etna in Sicily, which drew tourists who made the ascent partly to admire the colours of sunrise from the inn erected near the summit (Caspari, 1940: 161), and partly because of its mythological background: the giant Egkelados (enemy of the Olympians) and Typhon the monster were said to live in the volcano, where the forges of Vulcan (God of fire, Roman equivalent to Hephaistos) were installed. Once more, one can see that Augustan tourism is often linked to mythology, or a least to a mythological past: as noted by Cotterell (1980: 282): 'the Romans of the Augustan Age were a nation who lived in the past'; at a tourist level, it means that, as Dudley put it, the Romans were going 'to classical and historical sites rather than to the picturesque' (Dudley, 1975: 225).

If Augustan tourists were not attracted by the mountains, the countryside did appeal to them. The Alban and Sabine hills on the East and Southeast of Rome (around Tusculanum) were quite popular. Cicero's dialogue *Tusculanae Disputationes* is set in an elegant villa on the Alban hills, offering some appreciable coolness in summer, and on the Sabine hills was located the famous farm that Maecenas gave to Horace. Most of those country retreats were luxurious country estates (beautifully decorated inside, with mosaics, fine furniture, paintings and outside well-tended gardens, fountains, statues) but the presence of huge surrounding farms was of vital importance (McKeever, 1995: 68–71). These estates were self-sufficient (with everything from food and wine to bakeries and bathhouses) thanks to the farm and, in a way, the luxurious *villa urbana* (where the owner lived when he visited the estate) was superfluous. However, some villas were built purely as luxury retreats without working farms attached. A good example is Hadrian's villa at Tivoli, extending over 120 hectares, containing all kinds of buildings inspired by Hadrian's favourite sights from his travels around Greece and Egypt (for example the replica of Canopus, an Egyptian town, with statues along a canal, as well as theatres, temples and libraries). It is true that Hadrian's villa dates back to the early second century AD and, therefore, does not belong to the period considered in this chapter, but similar (albeit less lavish) villas existed in the Augustan Age.

Augustan Destinations: Urban Tourism

In summer, Rome was a popular destination for non-Romans. In AD 1 the city of Rome had more than one million inhabitants and its facilities were attracting tourists who in Rome certainly did as the Romans: they would go to the baths and relax, play dice or board-games, attend chariot-racing or gladiators' fights in the Colosseum, pay a visit to a Greek restaurant, a concert hall or a shopping centre with fresh slaves from Armenia or Africa. Just as Romans travelled to visit sites and monuments linked to the past (be it a mythological past such as Olympia where Zeus and Cronos fought for the conquest of power, a heroic past such as the site of the Trojan war, or a human past such as Alexandria), tourists went to Rome for the sake of heritage, for example for the fig-tree at the foot of the Palatine Hill where the cradle holding Remus and Romulus was allegedly overturned or for the shepherd's hut where the twin founders of Rome were reputedly raised. And just as Romans used to journey to Greece and Egypt to admire buildings glorifying humanity's craft and genius, tourists to Rome were interested in the new Rome and her grandiose monuments, palaces and forums (such as Caesar's Forum and Augustus' Forum). Suetonius reports that Augustus boasted that he found Rome a city of brick and left it a city of marble (August 28: 3). Last but not least and in very modern vein: Rome by night. Like Pompeii, Rome had a system of lighting in the main streets since the early third century enabling '*flâneurs*' to go strolling safely at night (Homo, 1971: 583).

Augustan Special Interest Tourism

In Augustan society, three types of special interest tourism can be identified: health tourism, oracle tourism and games tourism. Medicine was not very well developed in Augustan society and the average lifespan of Augustans was about 40 years because of epidemics of disease that had no known cure. Doctors used to prepare soothing ointments and poultices for treating sores and when they had to perform operations there were no anaesthetics, so Augustans often travelled in the hope of finding some treatment. The journey itself was sometimes considered a possible treatment: Celsus (the medical authority of the Augustan Era) wrote that 'in the case of tuberculosis, if the patient has the strength, a long sea voyage and change of air is called for… For this purpose, the voyage from Italy to Alexandria is perfect' (*Artes* 3: 22: 8). According to Badger, this voyage lasted about 10 days (Badger, 1920: 137). Those who could not afford to sail to Alexandria could visit one of the several mineral springs (Aquae, literally waters), comparable to the modern spas that often are the descendants of Roman sites: Aquae Calidae has been rebaptised Vichy; Aquae Sextiae: Aix-en-Provence; Aquae Sulis: Bath; and Aquae Mattiacae: Wiesbaden. Mourre (1986: 4546) describes this form of health tourism, whose importance the Sicilian-Greek historian Diodorus attested: 'Many people throughout Sicily who are troubled with their own peculiar ills go to Lipari and by using the baths become healthy again in incredible fashion' (*Bibliotheke Historike* 5: 10).

When Augustans had a problem or a question, they used to consult oracles (which is linked to the fact that the Augustan society was marked by widespread superstition (McKeever, 1995: 118)). Apollo was the fortune-telling god par excellence; Romans would not hesitate to travel far away to consult one of his oracles, for example at Delphi (Greece), Delos (Aegean Sea) or Claros (Asia Minor). Other highly reputed oracles were Trophonius' near Lebadea in Greece, the temple of Fortuna at Praeneste near Rome and the diverse oracles of Heracles in Greece, all established in remote times (Casson, 1974). Health and religion were combined in the case of visits to Asclepius' sanctuaries. Asclepius was the Greek god of medicine, son of Apollo, whose cult arrived in Rome in the third century BC. In the Augustan Age, his three main sanctuaries were Epidauros in Greece (where the god was born), the Greek island of Cos (home of Hippocrates and his school of medicine) and Pergamon in Asia Minor (where the famous physician Galen practised). The procedure was very ritualised: the patient entered the sanctuary, took a bath to get purified, entered the god's temple, prayed, spread a pallet and laid down to spend the night there. While asleep they would wait for the god to visit them, and either be advised on what treatment to take, or be magically cured (Edelstein & Edelstein, 1945: 240). On the walls of the dormitory were plaques inscribed with testimonials to the god's effectiveness. Pausanias described that 'on these plaques are engraved the names of men and women who have been healed by Asclepius, together with the disease from which each suffered, and the manner of the cure' (*Periegesis Hellados* 2.27.3). The belief that Asclepius would be benevolent enough to cure those who visited his sanctuary shows how tourism was linked to religion and health; this mix of health tourism and religious tourism illustrates how human structures (the dormitory, the management of thousands of visitors) had to adapt to collective faith in a way quite comparable to Lourdes today, yet it is not appropriate to design visits to Asclepius' sanctuaries as pilgrimage because visitors were never part of a collective movement but kept their individuality (as opposed to religious ceremonies when 'conventional social ties are suspended, an intensive bonding *communitas* is experienced' (Urry, 1990: 10)).

Sports tourism, travelling to attend games, was quite common in Augustan society. Augustans enjoyed many forms of games such as athletics (the traditional Greek games: the Olympics in honour of Zeus, the Pythian Games for Apollo or the Isthmian Games for Poseidon) or more recent innovations, those organised by emperors for public entertainment featuring chariot racing, boxing, theatrical performances and gladiators' fights (Fredouille, 1992: 105). McKeever compared Roman supporters' fervour with 'the fervour of today's football fans' (McKeever, 1995: 104). The Romans too wanted good spectacles and their emperors had huge stadia built for them: the Colisseum (capacity 50,000) and the Circus Maximus (250,000, much more than any existing stadium). In chariot-racing, collisions were particularly appreciated (dramatic confusions of wheels and broken limbs). Gladiators' games were very popular, when gladiators fought each other (or wild animals) to the death: blood, representations of cruelty and violence, somehow reminiscent of the *clou du spectacle* of Sparta's yearly festival in honour of Artemis – the whipping of young Spartan boys, a spectacle all the more sadistic since some boys died under the lash. Many sources mentioned these games and Philostratus (*Life of Apollonius* 6: 20), Plutarch (*Lycurgus* 18.1) and Cicero (*Tusc. Dip.* 2: 34), offer evidence that some writers felt that there was something peculiar in tourists' enthusiasm for this type of entertainment.

Tourism as Interpretation: Augustan Tourist Guides

Guide-books existed in the Augustan Age (a very popular one was Pausanias' *Guidebook of Greece*) but most of them were preparatory readings. Books were then handwritten on thick papyrus or leather sheets, thus quite heavy to carry. In the absence of handy guide-books, Augustan tourists would hire guides. Finding a guide seemed very easy: 'I was going around the colonnades, in the sanctuary of Dionysus', said a character in one of Lucian's satirical sketches, 'examining each one of the paintings, and right away two or three people ran up to tell me about them for a small fee' (Lucian, *Amores* 8). Tourists merely had to wait for potential guides to offer them their services. Augustan satirists featured guides who were not much appreciated, as shown by this prayer: 'Zeus, protect me from your guides at Olympia, and you, Athena, from yours at Athens' (Varro as quoted by Nonius, 419: 4). Augustan guides shared with some modern ones the inability to stop talking once launched on a subject: about a group visiting Delphi, Plutarch wrote that 'the guides went through their standard speech, paying no attention whatsoever to our entreaties to cut the talk short and leave out most of the explanations on the inscriptions and epitaphs' (*Moralia* 395a). The Greek Plutarch (46–120) lived just after the Augustan period, yet his comments on travel and tourism are very valuable: in the same text, about a Greek traveller he met in Delphi, Cleombrotus of Sparta, he wrote that this man had been 'wandering about Egypt and around the country of the Troglodytes' and had sailed 'far down the Red Sea, not for trade but because he loved seeing things and learning about them': the perfect example of a tourist.

Guides also had an important function as culture brokers. Augustan tourism was not really cross-cultural tourism (that would require from guides that they translate aspects of a culture for those from a different culture): it took place within a generic frame of cultural reference, the Roman-Hellenistic world. To develop further an example mentioned earlier, Augustans visiting the temple of Ptah in Memphis could understand several things (because Ptah was assimilated to Hephaistos and Vulcan) but some aspects were foreign to them (for example hieroglyphs). For this reason, they needed guides not as mentors (because the spiritual dimension was not the key issue) but as information-givers. The important distinction made by Cohen (1985: 5–29) between information and interpretation is relevant here: the communicative role of Augustan tourist guides did not involve interpretation but only explanation in a narrative way, mainly reciting mythological stories: 'Abolish fabulous tales from Greece, and the guides there would all die of starvation' (Lucian *Philopseudes* 4). Pausanias (2: 23: 5–6) indeed confirms that Augustan guides were primarily story-tellers: 'the guides at Argos know very well that not all the stories they tell are true, but they tell them anyway'. Questions of authenticity and gullibility are raised here again. Did Augustan tourists believe all the stories they were told? Did they believe that they were shown the cave where Zeus was born (in Crete), for example? Pliny often used a character called Caius Licinius Mucianus, a gullible sightseer who believed everything the guides told him: a spring that could flow with wine or a special elephant that had learned to speak and write Greek, which proves that, at times, the guides' words became more important than the sites themselves or, as Horne put it: 'What matters is what [visitors] are told they are seeing. The fame of the object becomes its meaning' (Horne, 1984: 10).

The Augustan Tourist Gaze

The Augustan tourist gaze, to use Urry's famous phrase, was a gaze of curiosity – as were probably all tourist gazes. Urry wrote that '[W]hen we go away we look at the environment with interest and curiosity' but surely all Ancient authors could have written the same. Although the Roman mind was deeply concerned about moral seriousness and respect for the past and its tradition, its curiosity had few limits, hence all the expeditions launched towards and over the empire's borders to discover the unknown (Cotterell, 1980: 283). In the same way, tourists and travellers were always willing to be initiated into new cults, which in our context would mean that all visitors to Bangkok would be Buddhists when they came home. The Augustan tourist gaze is curious towards what is far, not near, as illustrated by Pliny (*Epistulae* 8: 20: 1–2) who wrote in the late first century AD:

> We travel long roads and cross the water to see what we disregard when it is under our eyes… There are a number of things in this city of ours and its environs which we have not even heard of, much less seen ; yet, if they were in Greece or Egypt or Asia, we would have heard all about them, read all about them, looked over all there was to see.

Travelling was motivated by the desire to know more about remote and different things, no matter how interesting one's own neighbourhood might be. Another modern comparison is possible here, as the Augustans were like the New Yorker who has ascended the Eiffel Tower twice but will never visit the Statue of Liberty. The Augustan tourist gaze paid attention only to objects considered worthwhile: it was a selective, intellectual gaze that expected some quality from the objects gazed at. Travel in search of such satisfactions necessitated an adequate transport system.

Transportation Issues

The famous network of Roman roads was first developed for military purposes (the army built roads as they conquered new lands, then they were used for trade and tourism as well (McKeever, 1995: 90)). 'To manage their empire, the Romans built a magnificent network of roads, on which they could travel as much as 100 miles a day using relays of horses furnished from rest posts five or six miles apart' (McIntosh & Goeldner, 1995: 24). This is comparable to the fact that in the USA 'the national system of interstate highways … and the jet airline have both been tremendous boons to tourism, yet neither was developed expressly for that purpose' (McIntosh & Goeldner, 1995: 24), as another example of applying military technology to civilian use as a feature of modernity. Romans were very proud of their roads, even if they were not as safe as they were admirable. In one elegy (3, 16), the poet Propertius relates how at midnight he once received a note from his beloved Cynthia who was sending for him, yet he hesitated, arguing that travelling at night could be dangerous (because of bandits and highwaymen), before he romantically realised that for lovers all roads would be safe at any time.

Voyaging was not much safer because the sea had its dangers as well. In the Augustan age there were no longer any pirates since Pompeius Magnus defeated them in 62 BC, but tempests and shipwrecks were unavoidable. Augustan literature has numerous pieces proving that the Romans were afraid of water and rather nervous when it came to sea voyages. Propertius wrote several poems about shipwrecks, for example the elegies 2, 26 or 3, 7 about his friend Petrus who disappeared in a tempest at sea on his way to Pharos: the poet developed the idea that sailing off means heading for one's death, voyages being evil inventions. In the same way, it is significant that Virgil's *Aeneid* began with the long, colourful description of a tempest. Yet despite these dangers and the logical apprehensions, travel and tourism were very popular in the Augustan society, in two ways. First, they concerned most people and not only an elite. Urry rightly wrote that 'in Imperial Rome a fairly extensive pattern of travel for pleasure and culture existed for the elite' (Urry, 1990: 4), yet if the Augustan Grand Tour was reserved to a minority, a large number of Romans went on holidays in summer. No statistics are available and quantifying this phenomenon is difficult but the phrase 'mass tourism' may not be entirely inappropriate. Second, travel and tourism were very much enjoyed and appreciated and, as such, appear as an important cultural feature of the Augustan society, rather neglected by most authors, if not all.

Conclusion: The Modernity of Augustan Tourism

This chapter has outlined numerous similarities between Augustan tourists and contemporary tourists, from their gaze and motivations to their concern for safety and entertainment. Yet the modernity of Augustan tourism goes beyond that, reaching a structural level in the relationship between Augustan tourism and Augustan society. The Augustan case study shows that tourism provides solid information and evidence on a society's level of sophistication, notably in terms of time management and social organisation. Tourism could grow in Augustan society because its social system was organised in order to make Roman citizens' time as free as possible, most productive activities (except law and politics) being assigned to slaves, freedmen or colonised peoples. *Otium* became the mission statement of a society of leisure: 'Under the Empire, the Roman population is busy with only two things: eating and having fun', and it is interesting to see that the more *otium*-oriented the Augustan society got, the more it became a society of leisure (where tourism became more developed) (Hacquard, 1952: 156). The modernity of Augustan tourism is reflected in the way in which the development of tourism depends on social structures. In Roman times indeed, tourism reflected society as a whole: the emergence of tourism in the last part of the Republic corresponded to cultural progress (as reflected in literature and the arts in general), the climax of tourism with its numerous forms and its popularity in the Augustan age corresponded to the acme of Latin culture, while 'the decline of the empire was accompanied by the decline of tourism. The wealthy class was greatly reduced, roads deteriorated and the countryside became overrun with bandits, thieves and scoundrels, making travel unsafe' (McIntosh & Goeldner, 1995: 24). Literature abounds on the combined reasons for the Roman decadence and the fall of the empire but it is certain that the overwhelming importance of *otium* and pleasure were significant factors, which is interesting for the present analysis since *otium* and pleasure were the dynamics of Augustan tourism. It would then be interesting to examine if this life-cycle is only typical of the Augustan society or could also be identified, for example, in the brilliant Maya civilisation of the eighth and ninth centuries or in the prosperous era of Edo in Japan (1615–1868). This could be the subject of similar case studies, further testing this model of a dialogical parallel between a society's development and the development of travel and tourism within it.

References

Latin authors do not appear in the bibliography: mentioning page or year of publication would not be useful; the exact localisation of the text (e.g. Propertius 1, 11, 30: book 1, piece 11, line 30) makes it possible to find the quoted passage in any version.

Badger, R.G. (1920) *Travel Among the Ancient Romans*. Boston: The Gorham Press.

Boorstin, D.J. (1962) *The Image*. London: Weidenfeld & Nicolson.

Bosi, R. (1979) *Le Grand Livre de l'Archéologie*. Paris: Editions des Deux Coqs d'Or.

Braund, D.C. (1985) *Augustus to Nero: A Source Book on Roman History 31 BC–AD 68*. London: Croom Helm.

Cary, Max (1940) *Life and Thought in Greek and Roman World*, London: Methuen.

Cambridge Ancient History (1996) *Volume X 'The Augustan Empire'*. Cambridge: Cambridge University Press.

Caspari M.O.B. (1940) *Life and Thought in the Greek and Roman World*. London: Methuen.

Casson, L. (1974) *Travel in the Ancient World*. London: Allen & Unwin.
Cohen, E. (1985) The tourist guide. *Annals of Tourism Research* 12, 5–29.
Cotterell, A. (ed.) (1980) *The Penguin Encyclopaedia of Ancient Civilisations*. London: Penguin.
Daremberg, C. and Saglio, E. (1899) *Dictionnaire des Antiquités Grecques et Romaines*. Paris: Hachette.
D'Arms, J. (1970) *Romans on the Bay of Naples*. Cambridge, MA: Harvard University Press.
Dudley, D.R. (1975) *Roman Society*. London: Penguin.
Edelstein, E. and L. (1945) *Asclepius: Collection and Interpretation of the Testimonies*. Baltimore, MD: Johns Hopkins University Press.
Ehrenberg, V. (1976) *Documents Illustrating the Reigns of Augustus and Tiberius*. Oxford: Clarendon Press.
Frebaugh, W.C. (1923) *The Inns of Greece and Rome and a History of Hospitality from the Dawn of Time to the Middle Ages*. Chicago: F.M. Morris.
Fredouille, J.C. (1992) *Dictionnaire de la Civilisation Romaine*. Paris: Larousse.
Hacquard, G. (1952) *Guide Romain Antique*. Paris: Hachette.
Hammond, N.G.L. and Scullard, H.H. (1970) *Oxford Classical Dictionary*. Oxford: Clarendon Press.
Homo, L. (1971) *Rome Impériale et l'Urbanisme dans l'Antiquité*. Paris: L'Evolution de l'Humanité.
Hopkins, K. (1978) *Conquerors and Slaves*. Cambridge: Cambridge University Press.
Horne, D. (1984) *The Great Museum*. London: Pluto.
MacCannell, D. (1976) *The Tourist*. London: Macmillan.
Mau, A. (1899) *Pompeii, its Life and Art*. New York: Macmillan.
McIntosh, Robert W. and Goeldner, Charles R. (1995) *Tourism: Principles, Practices, Philosophies* (9th edn). Chichester: John Wiley & Sons.
McKeever, S. (1995) *Ancient Rome*. London: Dorling Kindersley.
Mourre, M. (1986) *Dictionnaire Encyclopédique d'Histoire*. Paris: Bordas.
Oxford Latin Dictionary (1968) Oxford: Clarendon Press.
Tucker, T.G. (1910) *Life in the Roman World of Nero and St Paul*. London: Macmillan.
Treble, H.A. (1930) *Everyday Life in Rome in the Time of Caesar and Cicero*. Oxford: Clarendon Press.
Urry, J. (1990) *The Tourist Gaze*. London: Sage.
Van den Berge, P. (1994) *The Quest for the Other*. Seattle: University of Washington.

Chapter 5

A Century of Tourism in Northern Spain: The Development of High-quality Provision between 1815 and 1914

CARLOS LARRINAGA

Introduction

To draw a better-defined picture of the phenomenon of tourism in south-western France, Michel Chadefaud established a model for analysis that may be useful to us as a general starting point for the study of the phenomenon of tourism in northern Spain in our period (Chadefaud, 1987: 16–20). According to Chadefaud, in industrial societies there is a twofold division between '*predominant* social class groups' and '*dominated* social class groups' (emphases in original). This means that the principal ideas and beliefs of these societies derive from the social group associated with the classes that control powers that are, for example, economic, religious or juridical in nature. This 'dominant ideology' impregnates all activities and human behaviour both in and out of the work period (for a critical analysis of this Gramscian concept, see Abercrombie *et al.*, 1980, 1990). Activities such as stays at spas, sea bathing and, later, sunbathing were articulated by these predominant classes.

This social demand, made up of needs in which objective and subjective elements mingle, is channelled by way of perceptions composed of images, speeches, etc. or in what in Chadefaud's language is referred to as 'performances'. If they are lasting, these elite performances may acquire the strength of a myth that serves as a reference or model for the *dominated* classes. Nevertheless, this is not a myth in the sense of a belief based on ignorance or credulity but in terms of language, word, communication system or message. Insofar as they maintain their power, such myths closely maintain the performances that feed a growing social need. In this way, we reach the concept of the 'product', which is easy to define for present purposes because it is articulated on three elements: lodging, transport and leisure.

Once this point has been made, we need to understand the relationship between the two terms of the binomial, *myths–products*. Taking the approach of 18th and 19th century idealists and leaving Marxist materialist analysis to one side, Chadefaud does not grant 'economic structure' an exclusive role in the appearance of these types of products. On the contrary, he intentionally places 'ideological structure' at the head of his reasoning because, as he says, 'manufactured' goods are not converted into 'products' if they do not correspond to the will to consume them and if they are not compatible with deeply rooted expectations: in other words, if social demand is lacking.

According to this author, the links between 'tourist products' and 'myths' are therefore marked by oscillation and interaction between them. He thus suggests the hypothesis that these 'myths' may have exerted an influence on both the definition and the very development of tourist products. The impact of a product on space gives rise to what he calls 'space production'. When speaking of 'stereotyped space', he suggests the hypothesis that a tourist space represents the projection into space and time of the ideals and myths of the wider society. In this way, one effect of the tourism function may be to bestow a privileged economic situation upon a given space.

To this hypothesis scheme, as he himself refers to it, Chadefaud adds the diachronic dimension, that of time, and, as such, defines three major periods (Chadefaud, 1987: 20–1):

(1) the product creation phase: the initial period in which the first elements of the 'myth–product' binomial are located in space. An immaterial offer is generated by way of mental representations aimed at potential clients. This encourages the creation of material provision (lodging, equipment, etc.).
(2) The product maturation process, characterised by the product expansion and elaboration stages. This maturation period is defined by the accumulation of investment that develops the offer of lodging, transport and leisure.
(3) The product's obsolescence period: different alterations (other myths, change in needs, competence, etc.) generate incompatibility between the demand and the offer. This leads to the third phase, which is characterised by the phasing out of the product and its material space.

(This is a similar concept to the resort product cycle: [Agarwal, 2002].)

Taking this analytical scheme as a basis, we intend to study the configuration of the tourist space associated with the northernmost provinces of Spain. Specifically, we aim to study the way in which provision of high-quality for tourists was created on the Bay of Biscay coast and, indeed, how it became the most important tourist area of its kind in Spain in the second half of the 19th century.

The Birth of the Myth

One of the most important features of the north of Spain, especially the regions of Cantabria, the Basque Country and Navarre – the three territories we have selected in this study – is the abundance of water. In contrast with the interior of Spain, where rainfall is scantier, the Bay of Biscay coastline and part of Navarre have an Atlantic climate with plenty of rainfall. This factor, along with these provinces' mountainous terrain, makes for a landscape that is different from that of the *meseta* or central plateau, which is flatter and much less humid.

Furthermore, Cantabria and the Basque Country are coastal areas beside the Atlantic Ocean and have plenty of beaches. Although Navarre is not on the coast and lies at the foot of the Pyrenees, it has one thing in common with the other two regions: an abundance of spas. The coastal Basque provinces of Guipúzcoa and Vizcaya are also the provinces of Spain that have most mineral water springs. Alava, Navarre and Cantabria also have well above the Spanish average (Anuario Oficial, 1877: 258, 1890: 588).

There are two elements – beaches and thermal waters – that can play an important role in the birth of particular myths. Although some Spanish spas certainly started up at the end of the 18th century, the truth is that most of them were put into use in the 19th century, when sea-bathing also began to develop in Spain.

Water treatments for ailments and illnesses had been widely practised since the days of antiquity. Basically, two forms of classical application are involved: hydrotherapy and the use of water as the direct conveyor of heat, cold and other intermediary temperatures by way of its application in the form of baths, showers, hosing, percussion etc.; and hydrology, which is the study of the composition of mineral waters which are supposed to have substances which have beneficial effects on the body.

It was not until the 18th century that hydrotherapy was studied in a scientific way as another field of medicine. The critical, reforming, lay and rationalist spirit of the Enlightenment doubtlessly made a major contribution to this. As Alain Corbin has pointed out, natural theology must have had a major role in leading Nature and the sea to be seen in quite a different way (Corbin, 1988: chap. 2). In the light of predominant rationalist thought, many intellectuals and medical practitioners were attracted to the natural sciences and published many treatises on the beneficial effects of both mineral and sea waters.

In this way, confidence in the curative properties of water spread throughout Europe in the first half of the 19th century. Alongside this process, the hygienist paradigm grew in importance. One must not overlook the fact that hygienism was a tendency developed by different doctors from the end of the 18th century. It consisted of pointing out the great influence exerted by social and environmental surroundings on the genesis and evolution of illnesses. In the case of medicine, hygienists turned their attention to the natural environment and its possible connection with the pathological problems of the individual. Hence, the importance granted to particular geographical conditions (mountains, sea, etc.) and the curative power of water.

In the mid-19th century decades, this hygienist paradigm was in full swing. Medical topographies contributed greatly to its success. Although it is true to say that these works had a limited readership, they exerted a considerable influence on the privileged classes of Spanish society, who were the first to come to enjoy the waters. In this sense, the north of the peninsula had exceptional qualities. The lush vegetation, green fields, mountains, plentiful beaches, mild and even cool temperatures, the sea breezes and the abundance of thermal springs were all elements that could not go unnoticed in the hey-day of hygienism. We are, therefore, in the first phase defined by Chadefaud, in which myths are created (Gil y Fresno, 1879, is a clear example). There are myths involving the curative properties of water, both thermal and marine, and involving the Atlantic climate itself, in comparison with the continental climate (which is more extreme in temperature range and less rainy). These elements soon became representations that took on the strength of a myth.

The evoked representations correspond to the attribution of the senses, with the period's mass media (travel books, guide-books, doctors' writings, iconography, etc.) together with certain characters, playing a key role in its propagation. All these publications, along with a particular line in regional literature (for example, José María Pereda or Amós de Escalante in Cantabria), became excellent propagation agents for this region's tourist image, which was also strengthened by visits from members of the royal family and the high aristocracy.

The large number of mineral springs in the north of Spain formed the basis for a boom in spa-building, which began in the early 19th century.

On this question, and with reference to Guipúzcoa, Urquía has suggested three reasons to explain the boom in water therapy at this time:

(1) breakthroughs in chemical investigation that allowed for a better knowledge concerning the composition of medicinal waters;
(2) the lack of effective curative resources for certain ailments, especially chronic ones; and
(3) fashion imposed by the aristocracy. (Urquía, 1992: 180–1)

To these reasons, one must also add improvements in transport, an increase in the standard of living and the progressive secularisation of Spanish society. In the case of Cantabria, there has also been a tendency to point to the economic crisis that this region had been suffering since the 1860s, when the colonial trade in flour – the local bourgeoisie's principal business until then – started to decline. Tourism was then to be seen as a new source of wealth in which to invest (Hoyo, 1993; Ortega Valcárcel, 1986; Martínez Vara, 1983; San Pedro, 1993).

From the beginning of the 19th century, we know that the first bathers were using new infrastructures in spas on the north coast, such as Cestona in Guipúzcoa, Molinar de Carranza in Vizcaya and Puente Viesgo in Cantabria. In the mid-19th century, Francisco de Paula Madrazo bore witness (in his book *Una espedición á Guipúzcoa en el verano de 1848*) to the places in Guipúzcoa that were then starting to receive visitors. He not only refers to spas (Arechavaleta's Baños Viejos, Santa Agueda in Mondragón and Cestona) but also to coastal towns such as Deva and San Sebastián. (Madrazo, 1849). According to Madrazo, the spas of the Basque provinces were the best 'in that movement of progress and perfection' in Spain, even managing to 'stand comparison with the best abroad' (Madrazo, 1849: 13).

As regards seaside tourism, it was not until the 1820s and 1830s that the first bathers, especially from Madrid, visited the northern coast. The beaches of Abra in Vizcaya, and those in Guipúzcoa, or even in Santander, were soon to become the favourite spots for these new summer tourists. In all these cases, it was even possible to combine spa water bathing with sea-water bathing on the beaches, given the proximity of the sites where they could be practised.

In any case, an evolution can be seen in the therapeutics of sea bathing. Two distinct periods may be defined. In the first, the system was very similar to that practised in spas insofar as sea water, either cold or heated, was poured into bathtubs in which clients bathed. At a later stage, bathing was practised directly in the sea. To this end, a whole series of infrastructures were elaborated. Likewise, dates for the beginning and end of the season were scrupulously established, as were the lengths of each immersion in the sea and the overall number of immersions, the most suitable bathing times, precautions on entering and leaving the water and the best diet for bathers.

By the 1820s, San Sebastián must have already become the favourite bathing station for Madrid society. In this sense, Rafael Aguirre refers to two contemporary texts. The first is by Samuel Edward Cook, who wrote in 1831 that in summer San Sebastián was a very popular city for bathing on the fine sands of the beach, for which purpose many families came from Madrid (*Handbook*). The second is by Henry Wilkinson who pointed out in 1838 that before the civil war San Sebastián was a fashionable spa visited by the Royal family (*Sketches of Scenery in the Basque Provinces of Spain)* (Aguirre, 1995: 88–9).

Improvements in the road network and in the means of transport themselves between the mid-18th and mid-19th century must have contributed to increasing the number of travellers heading from Madrid to the north coast, especially San Sebastián. Among these, the royal family itself stands out. Their presence also led to the promotion of these regions as health havens, thanks largely to their waters and the characteristics of their climate. Prince Francisco de Paula Antonio, the brother of Fernando VII, is known to have bathed on San Sebastián's Concha beach in 1830 and 1833. Queen Isabel II did the same in 1854 and 1865. In 1859, the Emperor and Empress of France, Napoleon III and Eugenia de Montijo visited San Sebastián from their summer home in Biarritz. Isabel II, Francisco de Asís and their children visited the Santander beaches in 1861.

To sum up, one may say that, in the mid-19th century, when the hygienist paradigm was in its hey-day in Spain, a myth had been evolving on the north coast, encouraging the development of a system of communication based on representations capable of attracting increasing demand. Logically, this demanded new investment and infrastructures. It was a question of creating a new tourist product based on a particular market. To adopt Chadefaud's terminology, there was a progression from mere mental representations to a tangible material offer.

Spas and Seaside Resorts in the North of Spain

We have already pointed out that both the Basque Country and Cantabria had a marine coastline as well as numerous mineral water springs, a factor that contributed to diversify their offerings since marine and mineral waters could be enjoyed in both regions. We have seen that this area of northern Spain had abundant mineral waters, Guipúzcoa and Vizcaya being the most favoured provinces. Obviously, this does not mean that all were in use or exploited for therapeutic ends, although many of them were. We may take 1877 and 1889 as reference years because very complete and useful mineral water guide-books – *Anuarios de las aguas minerales de España* – were published then. According to the data supplied by these guides, there were 143 spas in 1877, of which 32 were to be found in our study zone, that is to say, Cantabria, the Basque Country and Navarre. Ontaneda and Alceda, in Cantabria, are considered as a single spa although they really count as *two* neighbouring establishments. This figure stands for 23.4% of the overall total. It is nonetheless interesting to point out that for a surface area of 23,000 km^2 in these provinces, 32 spas implies one for every 718 km^2. In contrast, in Continental Spain's 500,000 km^2 (excluding offshore islands) the 143 thermal sites means one per 3496 km^2. The difference is striking and enables us to speak of an important concentration of spas in this area.

By 1889, however, the number of spas in Spain had increased – there were now 188 – of which 45 were situated in our study area. In this figure we include Corconte, a spa within the administrative limits of the province of Burgos but closely linked to the economy of Cantabria. This gives us a proportion of 23.9% of the overall total. Thus, at the closing stages of the 19th century, almost one-quarter of all Spanish spas were to be found in these three provinces. This gives us an idea of their importance in relation to the limited surface area they occupy (Larrinaga, 2003).

It was on this very north coast that the principal sea-bathing sites of Spain were developed. In this sense, the case of San Sebastián is especially significant. In general, if we stick to the chronology given by Walton and Smith, sea bathing in this city was quite a late phenomenon in relation to other countries in Western Europe. Indeed, these authors speak of almost a century's delay with regard to England, about 50 years in comparison with France (Boulogne) and somewhat less with regard to Belgium (Ostende). However, the difference would be even smaller in comparison with Holland and Germany (Walton & Smith, 1996: 36).

Apart from San Sebastián, other maritime tourism sites slowly became more important, especially Santander. The presence of different members of the royal family and the Madrid- and Castile-based aristocracy converted it into the other major tourist centre on the Biscay coast. Sea-bathing also began to spread in Vizcaya from the 1860s. As a result of the economic growth of Bilbao, an increase in tourism was to be seen on the beaches beside Las Arenas, Algorta and Portugalete.

Some sites close to Bilbao, however, were to end up becoming victims of industrial and urban development. This was to be the case of Portugalete where the beach eventually disappeared at the beginning of the 20th century as a result of the construction of the coast road to Santurce. On the right-hand side of the estuary, however, several interesting tourist sites sprang up in the last third of the 19th century. These were sites near Bilbao's industrial area but they had much lower population densities and a higher standard of living and landscape quality. The birth of these centres was directly due to hygienist theories that were popular at the time. Las Arenas was largely converted into a district for Bilbao's high society rather than a tourist resort in the accepted sense of the word. The same occurred at Neguri and Guecho. Algorta, however, ended up as a resort for day-trippers from Bilbao (Beascoechea, 2002; Walton & Smith, 1996: 40). In addition, the fact that the industrialisation process was basically centred on the Bilbao's Nervion estuary meant that little by little, other towns on the coast of Vizcaya were also promoted. This was the case with Plencia, Górliz, Baquio, Mundaca, Pedernales and Ondárroa.

As happened in Vizcaya, tourist resorts of lesser importance also sprang up along the coasts of Cantabria and Guipúzcoa. In this province, sea-bathing in Deva and Zumaya was closely linked to the spas of Cestona and Alzola. Closer to San Sebastián, Zarauz had begun to receive its first bathers at the beginning of the 19th century. Particularly significant in this sense was the presence here of the important progressive politician Pascual Madoz in 1846, as well as that of Queen Isabel II in 1854 and 1865. As Walton & Smith (1996: 53) put it:

> By 1914, indeed, a seaside resort system or holiday region was emerging in earnest around San Sebastián, with a variety of smaller resorts in easy reach of the provincial capital for entertainments and festivities, while they in turn provided attractive days or afternoons out for San Sebastián's visitors.

The Cantabrian and Basque Provinces as a Tourist Product

In the light of what has been said, these northern provinces clearly had the necessary elements for their configuration as a tourist product. The existence of thermal and maritime waters and the climate, which was considered benign by the hygienists of the period, all favoured, as we have seen, the creation of a series of myths that, from the mid-19th century onwards, led to the appearance of a tourist product as such. As Chadefaud suggests, it found physical expression in terms of lodging, transport and leisure.

The *Anuarios* of 1877 and 1889 allow us to classify spa accommodation into the following categories: very good, good, average or middling, bad, very bad or awful, undefined, unregistered and closed. Of the 32 spas that existed in 1877, only one, Urberuaga de Ubilla (Vizcaya) had 'very good' installations. Along with La Puda in Barcelona, it was said to be the best spa in Spain in that year. A further 12 had good infrastructures and 11 were average. One cannot be classified along the lines suggested by the *Anuario* because full data are lacking. In the remainder, resources were bad or very bad. This gives us the following balance: of 32 establishments, 12 had good installations, that is to say 37.5%, in comparison with the figure of 20% for the whole of Spain.

In 1889, of the 45 spas on record, seven had very good, 22 good and eight average installations. As may be noted, improvements were significant since almost 65% of the spas in these provinces had good infrastructures whereas in Spain taken as a whole, only 34% had the same condition. It is thus the case that, in general, Spanish spas improved their hydrotherapeutic resources towards the end of the 19th century. But it was in Cantabria, the Basque Country and Navarre that this phenomenon took on greater proportions, even though the latter two regions had been severely affected by the Second Carlist War in the mid-1870s, a factor that contributed to the absence of clients as well as to a temporary deterioration of their installations, as at (most obviously) the Santa Filomena de Gomillaz spa in Alava.

Investment in these spas must exclusively be put down to their private owners. Only the Barambio spa, in Alava, belonged to the municipality of Lezama but its conditions were so deplorable that it had to be closed to the public. In the majority of cases, it was the individuals or family owners that carried out improvements on the establishments. It is significant that very few companies took over these kinds of centres, which continued to be basically family-run businesses. Not until 1899 do we note the existence of five societies and four investment groups whose memberships seem to extend beyond immediate family members.

These investment and improvement operations were not confined only to the spa installations themselves, most of which had lodging facilities. As time went on, especially at the turn of the century, other hotel infrastructures were built in the vicinity of the spas. It was initially very common practice to take lodging in the spa itself, if rooms were available, or in private homes, inns or hostels nearby. Subsequently, however, the number of hotels grew in answer not only to increased demand but also as a result of general economic growth. This seems to be true of Cantabria, where the capital that the bourgeoisie invested in leisure activities transformed the spa world (Luis Gómez *et al.*, 1989: 93). In this sense, the inauguration of the *Gran Hotel* (or principal hotel) called for large-scale investment. In some cases, the construction of hotels was carried out simultaneously or shortly after the development of the spa, as occurred at Otaneda, Alceda and La Hermida, all three of which are in Cantabria. In the remaining spas of this province, the *Gran Hotel* was to be built at a later stage.

Nonetheless, investment was not only concentrated on the *Gran Hotel*. Other more modest, lower quality hotels were also built for less privileged social groups. This process added to the increased social hierarchisation that had marked the spas from the outset. In any case, these cheaper hotels enabled a diversification of provision to take place. An important portion of the middle classes still went to spas at the outset of the 20th century, albeit for reasons of health rather than for leisure purposes (Luis Gómez *et al.*, 1989: 91–107; San Pedro, 1993: 89–95).

Obviously, hotel provision was not centred only on the spas themselves. Fashionable coastal sites also drew this kind of investment in infrastructures. In this sense, San Sebastián and Santander stand out, being the two most important sea-bathing city resorts in Spain.

By the mid-1860s, San Sebastián had become the most important tourist centre in Spain (Larrinaga, 1999: chap. 6; and for an introduction in English, Walton, 2002). With the construction of the old city's new extension (*Ensanche* district), modern luxury buildings were built, some of which were to be hotels that came to satisfy an increasingly demanding clientele. Some of these new establishments may be put down to the initiative of old San Sebastián hotel proprietors who had sold their premises in the old part to set up new establishments in the *Ensanche*. This was to be the case, for example, of the Hotel Ezcurra (1870) or the Hotel Bermejo (1884). However, the most luxurious and elegant ones were initiated by French capital (Hotel de Inglaterra in 1881 and Hotel Continental in 1884). Alongside these new hotels, and others created in this period, many bed-and-breakfasts and hostels, mostly in the old part of San Sebastián, continued to exist. These provided more modest accommodation for less privileged social classes. As from the end of the 1870s, elite tourism coming to San Sebastián opted for the new hotels of the *Ensanche*. They were more comfortable, modern and expensive (Luengo, 2000: 71).

Of all these establishments, the most important was undoubtedly to be the Hotel María Cristina, a luxury hotel constructed for the company 'Fomento de San Sebastián'. It did not open until 1912. That very year, that same company inaugurated the Victoria Eugenia Theatre. They were two emblematic buildings set beside the River Urumea, in San Sebastián's *Ensanche* area, both of them designed to cater for high-quality tourism. The María Cristina Hotel represented in San Sebastián what the Hotel Real (1916) was for Santander or the *Gran Hotel* for each of the spas (Garate & Martín Rudi, 1995: 137–9; Larrinaga, 1999: 588–9; Rodríguez Sorondo, 1985: 159ff.).

In Santander, the principal area for expansion and tourist development was the Sardinero beach area. As early as 1849, when cholera threatened the spas of Europe and Guipúzcoa, 3000 people went to the capital of Cantabria for their sea-bathing (Sazatornil, 1994: 32). It was then that the first 'fonda' (boarding-house) was built in the area. From then on, the number of visitors increased, especially after 1861, when the royal family stayed at El Sardinero for four weeks. Three years later, a new road joined the city with El Sardinero, the Paseo Menéndez Pelayo and many small hotels and hostels were springing up along it to cater for bathers. This initial impulse was consolidated in 1868 when the brothers Arturo and César Pombo were granted the right to exploit the bathing facilities on El Sardinero's first beach. Their father, Juan Pombo, was also to start the works on the Gran Hotel, later renamed Hotel Sardinero, and shortly after, in 1870, he built the area's first casino (Ortega Valcárcel, 1986).

During the Second Carlist War (1872–76), which was fought mainly in the Basque provinces and which put several competitors out of action, Santander became the principal tourist resort of the country; however, but once the fighting was over, San Sebastián recovered its former leadership. This was to be no obstacle to the development of an important tourist complex on El Sardinero's beaches, thanks largely to the investment made by the Pombo family. Until 1897, this family owned not only the bathing gallery, the Gran Hotel and the casino at El Sardinero but also the Hotel Castilla, the Hotel Hoyuela, the Hotel Paris and a steam-powered tram that was inaugurated in 1892 (Gutiérrez Colomer, 1973: 435). However, the end of the century crisis associated with the loss of the colonies in 1898 was to be more serious in this city than in San Sebastián and this had a negative effect on the Pombo businesses on El Sardinero. It was then that a group of Santander businessmen took their place with a view to trying to promote the local and provincial economy by way of tourism.

One of the keys to future growth lay in an offer made by the City Council to King Alfonso XIII and his wife Victoria Eugenia to build a new palace on the Magdalena peninsula, near El Sardinero. This offer was accepted in 1908 and the palace was inaugurated in 1913. From then on, Santander also experienced an official annual royal visit, a privilege San Sebastián had enjoyed for many years, as Queen María Cristina, mother of Alfonso XIII, spent her summers in San Sebastián from 1887 until her death in 1929, with the sole exception of 1898, the year of the Spanish American war. This factor contributed greatly to the touristic development of the city: small summer palaces were built on El Sardinero and the luxurious Hotel Real was inaugurated in 1916 (Gil de Arriba, 1992; Pozueta, 1980; Sazatornil, 1994).

The second of the elements to consider when delineating a tourist product is transport. Indeed, Cantabria, the Basque Country and Navarre greatly improved their communications from the mid-19th century period onwards, thanks basically to the railway (Valero, 1991). Although it is true that from the end of the 18th century great progress had been made in the road system, with a basic view to improving the connection between the north coast and the central Spanish *meseta* (plateau), the truth is that the railway introduced outstanding changes insofar as tourist travel was concerned. Indeed, after the introduction of the 1855 Railway Law, this new means of transport developed greatly. Ten years before the law was passed (1845), the government had granted the marquis of Remisa the right to build the Santander–Alar del Rey line, where it joined the Castile Canal, an important communications and commercial artery between Santander and Reinosa. In 1864 the whole of the line was opened. This line was to be awarded to the Compañía del Norte in 1874, a company which already possessed the track between Alar and Venta de Baños, where it linked up with the Madrid–Irún–Paris line.

Thanks to the aforementioned 1855 Railway Law, the French financial group led by Emile and Isaac Péreire took control of the Northern line. This led from Madrid to Irún by way of Valladolid, Burgos, Vitoria, Alsasua, Zumárraga and San Sebastián. In Miranda de Ebro, it linked up with the Tudela–Bilbao line. Bilbao-based businessmen, on seeing that the Northern line was not to reach Vizcaya, decided to promote a railway that would link their capital with Tudela, in Navarre, and thus enable access to the rich agricultural markets of the mid Ebro valley. This railway was inaugurated in 1863 and, 15 years later, this was also taken over by the Compañía del Norte (González Portilla *et al.*, 1995; Novo, 1995; Tedde de Lorca, 1978; Various authors, 1998).

These great lines logically served to unite Madrid and the Spanish hinterland with the north coast. Santander and San Sebastián were the places to benefit most from the tourism point of view. Not surprisingly, it was in this latter city that the Madrid–Paris line was to be officially inaugurated in August 1864. Not only did the beaches of these cities benefit, the neighbouring spas also did. Those at Ormáiztegui and Gaviria, in Guipúzcoa, Caldas de Besaya in Cantabria, Zuazo and Nanclares de Oca in Alava, La Muera de Arbieto in Vizcaya or Alsasua in Navarre were all very close to these major railway lines. Likewise, the Soria–Pamplona line was near the spa of Fitero, in Navarre. To reach the other establishments, it was necessary to combine the train with another means of land transport. In this sense, the stations of Vitoria, Zumárraga and Tolosa were particularly important as railheads for spas in Guipúzcoa.

At the turn of the century, narrow-gauge trains became more important as a means of improving transport. The economic boom these northern provinces underwent over the course of these decades generated new necessities in transport that broad-gauge railways could not satisfy: for reasons of topography and traffic, cheaper lines were needed to extend the network beyond the main river valleys. This was reflected in the Secondary and Strategic Railway Law of 1908, which encouraged the extension of the narrow-gauge network. In this way, narrow-gauge railways enabled the smaller tourist towns of Cantabria and the Basque Country to remain competitive and indeed to increase the number of visitors (Larrinaga, 1999: 106–22; Macías, 1994; Ormaechea, 1989;).

The coastal lines built between Santander, Bilbao and San Sebastián and extending as far as Hendaye (France) in 1913 facilitated tourist travel between the different beach resorts of the northern coast. Apart from the capitals, other coastal places such as Zarauz, Zumaya or Deva, in Guipúzcoa, were served by this system. Some spas also benefited, such as Cestona, Alzola and San Juan de Azcoitia in Guipúzcoa; Cortézubi, Molinar de Carranza and Zaldívar in Vizcaya and Solares and Liérganes in Cantabria.

In general, means of transport in this part of Northern Spain were both good and plentiful in comparison with other parts of the country. Along with the railways, a good road network must be mentioned, a factor that greatly facilitated access to different tourist resorts, especially those spas that were far from the railway lines as was the case, for example, of Sobrón in Alava, Betelu in Navarre, Urberuaga de Ubilla in Vizcaya, Santa Agueda in Guipúzcoa or Puente Viesgo, Ontaneda and Alceda in Cantabria. All transport improvements carried out in these regions from the mid-19th century period made their own contribution to tourist development.

The third and last element to be taken into account in the development of the tourist product is leisure. The perception of this concept obviously changed significantly between the mid-19th century period and the turn of the century. Entertainment at Spanish spas, even ones situated in the North, was very limited, even in the 1880s. In general, they only included reading rooms, card games, billiard tables and walks in the spa gardens or surrounding areas. Only a few of them had a casino (for example, Caldas de Besaya) or a dance hall. However, from the turn of the century onwards, leisure offerings changed considerably and practically all spas in these regions tried to incorporate as many attractions as possible. This must be seen as a logical step if we bear in mind that by then, the hygienist paradigm had begun to falter and most bathers no longer came to these centres to be cured alone but came rather in search of entertainment.

This is perfectly clear in the development of the seaside resorts, especially Santander and San Sebastián. Regarding the latter city, the need to introduce a casino to widen the leisure and entertainment available to visitors soon became apparent. Entertainments had previously been limited to walks in the city's parks, concerts, theatre, day trips to nearby villages and cafe chat. Two private casinos were thus opened in the city in 1869: the Kursaal and the Indo (Sada & Hernández, 1987; Walton, 2003). Nonetheless, the idea of making a grand casino that would really put San Sebastián on the map was never dismissed. At the end of 1869, the board of the Kursaal casino made an agreement with the City Hall to construct a building near the beach. After various years of works and negotiations – a process interrupted by the Second Carlist War – the Gran Casino of San Sebastián opened to the public in July 1887.

Apart from the roulette wheels and other forms of casino gambling, other entertainments were also promoted to attract tourists to the city: bullfights, rowing and sailing regattas, children's games, *pelota* matches, all kinds of musical shows and dances, as well as horse- and car-racing at a later stage. Indeed, a whole range of activities were introduced, all of which aimed at attracting as many holidaymakers to the city as possible, as well as lengthening the tourist season as much as possible (Castells, 2000: 330–40; Larrinaga, 1999: 505–18).

Conclusions

At the beginning of the 20th century, the coastal provinces of the north of Spain were undergoing a maturation process at a time when their configuration as tourist products had already been consolidated. After a few years of investment within the context of 'precapitalist production', true changes in scale were to be introduced from the mid-19th century onwards. Apart from the afore-mentioned climatic advantages and infrastructures – especially that of the railways – it was the frequent presence of the royal family and the country's privileged classes that made the northern coast fashionable. This meant that a step forward was taken, in which investments on a novel scale of 'capitalist production' were made. It was the moment in which large hotels, casinos, theatres, villas, parks, promenades, recreation grounds, squares, avenues, etc. were built, thus configuring a new tourist product that stood out for its offer of quality.

By 1914, then, Cantabria and the Basque Country had become the most important tourist destinations in Spain. Nevertheless, we cannot speak in terms of absolute homogeneity, for diverging tendencies did indeed exist between spa and sea-bathing tourism. Thus, when the hygienist paradigm suffered a crisis, the number of visitors to spas began to decrease. However, the beaches of Santander and San Sebastián, on consolidating their leisure provision, saw the number of visitors they received increase considerably. A certain transfer can be seen of bathers from the mineral water spas to the coast, where tourist attractions were ever greater in number. Detailed evidence on this can be found in successive editions of the *Anuario oficial de las aguas minerales de España*. But the new focus on entertainment and consumption as well as the pursuit of health, in an increasingly sophisticated seaside setting, was to remain dominant throughout the 20th century.

References

Abercrombie, N., Hill, S. and Turner, B.S. (1980) *The Dominant Ideology Thesis*. London: Allen and Unwin.

Abercrombie, N., Hill, S. and Turner, B.S. (eds) (1990) *Dominant Ideologies*. London: Allen and Unwin.

Agarwal, S. (2002) Restructuring seaside tourism: The resort lifecycle. *Annals of Tourism Research* 29 (1), 25–55.

Aguirre, R. (1995) *El Turismo en el País Vasco. Vida e Historia*. San Sebastián: Txertoa.

Anuario oficial de las aguas minerales de España (1877, 1890).

Beascoechea Gangoiti, J.M. (2002) Veraneo y urbanización en la costa cantábrica durante el siglo XIX: las playas del Abra de Bilbao. *Historia Contemporánea* 25 (2), 181–202.

Castells, L. (2000) El turismo y la corte. In M. Artola (ed.) *Historia de Donostia-San Sebastián*. San Sebastián: Ayuntamiento de San Sebastián, Fundación BBVA y Nerea.

Corbin, A. (1988) *Le Territoire du Vide. L'Occident et le Désir du Rivage. 1750–1850*. Paris: Aubier.

Chadefaud, M. (1987) *Aux Origines du Tourisme dans les Pays de l'Adour*. Pau: Université de Pau.

Garate, M. and Martín Rudi, J. (1995) *Cien años de la vida económica de San Sebastián (1887–1987)*. San Sebastián: Instituto Dr. Camino de Historia Donostiarra.

Gil y Fresno, J. (1879) *Guía hidrológica-médica de Vizcaya*. Bilbao: Juan E. Delmas.

Gil De Arriba, C. (1992) *Casas para Baños de Ola y Balnearios Marítimos en el Litoral Montañés, 1868–1936*. Santander: Universidad de Cantabria and Fundación Marcelino Botín.

González Portilla, M., Montero, M., Garmendia, J.M., Novo, P. and Macías, O. (1995) *Ferrocarriles y Desarrollo. Red y mercados en el País Vasco, 1856–1914*. Bilbao: Universidad del País Vasco.

Gutiérrez Colomer, R. (1973) *Santander 1875–1899*. Santander: Diputación Provincial de Santander.

Hoyo, A. (1993) *Todo mudó de repente. El horizonte económico de la burguesía mercantil en Santander, 1820–1874*. Santander: Universidad de Cantabria and Asamblea Regional de Cantabria.

Larrinaga, C. (1999) *Actividad económica y cambio estructural en San Sebastián durante la Restauración, 1875–1914*. San Sebastián: Instituto Dr. Camino de Historia donostiarra.

Larrinaga, C. (2003) Le tourisme thermal dans l'Espagne de la Restauration, 1875–1914. In L. Tissot (ed.) *Development of a Tourist Industry in the 19th and 20th Centuries: International Perspectives*. Neuchatel: Editions Alphil.

Luengo, F. (2000): *San Sebastián. La vida cotidiana de una ciudad*. San Sebastián: Txertoa.

Luis Gómez, A., Gil de Arriba, C., San Pedro, A. and Herrero, J.J. (1989) *Aproximación histórica al estudio de los balnearios montañeses (1826–1936)*. Santander: Cámara Oficial de Comercio, Industria y Navegación de Cantabria.

Macías, M.O. (1994) *Ferrocarriles y desarrollo económico en el País Vasco (1914–1936)*. Bilbao: UPV.

Madrazo, F. de P. (1849) *Una espedición á Guipúzcoa en el verano de 1848*. Madrid: Imprenta de D. Gabriel Gil.

Martínez Vara, T. (1983) *Santander, de villa a ciudad*. Santander: Ayuntamiento de Santander and Librería Estudio.

Novo, P.A. (1995) *La ordenación ferroviaria del País Vasco. Mercado y ordenación del territorio*. Bilbao: UPV.

Ormaechea, A.M. (1989) *Ferrocarriles en Euskadi, 1855–1936*. Bilbao: ET/FV.

Ortega Valcárcel, J. (1986) *Cantabria 1886–1986. Formación y desarrollo de una economía moderna*. Santander: Cámara de Comercio, Industria y Navegación de Santander.

Pozueta Echevarri, J. (1980) El proceso de urbanización turística. La producción del Sardinero. Doctoral thesis, Universidad de Cantabria, Santander.

Rodríguez Sorondo, M.C. (1985) *Arquitectura pública en la ciudad de San Sebastián (1813–1922)*. San Sebastián: Grupo Dr. Camino de Historia Donostiarra.

Sada, J. and Hernández, T. (1987) *Historia de los casinos de San Sebastián, siglos XIX y XX*. San Sebastián: Nuevo Gran Casino del Kursaal.

San Pedro, M.A. (1993) *El balneario de Puente Viesgo, 1796–1936*. Santander: Universidad de Cantabria y Fundación Marcelino Botín.

Sazatornil, L. (1994) El Sardinero. De casa de baños a ciudad-balneario. In *Baños de Ola en el Sardinero. Exposición*. Santander: Ayuntamiento de Santander.

Tedde de Lorca, P. (1978) Las compañías ferroviarias en España (1855–1935). In M. Artola (ed.) *Los ferrocarriles en España, 1844–1943*. Madrid: Banco de España.

Urquía, J.M. (1992) El agua como remedio. *Cuadernos de Sección. Ciencias Médicas*, No. 2.

Valero, A. (1991) Chemin de fer et tourisme. L'exemple de Norte Principal. *Mélanges de la Casa de Velázquez*, XXVII (3).

Various Authors (1998) *150 Años de los Ferrocarriles en España*. (Vol. I). Madrid: Anaya.

Walton, J.K. (2002) Planning and seaside tourism: San Sebastián, 1863–1936. *Planning Perspectives* 17, 1–20.

Walton, J.K. (2003) Tourism and politics in elite beach resorts: San Sebastián and Ostend, 1830–1939. In L. Tissot (ed.) *Construction of a Tourist Industry in the 19th and 20th Centuries*. Neuchatel: Editions Alphil.

Walton, J.K. and Smith, J. (1996) The first century of beach tourism in Spain: San Sebastián and the *Playas del Norte* from the 1830s to the 1930s. In M. Barke, J. Towner, and M.T. Newton (eds) *Tourism in Spain. Critical Issues*. Wallingford: CAB International.

Chapter 6

Japanese Tea Party: Representations of Victorian Paradise and Playground in The Geisha *(1896)*

YORIMITSU HASHIMOTO

The Missing Link between *The Mikado* (1885) and *Madame Butterfly* (1904)

The Geisha: A Story of a Tea House (1896), by Owen Hall and Harry Greenbank, is the missing link between the two plays *The Mikado* (1885) by Gilbert and Sullivan and *Madame Butterfly* (1904) by Puccini. For the Victorians, the performance became a virtual tour of Japan after the successful 'Living Display' in the Japanese Village located in Knightsbridge in 1885 and other World Fairs like the one held in Chicago in 1893. In these 'exhibitions', the tea-serving girls, dressed in Japanese folk costume (the kimono), had fuelled the craze for Japanese art and customs, also referred to as Japonism. W.S. Gilbert actually visited Knightsbridge and utilised what he observed for his best known work, *The Mikado,* particularly 'a charming Japanese tea-girl' who knew only two words of English: 'Sixpence, please', the charge for a cup of tea. He employed her to communicate the Japanese way of using a fan and walking when wearing a kimono (Fitz-Gerald, 1924: 107–9). Most of these recorded backstage episodes were vividly reproduced in Mike Leigh's movie, *Topsy-Turvy* (1999).

The Geisha was one of the typical by-products of the 'Japanese tea-girls' craze. Audiences would go to the theatre and 'experience' Japan through the eyes of British officers and female tourists in leading roles on stage, using the kimono and various Japanese objects to suggest an exotic Japanese teahouse. This imaginary chrysanthemum tour was, as in a contemporary review, 'a feast in colour' (*Illustrated London News*, 1896: 572). How did *The Geisha* represent Japan and what did the British audience expect to see in Japan? And how did Japan respond to this tourist demand? In this chapter I will argue that this little-known and unstudied but extremely popular musical in the West at the turn of the century illustrated a typical version of the British tourist gaze in relation to imperialistic desire, particularly in terms of fortification of the borders between race and gender.

The story is anglocentric and phallocentric, in keeping with its time. After the arrival of HMS *Turtle* in Japan, British sailors are welcomed by geisha girls in a teahouse. Apart from the geisha girls, the Chinese proprietor of the teahouse, Wun-hi, hires as an interpreter a French girl, Juliette, who would like to marry a rich man. An officer on the ship, Reggie, has a fiancée called Molly. She and her female friends arrive as tourists in Japan at the same time. They discover that Reggie is fascinated by a well-known geisha, O Mimosa San. In order to regain his love, Molly disguises herself as a geisha, Rolly-Polly-San. Meanwhile, the local governor Marquis Imari tries to obtain O Mimosa San from her betrothed Katana, and threatens Wun-hi that he will seize the 'license' of the teahouse if he does not agree to sell all the geisha girls at an auction. The leader of the female tourist party steps in to buy O Mimosa San instead but the result is that Imari chooses Rolly-Polly-San instead. Then British 'maids and men unite' (Hall, 1949: 66. Future page references to this text will be presented in parentheses) with each other to rescue Molly. At the wedding, Juliette replaces Rolly-Polly-San, while Molly in fortune-teller disguise threatens Imari with an ominous prediction. Imari finds out that the bride is Juliette but accepts it and all ends happily; in the end, both O Mimosa San and Rolly-Polly-San get to marry their betrothed.

This operetta became very popular and was presented in the West End 760 times between 25 April 1896 and 28 May 1898, even more performances than *The Mikado*. Kurt Gänzl researched *The Geisha*'s worldwide performance history in detail and ranked it as the first internationally successful British musical (Ganzl, 1997: 113–14, 1986: 619–22). *The Geisha* was received so favourably wherever it went, in the English-speaking world and across Europe, that Anton Chekhov mentioned its first performance in Yalta, Russia in his famous short story 'The Lady with the Dog' (1899) (Chekhov, 1984: 16) and Baden-Powell, later the founder of the Boy Scout movement, joined a local amateur club to play the role of Wun-hi in Simla, India in 1897 (Jeal, 1989: 196). As the operetta enjoyed international popularity, the Japanese word 'geisha' spread and became synonymous with Japan and the Japanese.

Literally geisha means a person who has a skill, and signifies a Japanese woman who is trained in the art of dancing, singing and providing entertainment. As the *Oxford English Dictionary* indicates, geisha was not documented in Britain until 1891, five years before the operetta *The Geisha*, and the word was still unfamiliar to the audience who were not confident about its pronunciation. Lest it be circulated wrongly as 'geesha', Arthur Diósy, the supervisor of *The Geisha* and the founder of the Japan Society, recommended a song to rhyme with 'Asia' (Adlard, 1990: 74). Thus, several popular songs connected 'geisha' with 'gay' and 'Asia' to confirm the correct pronunciation.

The Geisha was performed less frequently after the Great War and the complete libretto was not recorded in Britain until 1999. The temporary popularity seems to indicate that the performance of *The Geisha* was so closely connected with the late Victorian era and the then leading ideology of the British empire, that it would have appeared out of fashion or nostalgic after that. In the next section, I shall locate *The Geisha* in the dominant historical, ideological and cultural contexts of the late Victorian era.

Japan as a British Men's Paradise for Fighting and Flirting

The Geisha depicted Japan as a perfect paradise for British officers where men could be men and women dare not go beyond the pale. After HMS *Turtle* enters the treaty port, the geisha girls sing an opening chorus to tempt British officers into the teahouse (p. 4). Seeing the officers, the geisha girls sing a welcome song, 'Here They Come', to praise British manliness: 'Great big English sailor men! ... Fight with any man they please – Marry little English Miss, Flirt with pretty Japanese!' (p. 5). These lyrics, contrasting fight and flirt, seem to be a witty, if euphemistic, summary of British tourist desire in the colonies. The beginning of the operetta suggests everything: the geisha girls would devote themselves to entertain the 'Great big' British men, even if it is a temporary love, and British officers would interfere in the local situation, to fight against the despotic local king in this case, and save themselves to marry British women back home.

The idealised availability of geisha girls in a teahouse was widely circulated in Britain as the term gained currency in the 1890s. This myth was immortalised by French globetrotter Pierre Loti's *Madame Chrysanthème* (1887) based on his 'marriage' with a Japanese woman during his stay in Nagasaki. Loti was surprised at the submissiveness of little childish Japanese girls working in the teahouses and in travelogues he represented them as 'enchanting lithe dolls without a soul' (Littlewood, 1996: 120) best for temporary love. When he returns with fear that he 'might be leaving her in some sadness', he finds her checking to see if the money she had received was forged or not, and he decides to depart without pain. Instead of 'Guécha', Loti popularised the word mousmé ('young woman') of the teahouse in the Western world until the popularity of *The Geisha* drove out the alternative French formulation throughout the British Empire.

As the *Illustrated London News* review pointed out, *The Geisha* was significantly influenced by the English illustrated edition of Loti's book (1889). One of the geisha girls is named 'O Kiku San (Chrysanthemum)', obviously following Loti. Four of the five times 'mousmé' was used, it referred to 'French mousmé' implying Juliette. Naming other geisha girls 'O-some-flower-name-San' like 'O Mimosa San' (Miss Mimosa) is derived from Loti too. The most direct allusion to his book is in the comical duet 'The Dear Little Jappy, Jap, Jappy'. After the geisha Komurasaki San (Little Violet) utters the line 'Oh, no, geisha have nothing to do with love' (p. 8), an officer named Cunningham tells a story in a duet with her. This is an anglicised Loti story of miscommunication between 'a jolly Jack Tar' and 'a Dear Little Jappy, Jap, Jappy', in Nagasaki. Jack asks her to marry him in English but does not understand her reply 'Hai Kashikomari!'('Yes sir'). On his departure after this spectacular misunderstanding, he weeps at the loss of a bride, 'Till the captain and crew thought him cracky' (p. 9):

But that dear little Jappy, Jap, Jappy,
She has filled up the gappy, gap, gappy,
And has chosen instead
To be happily wed
To a Japanese chappy, chap, chappy! (p. 9)

While Loti depicts his 'marriage' with a mousmé only as a cash nexus, this duet with a geisha just after the first British contact with the native women indicates and intensifies the foolishness of taking the subsequent cross-cultural relationships seriously.

The 'gay' and 'Asia' operetta abounds with happy-go-luckiness of this sort. The similar opening choruses of *The Mikado* and *The Geisha* confirm that Japan was still seen as a distant and imaginary topsy-turvydom, as suggested by the imported curiosities which had been all the rage since the 1880s. In a concerted piece with officers, four geisha girls cheerfully confirm the entertainment of a teahouse and light-heartedly seduce the male British sailors into an Oriental extravaganza. 'If You Will Come to Tea',

We'll do our best
For an English guest
On an Asiatic spree
We'll dance and sing for you
Our repertory through,

And show you then,
You officer men,
What smart little girls can do. (p. 19)

Of course not all of the geisha girls in the musical are always easy-going. The prima geisha, O Mimosa San, sings two gloomy songs and laments the vanity of love. In the duet, 'The Amorous Goldfish', she kneels by the seated Fairfax and compares herself with a goldfish in a bowl; even if she loves an officer who looks inside the bowl and feeds her, he will forget 'his sad little pet' (p. 14) before long, and the goldfish will continue to fade away until someone carelessly smashes the bowl to leave it suffocating on the carpet. Fairfax's betrothed Molly envyingly and frenetically asks her if he loves her and O Mimosa San tries to comfort her by saying that 'All the foreign gentlemen who come here flirt with a mousmé or a geisha' but 'that does not mean real love' (p. 30). Molly, however, decides to be a geisha and enters the teahouse and O Mimosa San sings how miserable 'A Geisha's Life' could be. She poses a question, rather self-reflexively, 'Who sing and dance the livelong day?'.

As a matter of fact, O Mimosa San herself accepts the slave-like apprenticeship. Meeting her lover, soldier Katana (Katana means sword), she explains the reason why she could entertain the men without love just as a soldier could kill people in war without hate. How Mimosa accepts her place is well represented in 'Jewel of Asia', one of the most popular songs of the operetta. Carrying a parasol, Mimosa wonders about Fairfax's fiancée Molly Seamore who is jealous of Mimosa and who has disguised herself as a geisha. Mimosa reaffirms that geisha girls consort with British officers who will 'Marry little English Miss, Flirt with pretty Japanese' in the following aria. 'Jewel of Asia' depicts a geisha girl in a garden opening a gate to a foreigner who is passing by:

And I blush to relate
    That he taught Japan's fair daughter
To flirt and kiss
Like the little white Miss …
He call'd her the Jewel of Asia – of Asia – of Asia,
But she was the Queen of the Geisha – the Geisha, – the Geisha (p. 51)

Accordingly, she consents that it is merely a temporary affair before he returns home to meet 'an English lady' and 'declared how much he missed her'. The song ends with

It is just as they say, sir,
    You love for as long as you can,

A month or a week or a day, sir
Will do for a girl of Japan. (p. 51)

Although the line of 'he never even kissed her' is ambiguous and less suggestive of immorality to a British audience, the song is clearly repeating the same message from the opening chorus, i.e. that foreigners were welcomed and entertained by geisha girls in teahouses without regret or responsibility.

Against Miscegenation: The French Empire as Negative Example

It is really exceptional in *fin-de-siècle* Britain, however, to describe inter-racial affairs of whatever kind without their carrying any pain and price. Rudyard Kipling affords the best example. His two well-known short stories, 'Beyond the Pale' (1888) and 'Without Benefit of Clergy' (1890), illustrate how such relationships were taboo in British India at that time.

'Without Benefit of Clergy' would be the other extreme to *The Geisha*. It starts as *Madame Chrysanthème* does but ends quite differently. A British soldier buys his native mistress in India from her mother but unlike the mousmé or geisha, the Indian mistress does not understand that it is only a cash nexus. She wants and believes his love and tries to confirm it repeatedly like 'Thou wilt never cease to love me now? Answer, my king'. Her innocent question irritates him who only wants her temporarily for his lust. After a while he begets a boy but loses him shortly after the birth. His indifferent detached attitude to the death of his own child awakens his 'wife' to realise his intention. She regrets having attached herself to a British soldier who will not love her and their child. Then, instead of leaving for a safe area with the British soldier to escape from a cholera epidemic, she chooses to kill herself by staying and becoming infected. When she dies, the man suffers from a guilty conscience. Although India offers an exotic location for the military life and an obedient mistress who loves and respects the British soldier as a 'king', he has to pay for his 'fight' and 'flirt' in this story.

The reality of the colony, isolation, fatal sunshine and degeneration into 'native' ways, described by colonial officers and writers like Kipling and Conrad, disenchanted the late Victorian populace. The depressing depictions of inter-racial intercourse reflect the late British imperial and colonial policy of keeping a 'social distance' between the British and the rest. Unlike the 18th century, during the course of the 19th century there was a striking shift in attitudes concerning the native 'wife', or concubine, from permission to prohibition. In terms of India, the well-known memsahib society expanded particularly after the Mutiny in 1857 in order to 'maintain "civilised standards", especially sexual standards' (Hyam, 1998: 119, also 106–9 and chap. 5). In contrast, the French Empire continued to encourage 'concubinage for their administrators' (Hyam, 1998: 214) and Loti's works are a prime example of displaying 19th century sex tourism from Africa to Asia. Interestingly, this striking difference seemed to affect the 'French mousmé' Juliette in *The Geisha,* who in true French imperial style displays no misgivings about miscegenation and ingratiates herself with a native governor. She is depicted as a passionate Loti-like figure who says 'Men make love the same in all countries. There is only one language for love' (p. 9). Her object is to climb the class ladder, which is more important than racial difference and, in the course of the story, she becomes Marquise Imari. She tries to attract Imari's attention childishly by posing herself in front of him as though by accident. Knowing that Imari is going to obtain O Mimosa San in the auction, Juliette coaxes the leader of the British women tourists to buy her, which causes more trouble when Imari decides to marry Molly Seamore in her geisha disguise.

The xenophobic agenda, characteristic of the 1890s (Hashimoto, 2003b) is clear. The heroine is trapped by a thoughtless selfish French woman and an alliance between the British of both sexes protects a compatriot from a lewd Oriental despot. In terms of xenophobic attitudes towards miscegenation, the final marriage is perfectly well arranged: marrying evil with evil, British with British and Japanese with Japanese. These cross-class and cross-sex unions united against an alien were common in late Victorian melodrama, according to John M. MacKenzie. MacKenzie also indicates that the focus of the characteristic story shifted from class tension to race tension in the course of the 19th century and suggests that the Oriental villain was an externalised upper-class master (MacKenzie, 1984: 45). Considered from this point of view, in early 19th century melodrama Imari and Juliette's relationship would have been regarded as the result of an affair between master and servant and *Madame Butterfly* (1904) as a transmigration of *La Traviata* (1853).

La Geisha, which premiered on 8 March 1898, was never as successful in France as in other countries (Ganzl, 1994: 519). Focusing on Juliette, the reason for staging a mere four performances can easily be explained. The operetta transposed French Japonist works into an anglocentric teahouse garden and the transmutation of Loti's male narrator into the frivolous feminine figure of Juliette might have come across as a racial slur against the French imperial project, which was currently under extreme tension with the British Empire, such as during the Fashoda conflict in 1898. At this point, the use of the term 'geisha' instead of 'mousmé' is also a display of British political consciousness of empire, expressing its struggle for supremacy in a change of label; and the focus on the idea of the teahouse had strong associations with a product of Empire that had become, in many senses, Britain's national beverage.

Except for Juliette, the operetta *Geisha* carries no seed of future trouble caused by inter-racial 'marriage', as in other narratives in the late Victorian age. Apparently the teahouse is more refreshing and embracing than the idea of decadent and stagnant opium dens in Oscar Wilde's *The Picture of Dorian Gray* (1891) or Conan Doyle's 'The Man with the Twisted Lip' (1891) (Hashimoto, 2003a). The proprietor of the teahouse, pidgin-English-speaking and pig-tailed Wun-hi, is far from being a menace and is indeed presented as asexualised comic relief. Japan in *The Geisha*, as well, is sanitised and sterilised beforehand. The officer's flirtation will never develop into love or marriage in the operetta. Actually, in spite of several allusions to the teahouse as a brothel, there is no explicit mention of actual sexual intercourse, which the discourse of the public stage in the London of the 1890s would not have permitted, although Lieutenant Fairfax says to midshipman Stanley who wants to come to the teahouse, 'This is no place for little boys' (p. 7). Instead, the story of the teahouse is an archetypal boy-meets-girl story within 'civilised standards' to stabilise the distinction of race and gender. As 'The Amorous Goldfish' duet demonstrates, the British officers' affairs with the geisha girls do not go beyond the relationship between master and pet or a romanticised 'Little Mermaid' (original: 1837, English: 1846) narrative. The great divide between mammal and fish could never be crossed nor even blurred.

Mission to Civilise: Teaching Kissing to the Geisha

The exceptional song with sexually explicit content is 'The Kissing'. Speaking with O Mimosa San, Fairfax happens to find that there is no kissing in Japan. Surprised, he courageously tries to teach her what it is in a duet. He admires 'the nicest girl in Asia' but addresses that 'there is something missing' although 'English, French and German misses ... are all expert at kissing' (p. 16). Mimosa, then, asks him eagerly and curiously:

> Will you teach me, if you please?
> I believe I'm quick and clever,
> And I promise I'll endeavour
> In the task to do you credit,
> If your pupil I may be!

Teasing and tantalising her, Fairfax demands that she confirm her agreement. He mischievously pressures her by saying that he will not teach her if she is 'half afraid to try'. She makes up her mind and strikes a pose at his mercy.

Fairfax: And I give it to you – thus! [*Kisses her.*]
Mimosa: It has charms I can't explain
Fairfax: Which you never knew before! [*Laughing.*]
Mimosa: Teach me once, just once again!
Fairfax: Pretty pupils I adore. (p. 17)

Satisfied with the joy of teaching and studying, they chorus: 'Little maiden, Wonder-laden, Ev'ry day learns something more!'. Mimosa and Fairfax exemplify the culturally acceptable encounter between East and West according to Victorian values. Japan is exemplified as the traditional and timeless Orient or 'virgin' land waiting for the western male explorer and saviour. At the same time, the plot lacks the potential for this causing trouble as in other 1890s colonial stories. The duet is sensually and tactfully made to tickle the audience's curiosity while avoiding any contaminating inter-racial intercourse beyond the playfulness of the kiss.

In a broader context, the kissing duet is part of widespread discourses portrayed in travelogues and books on Japanology at the turn of the century. That the Japanese had no custom of kissing had already been touched upon in the 1880s in an article 'Recent Travels in Japan' (1880) (*Quarterly Review*, 1880: 329), and in the story *The Eastern Wonderland* (1882) (Angus, 1882: 68). This myth was endorsed by a naturalised Japanese, Lafcadio Hearn (Hearn, 1895: 101) and a Japanese Christian, Naomi Tamura. Tamura published the provocative account *The Japanese Bride* (1893) and claimed that, 'The Japanese never kiss on any occasion before the public to show their affection' (Tamura, 1904: 45).

As for the travelogues, *Japs at Home* (1892) is most noteworthy. The author Douglas Sladen was a friend of Arthur Diósy (Adlard, 1990: 130). While in Japan, Sladen visited Sir Edwin Arnold, author of *The Light of Asia*, a celebrated Japanophile who first used the word geisha in English. As an avid reader of Loti's *Madame Chrysanthème*, Sladen quoted several passages from the novel and depicted a Japanese girl who thought 'kissing the queerest custom ever invented' and learned 'to do it charmingly in a lesson or two' (Sladen, 1892: 153). This passage might have inspired the writer of *The Geisha* to introduce the kissing duet. According to an interview, Owen Hall, who had never been to Japan, 'read five and twenty books on the subject' before he wrote *The Geisha* (Adlard, 1990: 71–2). Closely connected with the travelogues and other fiction, the operetta *Geisha* intensified and spread this myth across the world, presenting Japan as 'kissable' as the globalisation of British manners and customs extended to the missionary dissemination of sexual practices.

The Angel in the Teahouse: Refuge from the New Woman?

Since the opening of Japan by the American Commodore Perry's gunboat in 1853 these innocent geisha and mousmés, allegedly ignorant of kissing, attracted a stunning number of visitors from the West (Lehmann, 1978: chap. 3; Littlewood, 1996: chaps 11–12). Geisha entertainment in teahouses had already become a not-to-be-missed tourist attraction in the 1890s. In 1897, an American in Japan sardonically described how the travelogues were spawned after cliché tours of temples and cities:

> A sojourn of a few weeks here makes the globe-trotter an author; …; while an attempt or two to use chopsticks at a tea house entertainment initiates him into the inner circles of Japanese home life. If he has a wife, her education is not completed until she has been photographed in a mis-fit *kimono,* …, she must be mistaken for a *geisha.* (Bowie, 1897: 18–19)

It is no exaggeration to say that no books on Japan in the late 19th century failed to give a specific mention to geisha girls. Mary Fraser, who had stayed in Japan as a British diplomat's wife, noted in 1899 'The books I have read on Japan have always had a great deal to say about the *musmë* … or the *geisha*' (Fraser, 1899: 346). This is reflected in *The Geisha* as well: 'English officers don't marry geisha', Mimosa tells Fairfax, 'you listen to my song, you look into my eyes, and then – you go away to your country and write a book about the pretty singing girls of Japan' (p. 15). Specifically, the creation of the myth of Japan as a flirtatious Utopia or corrupted Sodom might be tracked down to the first western contacts in the 16th century (Wilkinson, 1983: 46–7). But in what context were geisha girls regarded as attractive to the western gaze at the end of the 19th century?

The craze for the Japanese girl was, so to speak, a *fin-de-siècle* phenomenon. As the *Oxford English Dictionary* indicates, 'mousmé' was first used in 1880 and 'geisha' in 1891. The most passionate missionary is Sir Edwin Arnold who 'missed the Poet Laureateship because of the Oriental turn of mind', according to his appreciative reader Mahatma Gandhi (Gandhi, 1904: 296). Arnold admired a 'Gentle, and sweet, and debonair' Japanese girl in his well known poem, 'The Musmée' (1891), and, unlike his contemporaries, brought his Japanese wife to Britain.

The previously-mentioned Tamura criticised Arnold's lecture depicting Japan as where 'you begin to abandon the idea of original sin' (Tamura,

1904: 85) and hinted at the exploitation of women caused by their inferior place. The most interesting point is that Tamura internalised and repeated almost exactly how Christian missionaries had attacked the lewdness of the perceived Japanese lack of shame and awareness of original sin. In 1859, Laurence Oliphant, the attendant of Elgin's mission, shocked at the public brothels in Japan, remarked: 'There is nothing slovenly in the mode of administration here. Vice itself is systematised' (Oliphant, 1859: 494). This vice was, however, an acceptable substitute for taking a native wife in the eyes of imperial administrators across the British Empire around the turn of the century (Hyam, 1998: 142–8). While Victorian respectability flourished, international white or yellow slavery spread, and supplied the expansion of the British Empire. In 1922 Havelock Ellis recorded a British officer who had known perhaps 60 prostitutes. Like Fairfax in *The Geisha*, who went 'half round the world' 'on pleasure and on duty' (p. 48), he considered the Japanese the best because they were 'scrupulously clean, have charming manners and beautiful bodies, and take an intelligent interest in the proceedings' (Hyam, 1998: 133).

Obedience in the Japanese was praised by many others. A future famous MP wrote about women's traditional submissiveness as a key component of their character and praised their 'winsome and healthy little body' with 'the heart of an unspoiled child' (Norman, 1892: 178). Douglas Sladen also described the Japanese tradition which was regrettably undermined by 'European theories concerning the relation of the sexes' (Sladen, 1892: 159). There were ironical twists of the gaze between the east and the west in the course of the 19th century. While western visitors, through the 1880s, began to pay tribute to the innocent childlike dependent mentality of lack of sin and shame, which had been subject to criticism mainly by respectable Victorians in the middle of the 19th century, Tamura, the Japanese convert to Christianity, adopted their point of view and belatedly crusaded against this 'backwardness' in the 1890s.

The rediscovered virtue of the submissiveness of Japanese women coincided with the phenomenon of the 'New Woman' in England, who challenged male-oriented Victorian society by demonstrating that woman could do, or even do better, anything a man could do. Although the expression was first used in 1894, the trend that it expressed, together with a tendency to mock emergent feminisms, was increasingly evident during the 1880s (Ledger, 1997: 2–3). An example from Gilbert and Sullivan's *Princess Ida* (1884) illustrates this as it caricatures a woman's college. *The Mikado* also denigrates 'the lady novelist' as a 'singular anomaly'. In reaction to the emergent 'New Woman', the earlier ideal of 'The Angel in the House' seemed to be projected onto the Japanese geisha in the teahouse. Clive Holland's *My Japanese Wife* (1895) is a perfect example. This was one of the most popular Japonist novels with 60,000 copies being sold, according to the author's foreword to the American version. It was consumed as an English counterpart to Loti. A contemporary reviewer in *The Spectator* reproached it for plagiarism although the author denied it. In fact, the differences are few but interesting: a Cambridge man, fed up with English women's loss of femininity, does not abandon his Japanese wife but brings her to Britain.

The misogynistic attitude toward the idea of 'New Womanhood' throws new light on the late Victorian operetta. In *The Geisha,* Mimosa was contrasted with an English woman, Molly Seamore. Although there is no word of 'New Woman', Seamore suggested her independent characteristics. Her entrance represents how she is not fettered by old Victorian womanhood and, as a result, she behaves eccentrically. She enters in a manly, smart yachting costume drawing an empty rickshaw because she does not like to see the scantily-clad puller exerting himself in front of her. This lack of insight, which invites the audience to laugh at the absurdity, hints at the problems she will cause both among men of her own society and in Japan. Her friend, in contrast, describes her as 'a young lady with all modern improvements' who is 'quite able to take care of herself' (p. 33). In fact, she is so adventurous and curious that she travels around the world and penetrates into a teahouse disguised as a geisha to confirm her betrothed Fairfax's love. After becoming a geisha, Molly changes her name into Rolly-Polly San, which suggests a 'great big lady' rolled in a kimono. Rolly-Polly sings a part of 'Chon Kina' in the auction of the geisha girls.

> I'm the smartest little geisha in Japan,
> ...
> I can dance to any measure that is gay,
> To and fro in dreamy fashion I can sway,
> And if still my art entices,
> Then at extra special prices
> I can dance for you in *quite* another way!
> Chon Kina – Chon Kina
> Chon, Chon – Kina, Kina
> Nagasaki – Yokohama
> Hakodate – Hoi! (p. 38) (Emphasis in original)

Chonkina was a sensual game mainly played in Japanese teahouses. As it was highly welcomed by the western tourists, the Chonkina dance degenerated into a mere striptease (Linhart, 1993: 211–43). Apart from its sensual connotation, the song's message is explicit. Here an English modern shrew turns into a well-trained prostitute-like geisha who is willing to serve the men. But Lady Constance Wynne, travelling round the world in her yacht, is asked by Juliette to buy and save Mimosa from Imari and, as a result, Imari buys Rolly-Polly-Molly instead. Imari tries to persuade her by saying, 'You are going to marry! All girls marry, it is the natural finish to a spinster's education' (p. 44). She herself regrets her imprudence deeply in a song 'Toy Monkey' saying to herself 'Foolish little Molly, Punish'd for your folly' (p. 46). Wun-hi's playing on her surname Seamore reinforces the idea of her folly: 'Little Miss Sealess' or 'Miss Seamore or less' (p. 52). After these ordeals, she is saved to accept her place in the finale by her statement that 'I want a young man of my own' (p. 66).

The implication is clear: the plot puts a progressive woman in her rightful place by reconciling her to traditional Victorian values. Molly is punished by her transgression of boundaries, both male–female and British–Japanese. Following the geisha girls, she learns obedience but pays a price because she plays along the borderlands of race. A review of *The Geisha* performance in India is worth quoting; Molly is 'a sprightly thoughtless girl, full of fun and adventure without counting the cost either to herself or others'(Jeal, 1989: 196). It suggests that the British New Woman should behave like the stereotypical memsahib in India, who knows her place as the provider of support and services for male British imperial agents.

Real Victorian women, however, had gone and seen far beyond Molly Seamore. After the 1850s, a number of enterprising travellers, frequently 'spinsters', had advanced into a traditionally exclusive masculine domain. The party of Lady Constance in *The Geisha* was possibly based loosely on Lady Brassey, who wrote *A Voyage of the Sunbeam* (1878) recording her journey around the world, including Japan, in her yacht with her children. 'Molly Seamore' might have been an allusion to Eliza Ruhamah Scidmore, one of the representative Far East women travellers, although she was American. Scidmore's *Jinrikisha Days in Japan* (1891) also traced the cliché tour but she travelled alone with interesting views and twists from other, male globetrotters. While Molly is taught how to eat with chopsticks (p. 29) just like a typical tourist, Scidmore, unlike other travelogues, illustrates in detail the way of using them in her book (Scidmore, 1892: 88–9). In the frontispiece of the book, Scidmore seemed to enjoy her disguise in old Japanese court costume, not geisha-like, but a strange-looking kimono. These sophisticated tourist accounts may have helped to inspire the humorous portrayal of Molly Seamore.

In a broader context apart from this allusion, a serious controversy arose concerning the proposed entry of 21 women fellows to the Royal

Geographical Society in 1893. One of the nominated explorers, Isabella Bird, 'traversed districts into which no European had ever previously penetrated' and she lived with a Japanese male in a village of so-called native Japanese Ainu in 1878. Despite the reputation achieved by Bird and others, George Curzon, the future President of the Society and Viceroy of India, concluded that women were 'unfitted for exploration' (Birkett, 1992: 63) and the door was shut tight. Soon *Punch* acclaimed the decision in *A Song of the RGS*: 'let them [female Fellows of the RGS] darn socks, boil "taters" or make tea' (Checkland, 1996: 166). In 1895, Mary Kingsley who returned from a single exploration of 'virgin land' in West Africa, was subject to similar insinuations about being a 'New Woman' although she detached herself from the 'New Woman' movement. The representation of Molly in *The Geisha* should be placed in this context.

Molly's disguise repeated these women explorers' 'transgressive' penetrations of new societies. Geography and imperialism had been metaphorically and practically connected with masculinity, as the expression 'virgin land' illustrates (McClintock, 1994: 1–3). Adopting native disguise was, therefore, a metaphor of penetration into the harem-like teahouse. As is well known, Robert Burton entered the innermost sanctum of the Muslim world in 1853 by disguising himself to undertake a pilgrimage to Mecca. Almost at the same time, Robert Fortune adopted Chinese disguise in order to smuggle tea seedlings from deep inside China to India and contributed to the British domination of the tea market, previously a Chinese monopoly (Thurin, 1999: 32–5). Female explorers like Mary Kingsley had intruded into this masculine sphere of imperial mission. From this point of view, the kissing duet in *The Geisha* reinforced the idea that British imperial agents were an exclusively homosocial but heterosexual male group and reconfirmed the mission to civilise as masculine.

Japan as the Garden and Geisha: Putting New Japan in the Old Place

Like some British women, the Japanese had already ceased to be silent subjects to the British male-oriented empire since the 1880s. As industrialisation developed, the Japanese government inaugurated the westernisation of the nation, such as the proclamation of the constitution (1890) and the imperial war with China carried out in the name of protecting the independence of Korea (1894–95), in emulation of European imperial expansion. The victory over China, considered as a demonstration of the achievement of Japan's civilisation, was caricatured in *Punch* as 'Jap the Giant-Killer' (29 September 1895). At the same time, a number of

Japanese tried to accelerate the emergence of modernity from a despotic Oriental past. The Chon Kina dance to the tourists, for example, was banned as a racial slur in 1891. About two months before *The Geisha*'s first performance, an English magazine was inaugurated to propagate the mission of the new Japan. According to Eigo Fukai, the editor of *The Far East*, its purpose was to widen the definition of civilisation and establish a mutual relationship to supersede enforced inequality in economic and political relations within the international community (*Far East*, 1896 [20 February]: 8 [20 December]: 2).

However, westernisation or modernisation has been unpopular among tourists since the Victorian age, as it dilutes the 'otherness' of 'exotic' destinations. Douglas Sladen expressed his wishes frankly and directly: 'Never grow up! And may Japan never grow up out of its old delightful status of a "Nation at Play"' (Sladen, 1892: 317). Thus, the Japan of *The Geisha* should be a 'happy' and 'gay' Asia, simply a pleasure garden where the visitors could gather chrysanthemums as they want. The pervasive metaphor of garden and geisha explains why the operetta was set in the garden and why almost all geisha girls were named after a flower.

These festivities of 'human flowers', however, were 'considered by native observers as evidence of extreme vulgarity', as Lafcadio Hearn observed in 1894 (Hearn, 1894: 528). A member of the Japan Society, Osman Edwards, quoted Fukai's lament for such a representation of Japan: 'Our country is simply a play-ground for globe-trotters, our people a band of cheerful, merry playfellows' (Edwards, 1901: 4). Commenting on *The Geisha*, Fukai admitted that 'Light-hearted friends of Japan find in these lines the most happy features of the country, and overlook the gross injustice done in the play to the Japanese nation'; and regretted that Japan was still depicted as the stereotypical Oriental society where a despot like Marquis Imari tyrannises and the slave trade continues in spite of the constitutional state (Edwards, 1899: 144). On balance, Diósy, the producer of *The Geisha*, after hearing the words of Fukai, explained how he could not help but submit to 'the demon of stage convention' and the obstinacy of the actresses. Further, he added: 'The play did not offend the Japanese; they treated it as a joke', taking an example of his friend, a Japanese naval officer who had gone to see it several times with the whole crew (Edwards, 1899: 161).

It seemed to be, however, beyond a joke for some performers and audiences. After 9 September 1898, *The Geisha* was regularly staged in America. At the time, an anonymous actress, who was asked to sing in a quartet, lay on the floor crying and complaining about the 'stupidity of the *Geisha*'. The manager agreed with her but explained that he had to think of the financial side of the affair. That was the last straw and she fled to Europe where she happened to see a performance of a real geisha, Madame Sadayakko. There and then Isadora Duncan inaugurated the modern dance movement (Duncan, 1996: 35, 71–2).

The similar 'imbecility of the thing' was differently deplored by a Japanese audience. Yone Noguchi, a Japanese poet who lived in America at the turn of the 20th century, took on the guise of a Japanese woman, Miss Morning Glory, as he described an American girl imitating Chon kina dance in 1902.

> I was sorry, thinking that she might regard me as an uncivil Jap.
> 'Chon kina! Chon kina!'
> Thus Dorothy repeated. It was a Japanese song, she said, which the geisha girls sung in '*The Geisha*.'
> ....
> I presume that '*The Geisha*' is practising a plenteous injustice to Dai Nippon [Great Japan].
> I recalled one Merichen[American] consul who jolted out that same song once at a party.
> He became no more a gentleman to me after that. ('Miss Morning Glory', 1902; 70)

This indicates the way in which *The Geisha* reinforced the American image of Japan (British Library, n.d.), and how difficult it was for Japanese men to speak for themselves in the American commercial publishing world. Noguchi knew that a Japanese male poet's straight criticism would not be accepted nor considered in America, so he borrowed the sugar-coated Japanese girl's mouthpiece, even though this was the kind of feminisation of Japan he himself criticised.

The Diary of Miss Morning Glory (1902) produced another unexpected dividend. Yone Noguchi hired a woman, Leonie Gilmour, who checked his work and arranged its publication as an agent. This cash nexus between writer and informant became intimate. Yone Noguch, however, left her to go back to Japan in 1904 and, before long, Gilmour had a child, 'without benefit of clergy' as it were. The child became Isamu Noguchi, a leading modern sculptor (Duus, 2004: 20–31). Isamu Noguchi and Isadora Duncan, who inspired modern art by crossing the east–west border, might be unexpected by-products of *The Geisha* performances. In other words, *The Geisha* went beyond its Victorian limitation, prohibition of miscegenation, to bring about cultural and racial hybridities above the sphere of the British Empire.

This phenomenon of hybridities and the Japanese nationalistic backlash were contemporary with a political partnership: the Anglo-

Japanese alliance of 1902. By this union, Japan managed to achieve parity with the western powers and began to reject the image of the geisha. In 1901, geisha Madame Sadayakko's performances in London, as well as the writing of Yone Noguchi, exploited the previous Japonism but changed the direction slightly, based on their own Japanese authenticity. A critic of *The Times* wrote, 'With real Japan before us, the last thing we wish to be reminded of is the sham Japan of cockney invention' (Downer, 2003: 185).

The Russo-Japanese war, assisted by the Anglo-Japanese alliance, was a turning point. After the Japanese victory over Russia in 1905, the Japanese government considered the Japanese prostitution network for overseas visitors as a national disgrace and prohibited it. In the world of caricature too, the masculine samurai sword-bearing man became more commonly used as an icon, replacing the little Jap or geisha girl. As the author of *My Japanese Wife* (1895) regretfully noted in 1907, 'Japan can no longer be thought of as what a humorist once called "the kingdom of the two G's – the land of gardens and geishas"' (Holland, 1907: 23).

The transformation from garden to empire was expressed by the nature of the teahouse in the Japanese National Industrial Exhibition of 1903. A Japanese bureaucrat, Hirokichi Mutsu, contributed to an American magazine a report to describe 'Japan's wonderful progress' including the following:

> Dainty maidens of that beautiful island, attired in their picturesque native costume and speaking but little of our own language, serve the visitor a cup of the celebrated oolong tea at the very moderate charge of two and a half cents. (Mutsu, 1903: 119)

This referred to the teahouse of the Formosan building, named after the island which Japan acquired and 'civilised' after the Sino-Japanese war. The country of the 'Sixpence girl' in 1885 had moved on by 1903 to present teahouse girls from a colonised territory as an exotic attraction. Later Mutsu, because of his English wife, was despatched to London as First Secretary of the Japanese Embassy and appointed Commissioner to the Japan–British Exhibition of 1910 to try to bridge the two 'Island Empires' (Hotta-Lister, 1999: 49). Not surprisingly, a similar Taiwanese (Formosan) Tea House was opened in the Japanese–British exhibition to publicise how Japan had succeeded in civilising a foreign land (Watanabe, 1997: 126).

This shift in Japan's identity from the subject of empire to agent of empire would explain why *The Geisha* was forgotten so quickly at the beginning of the 20th century. As the popularity of *Madame Butterfly* (1904) suggested, more sadomasochistic sublimation was necessary to castrate the rising sun: obedience became fanatic self-sacrifice to turn the potential

Japanese menace into self-destruction. The alteration of the status of Japan was unexpectedly alluded to in James Joyce's *Ulysses* (1922) set in Dublin on 16 June 1904. With several references to the ongoing Russo-Japanese war, Joyce effectively contrasted the uneasy news and a song of *The Geisha*, 'Jewel of Asia'. This suggested that after the Great War, *The Geisha* became a nostalgic representation of Asia as the gay geisha or the jewel of the imperial crown.

Disillusion and disenchantment had spread over Britain through the Great War. In 1921, a year before Joyce's *Ulysses*, Britain and Japan decided at the Washington conference not to maintain their diplomatic alliance. At the same time, British diplomat Ashton-Gwatkin anonymously published a timely best-selling novel *Kimono* dealing with the issue of international marriage between a British nobleman and a Japanese woman. The British man on honeymoon in Japan, goes to a Japanese brothel secretly with his friends before his first night with his new bride and happens to see the 'national dance', Chon kina.

> *Chonkina, Chonkina, Chon, Chon, Kina, Kina,*
> *Yokohama, Nagasaki, Hakodate – Hoi!*
>
> The refrain of an old song was awakened in his mind by the melodious name of the place.
>
> ....
>
> She [geisha girl] peeled them[drawers] off with an affection of modesty, which was indecency's climax. Then, grotesquely nude, she posed in the middle of the group, a flat denial of all the canons of Hellenic beauty .... The secret of Venus had been for him, as for many men, an inviolate Mecca towards which he worshipped .... [But] An overgrown embryo she seemed, a gawkish ill-moulded thing .... was she [his wife] like this? (Paris, 1921: 57, 64–5)

He was disgusted with 'the butterfly women of the traveller's imagination' and he felt the distance between these women and his new wife who was brought up and educated in Europe separated from the homeland. This modified version of *My Japanese Wife* presents the reverse side of *The Geisha*. Geisha as the effeminised Japan is revealed in the novel as invalid and as a 'reality' that it is harmful to know. The message is, as it were, 'scratch the kimono and you'll find the naked truth about Japan'. The fear of miscegenation is, therefore, intensified, based on the belief that nature runs deeper than nurture. *Kimono* indicates that the happy-go-lucky geisha girls were out of date by the 1920s, when the stereotype of the Oriental woman was polarised between the tragic suicidal Madame Butterfly and the Oriental femme fatale, the Dragon lady.

Conclusion

The operetta *The Geisha* owed its success at the turn of the century to its intimate connection with the contemporary context, as the boundaries of race, gender and class were destabilised by various challenges. It reveals the British political unconscious intention to restore patriarchal law and order from anarchy, arising from the emergence of the subversive new woman as well as the rising new Japan from the 1880s. At this point, although inspired by a French globetrotter's travelogue, *The Geisha* was tailored into contemporary British taste, in which a French agent of imperialism was reduced and effeminised as the sexually loose girl Juliette. Her transgressive ambition to climb the class ladder, regardless of race, is a vestigial survival of the class conflict theme of early Victorian melodrama, which is transformed with a racial twist through marriage to a native nobleman. But the theme of the operetta is less about an attitude towards miscegenation than the imperilled virtue of an English progressive woman in the hands of a local despot, in reaction to which the marriage of British man with British woman seemed the only rightful and natural outcome. The rescue of the adventurous modern woman from the menacing Oriental, however, helps to return the subversive women to her rightful submissive place. A similar feminisation of the New Woman can be seen in the new Japan, inaugurated by the imperial mission at the *fin-de-siècle*. The teahouses of submissive geisha girls are, therefore, the ideal prerogative sphere where racial and gender hierarchies are re-stabilised to reconfirm masculinity. The potential menace of a new Japan is minimised into an atavistic Oriental lord and innocent geisha girls who ask the British sailors to protect them from local tyranny and to civilise them. Like the example of the duet in which the British officer teaches a geisha how to kiss, *The Geisha* limits the British imperial mission to men, without violating the taboo against miscegenation. The perception of Japan as a playground (innocent or otherwise) for British men, however, metaphorically and practically, began to disappear with the modernisation that took place from the early 20th century, during which *The Geisha* became less popular and attractive. However, its considerable ephemeral popularity provides vivid reflection of and reinforcement for contradictory and conflicting British tourist, imperial and xenophobic desires during the transitional years of the late 19th and early 20th century.

References

Adlard, J. (1990) *A Biography of Arthur Diósy*. New York: Edwin Mellen.
Angus, D.C. (1882) *The Eastern Wonderland*. London: Cassell.

Birkett, D. (1992) *Mary Kingsley*. London: Macmillan.
Bowie, H.P. (1897) A foreigner's impressions of Japan. *Far East* 2, 18–21.
British Library (n.d.) Scrapbook of reviews of performances of *The Geisha*.
Checkland, O. (1996) *Isabella Bird*. Aberdeen: Scottish Cultural Press.
Chekhov, A. (1984) *The Russian Master and Other Stories*. Oxford: Oxford University Press.
Downer, D. (2003) *Madame Sadayakko: The Geisha Who Bewitched the West*. New York: Gotham Books.
Duncan, I. (1996) *My Life*. New York: Liveright.
Duus, M. (2004) *The Life of Isamu Noguchi*. Princeton: Princeton University Press.
Edwards, O. (1899) Japanese theatres. *Transactions and Proceedings of the Japan Society* 5, 141–64.
Edwards, O. (1901) *Japanese Plays and Playfellows*. London: Heinemann.
Far East: An English Edition of the Kokumin-no-tomo (1896) (Vols 1 and 2). Tokyo: Office of the Kokumn-no-tomo.
Fitz-Gerald, S.J.A. (1924) *The Story of the Savoy Opera*. London: Stanley Paul.
Fraser, Mrs H. (1899) *A Diplomat's Wife in Japan* (Vol. 1). London: Hutchinson and Co.
Gandhi, Mahatma (1904) The Edwin Arnold Memorial. In *The Collected Works of Mahatma Gandhi* (Vol. 4). New Delhi: Ministry of Information and Broadcasting, Government of India.
Ganzl, K. (1986) *British Musical Theatre*, Vol. 1, 1865–1914. London: Macmillan.
Ganzl, K. (1994) *The Encyclopaedia of the Musical Theatre*. Oxford: Oxford University Press.
Ganzl, K. (1997) *The Musical*. Boston, MA: Northeastern University Press.
Hall, O. (1949) *The Geisha: a Musical Play in Two Acts*. London: Emile Littler.
Hashimoto, Y. (2003a) Germs, body-politics and Yellow Peril: Relocation of Britishness in *The Yellow Danger*. *Australasian Victorian Studies Journal* 9, 52–66.
Hashimoto, Y. (2003b) Victorian biological terror: A study of 'the stolen bacillus.' *The Undying Fire: The Journal of the H.G. Wells Society, the Americas* 2, 3–27.
Hearn. L. (1894) *Glimpses of Unfamiliar Japan*. London: Kegan Paul.
Hearn, L. (1895) *Out of the East*. London: Osgood- McIlvaine.
Holland, C. (1907) *Things Seen in Japan*. London: Seeley.
Hotta-Lister, A. (1999) *The Japan–British Exhibition of 1910*. Richmond: Japan Library.
Hyam, R. (1998) *Empire and Sexuality*. Manchester: Manchester University Press.
Illustrated London News, 2 May 1896, 592.
Jeal, T. (1989) *Baden-Powell*. London: Hutchinson.
Ledger, S. (1997) *New Woman*. Manchester: Manchester University Press.
Lehmann, J-P. (1978) *The Image of Japan*. London: George Allen and Unwin.
Linhart, S. (1993) Chonkina – Ein Japanischer Tanz in Europaischen Schilderungen. In K. Antoni and V-M. Blummel (eds) *Festgabe fur Nelly Naumann*. Hamburg: Gesellschaft fur Natur- und Volkerkunde Ostasiens.
Littlewood, I. (1996) *The Idea of Japan*. London: Secker and Warburg.
McClintock, A. (1994) *Imperial Leather*. London: Routledge.
MacKenzie, J.M. (1984) *Propaganda and Empire*. Manchester: Manchester University Press.
'Miss Morning Glory'(Yone Noguchi) (1902) *The American Diary of a Japanese Girl*. Tokyo: Fuzanbo.

Mutsu, H. (1903) Japan's wonderful progress. *The Cosmopolitan* 36, 113–19.
Norman, H. (1892) *Real Japan*. London: T. Fisher Unwin.
Oliphant, L. (1859) *Narrative of the Earl of Elgin's Mission to China and Japan in the Years 1857, '58, '59*. Edinburgh: W. Blackwood.
Paris, J. (1921) *Kimono*. London: W. Collins.
Quarterly Review (1880), Vol. 150.
Scidmore, E.R. (1892) *Jinrikisha Days in Japan*. New York: Harper and Brothers.
Sladen, D. (1892) *The Japs at Home*. London: Hutchinson.
Tamura, N. (1904) *The Japanese Bride*. New York: Harper Brothers.
Thurin, S.S. (1999) *Victorian Travellers and the Opening of China*. Athens, OH: Ohio University Press.
Watanabe, T. (ed.) (1997) *Catalogue of Ruskin in Japan 1840–1940*. Tokyo: Cogito.
Wilkinson, E. (1983) *Japan Versus Europe*. Harmondsworth: Penguin Books.

Chapter 7

Radical Nationalism in an International Context: Strength through Joy and the Paradoxes of Nazi Tourism

SHELLEY BARANOWSKI

In June 1935, a self-described 'English admirer' of Adolf Hitler, Sir Benjamin Dawson, sent a letter to the Führer, convinced that preserving peace among nations and bettering 'the way of life of the great mass of the people' ranked at the top of Hitler's priorities. Dawson, who in addition to being part owner of a textile mill was chair of the Conservative party in Bradford, asked Hitler to support an international agreement that would guarantee workers a shorter workday without wage reductions. Dawson's appeal failed to produce the desired outcome. For fear of unsettling British public opinion, the German embassy in London informed the foreign ministry in Berlin that Dawson was not influential enough to warrant more than a polite, noncommittal response (Bundesarchiv Lichterfeld (BAL), R43II/546 a). Nevertheless, for all its naiveté and apparent disregard for the Nazi regime's racial and political violence, Dawson's letter underscores a feature of the Third Reich that contributed to fascism's appeal during the inter-war period, its promise to raise mass living standards, overcome the social divisions that liberal capitalism produced and, especially important to circles inclined to appeasement, undermine the Left.

What did a 'better' way of life mean? Dawson rightly emphasised a shorter workday for it occupied a vital place in international discussions on a family of issues that included mass production, leisure time and mass consumption. Yet if authoritarian and fascist regimes hardly stood at the forefront in implementing the eight-hour day (Dawson's optimism notwithstanding), they did draw attention for their solutions to the 'problem' of increased leisure time for workers. Sharing the belief of industrial psychologists and social scientists internationally as to the dangers of unregulated leisure, they distinguished themselves by deploying the state as the exclusive organiser of workers' free time (Cross, 1993; De Grazia, 1981: 237–44). Among the dictatorships, however, the Third Reich occupied a class by itself through its leisure-time and tourism organisation Strength through Joy (*Kraft durch Freude* [KdF]). The scale of KdF's activities and the size of its membership dwarfed its closest counterpart, the organisation that provided KdF's partial inspiration, the Italian Fascist leisure-time agency 'After Work' (*Dopolavoro*) (*Dopolavoro und Kraft durch Freude*, 1936). Moreover, among other honours, KdF won a trophy from the International Olympic Committee for its sports programmes and a prize at the 1937 Paris Exhibition for the architectural design of its resort, then under construction, on the Baltic. It even won grudging praise from the International Labour Office for providing 'the most extensive official experiment' in travel through its cruises, despite Germany's withdrawal from the League of Nations and KdF's contempt for the League's labour arm (Frohmann, 1976: 204; International Labour Office, 1939: 4; International Olympic Committee, 1994: 216). Such recognition testified to Nazism's success in convincing an international audience of the efficacy of its leisure policies. Among other tactics, KdF's leadership invited foreign guests to its annual meetings, treating their visitors to cruises through the Norwegian fjords and excursions to prime tourist sites in Germany. An Irish delegate to the Nazi-sponsored World Congress for Leisure Time and Recreation in 1938 remarked that no other industrialised nation had anything like Strength through Joy. Foreign delegates, he marvelled, were housed 'in one of those vast liners' (the brand new cruise ship *Wilhelm Gustloff*), 'which surpassed anything it is possible to imagine for comfort and luxury' (Auswärtiges Amt-Politisches Archiv R49245).

For an autarkic and virulently nationalist regime to have cultivated praise outside Germany for its tourism and leisure programmes is paradoxical. The explanation lies not only in the potential of those programmes for disarming foreign criticism of Germany but also in the pressure that existed within Germany to satisfy expectations for a better material existence. Thus, improving the standard of living, especially for working-class Germans, whom the Nazi party sought to lure away from 'Marxism', preoccupied the Nazi leadership even before the party took power. The Weimar Republic's nascent consumerism, despite its well-documented economic crises, the popular fascination after the First World War with American-style mass consumption and the campaign of the Left, the Socialists in particular, to improve working-class recreational opportunities and access to goods, meant Nazi leaders could not ignore popular desires, whatever their dislike of 'materialism' (Confino & Koshar, 2001: 135–6, 143–6; Nolan, 1994; Rogers, 1998: 370–1). The Nazi party's electoral appeal as the republic declined lay at least partly in its advocacy of social mobility through individual achievement (*Leistung*) and its assurance that a Nazi state would eliminate the class hierarchies that consumption defined. In their place, the party promised a 'national community' (*Volksgemeinschaft*) united by racial purity, rather than divided by social conflict; one in which all racially acceptable Germans, regardless of class or region, would share in a prosperous future (Fritzsche, 1998).

The Nazi takeover in 1933 yielded a second paradox, however, the tension between 'guns and butter'. War preparations assumed pride of place in the German economy, especially after 1936 with the institution of the Four-Year Plan, which explicitly envisioned autarky and imperial expansion. Of necessity, the Nazi regime curtailed wage increases and private consumption. Mass consumption lagged substantially behind that in the USA, a good illustration being the gap in personal automobile ownership, and noticeably behind that in Britain and France (Koshar, 2000: 119; Overy, 1994: 262–5). Curiously though, the growth in the sale of refrigerators, radios, cameras, and camping equipment proceeded apace until 1939. Although KdF's tourism largely ceased during the war, at least for civilians, commercial tourism persisted, complicating military mobilisation (Berghoff, 1996, 2001; Koshar, 2000; Mason, 1976; Overy, 1994). The conflicting claims of consumption and rearmament did not deter the Nazi regime from its central goal, the acquisition of 'living space' (*Lebensraum*) in the east, which would ultimately become the centre of a global empire. Nor did they push the regime into war sooner than it had planned, as Tim Mason's pioneering and influential study of Nazi social policy once suggested (Mason, 1993). Nonetheless, domestic political considerations did require a creative, if muted, accommodation to an emerging consumer culture. As the largest leisure-time organisation of its kind, what role did KdF play in the Third Reich's attempts to resolve the consumption dilemma? What was characteristically National Socialist in its answer to the internationally recognised problems of modernity?

Founded in November 1933 as compensation for the failure of its parent organisation, the German Labour Front, to become the exclusive bargaining agent for workers, KdF began inauspiciously (Spode, 1982: 28–9). Nevertheless, it rapidly became the most visible evidence of the regime's attempt to 'raise' working-class living standards and manage consumption so as not to jeopardise its racist and imperialist goals. To conform to that aim in fact, KdF's spokesmen described leisure as integral to raising productivity. Minds and bodies reinvigorated through respite would result in greater output on the job (Ley, 1943: 29–4). To be sure, KdF understood the attraction of material goods. The presence of its director of the office of Travel, Hiking, and Vacations, Bodo Lafferentz, on the board of directors of Volkswagen, Hitler's pet project for the masses, testified to that (Mommsen & Grieger, 1996: 133–54). Primarily however, KdF strove to provide party- and state-mediated, low-cost and less tangible forms of consumption that would open the 'cultural property' of the nation to workers. On the one hand, KdF would substitute for working-class recreational associations and programmes that the regime dissolved, including the tourism that the Socialists developed during the 1920s. On the other, it would compensate for the limited accessibility of commercial leisure by using its large clientele to negotiate lower prices for its offerings. Recognising that wages would likely not be raised, indeed claiming that doing so would fuel an insatiable 'materialism', KdF defined consumption as access to the cultural practices of the middle and upper classes: the theatre, the playhouse, the opera, sports such as sailing, horseback riding and tennis and especially tourism. By explicitly describing leisure programmes as consumer goods, KdF could claim to raise mass living standards without compromising rearmament and thus fulfil its promise to foster upward mobility. It would also do its part to undermine entrenched proletarian milieux that supposedly demoralised workers, weakening their stake in the nation.

Six divisions directed KdF's activities, which in addition to tourism covered organised sports, adult education, concerts, theatre, opera and light entertainment. KdF's purview extended as well to the rationalisation and 'aestheticisation' of the workplace through its office, the 'Beauty of Labour' (*Schönheit der Arbeit*) (Rabinach, 1979: 189–222; Weiss, 1993: 295–6). Taken together, KdF's various initiatives endeavoured to render workers less proletarian in habit and identity by encouraging them to appropriate high culture as their own, channelling them into the pursuit of middle-class pastimes and disciplining and sanitising working-class bodies. The bodily interventionism and explicit productivism of Strength through Joy appeared vividly in the Beauty of Labour, a project with roots in the ideas of Charles Fourier and the British 'Garden Cities' movement, and later, Taylorism (Rabinach, 1979: 197–200). As the division most directly concerned with work, it supported the claim of the KdF leadership that Strength through Joy was no mere leisure-time agency but one that addressed the complementarity of workers' 'creative lives' on and off the job. Desiring to transform workplaces into sites of efficiency, cleanliness and harmony between employers and employees, the Beauty of Labour energetically lobbied employers (it had no legal authority to compel them) to construct athletic facilities, modern toilets, washing and changing rooms, attractive dining rooms that would encourage workers to use silverware and china at meal times and scrupulously sanitary workplaces. Those initiatives endeavoured to lift morale and productivity, promote personal health and hygiene and eliminate all signs of the grime and exhaustion of manual labour.

The Nazi regime's economic and military priorities help to explain why the Beauty of Labour expected employers to cover the cost of plant improvements themselves. To avoid becoming a drain on the Reich treasury, KdF's operations became largely self-financing through a combination of tax abatements, subventions from its parent, the Labour Front and the contributions of its target audiences. Such cost control conformed to KdF's goal of improving living standards without succumbing to 'materialism'. For the Beauty of Labour, well-kept planted grounds, good lighting, clean changing facilities, tasteful dining rooms and lunchtime concerts would grant workers membership in the nation that possessions could not alone provide. Whereas, according to its glossy publication by the same name, construction workers in New York, the financial capital of the world's most advanced consumer culture, wolfed down their midday meals while sitting precariously atop a beam on the Rockefeller Center construction site, German workers – their hands and faces glowing and clean – dined at tables decorated with floral centrepieces, served by attractive waitresses (Essen & Essen, 1938: 446–50). In addition to deriding the 'Marxists' for terming plant improvements as collectively a capitalist diversionary tactic, the Beauty of Labour also strove to eliminate the signifiers of market-based consumption that not only violated the regime's aesthetic sensibilities but also held the potential for fuelling unacceptable levels of demand. It campaigned against advertising in the workplace, and especially in Germany's villages, which it sought to prettify in time to impress the presumed legions of foreign visitors, who would attend the KdF-sponsored World Congress for Leisure and Recreation in Hamburg and the summer Olympic Games in Berlin (Landeshauptarchiv Magdeburg, 1934–43). Despite pushing for the construction of better housing for workers, its publications insisted that such homes balance comfort with simplicity and not become sites of unrestrained consumption as depicted in Hollywood films (Eine nachdenkliche Geschichte, 1937). Consistent with the racially-inscribed way in which Nazism understood Germany's international position, threatened by Bolshevism from one side and American-dominated international capitalism on the other, the Beauty of Labour described the alternatives to its visions as 'Jewish', whether this meant the seemingly ubiquitous mass advertising in the smallest of villages, filthy working conditions that exacerbated the class partisanship of workers or the commercialisation of art (NSG Kraft durch Freude, 1936: 25–7; von Huebbenet, 1939: 39).

Strength through Joy's domestic and foreign tourism, however, easily emerged as its most popular programme, and it became emblematic of the Nazi regime's ambivalent nod to consumption. Just three months after its founding, KdF's first tours commenced; affairs that took tourists from Berlin, Dresden, Altona, Hamburg, Königsberg, Essen, Dortmund and Hannover to the upper Bavarian, Harz, Rhone and Silesian mountains as well as to the Bavarian and Thuringian forests. By 1936, KdF generated nearly 10 million overnight stays, over 11% of all guest overnights (Kahl, 1940: 7–8; Spode, 1982: 299). By 1938 furthermore, an estimated 43 million KdF trips had been taken, many of them by repeat travellers. In that last full prewar year, KdF's staff of approximately 140,000, most of them volunteers, mobilised 8.5 million tourists (Reichel, 1993: 245–6). The majority of the tours consisted of short excursions of up to three days, but the participation in the longer vacation trips and cruises was by no means negligible, amounting to approximately one and a half million out of 6.2 million vacationers in 1939 (Spode, 1980: 295). Strength through Joy claimed to increase access for ordinary Germans to the destinations that previously only the wealthy had enjoyed, examples being its voyages to the Portuguese island of Madeira, a favourite watering hole of the British aristocracy and wealthy middle class, or its cruises around the Italian coast and to other Mediterranean, Adriatic and Ionian ports. Moreover, for all its misgivings about hedonism and its insistence on austerity– the third- and fourth-class train compartments that transported KdF tourists provoked repeated, and understandable, complaint – KdF increasingly emphasised creature comforts that would become available to 'lesser-earning' Germans. The one-class liners that KdF commissioned, the *Wilhelm Gustloff* and *Robert Ley*, launched in 1938 and 1939 respectively, each contained libraries, swimming pools, smoking rooms, comfortably appointed cabins with hot and cold running water and generous sun-deck space (NSG Kraft durch Freude, 1938: 109–23, 1939c). The amenities planned for KdF's huge, 20,000-bed, resort on the Baltic, Prora, the first of five envisioned by the Labour Front's leader, Robert Ley, included a huge concert hall, billiards room, cinema, restaurants, two swimming pools (one with a wave-making machine) and again comfortable rooms, all of them facing the beach (Reichsamtsleitung Kraft durch Freude, 1938: 127–32; Rostock & Zadnièek, 1995; Spode, 1997: 7–47). Such projected 'luxury' would prove that Nazism delivered what the Marxists could only lamely imitate.

KdF insisted, however, that its tourism opposed mere pleasure-seeking and commercialism, consonant with the regime's repeated calls for sacrifice and self-restraint. It helped KdF's case that tourists and tourist promoters often claimed (as they still claim) serious purposes and deep meaning for their enterprises precisely to disguise the commercial nature of tourism development (Koshar, 1998: 323–40). 'Our vacation trips are not commercial undertakings', one KdF monthly bulletin intoned, 'but an occasion [*sic*] for the highest idealism' (NSG Kraft durch Freude, 1934). Motivations for tourism, such as contemplating the sublime, cultivating comradeship with one's fellow tourists, improving one's education by studying the architecture of ancient Greece, expanding one's horizons by visiting exotic locales, awakening one's historical consciousness and even acting out fantasies, appeared in KdF's monthly programmes and in the testimonials from tourists that such periodicals solicited. The language employed confirms Christoph Hennig's observation that tourism is the expression of dreams, fantasies and the imagination played out in 'reality'; i.e., the aesthetic experiences that renders tourism less like a commodity than other, more tangible, consumer goods (Hennig, 1999: 91–103). The KdF trip was, according to its periodicals, 'like a dream' or 'fantasy', a 'dream come true', or 'a fairy tale'. Taken together, KdF trips were 'unforgettable experiences' that provided opportunities to observe an alien culture, fall in love and find a life partner with another passenger in exotic settings and elevate oneself completely above the humdrum (NSG, 1934, 3; 1939d: 4–6). For those who wanted little more than frivolity or amusement, a category of tourist that KdF tour organisers presumed existed (and, as we will see, not without reason), KdF monthly programmes settled for straightforward and less ethereal proscriptions. Tourists were not to dress as if they were models in a fashion show, ridicule the customs and dress of others (especially other Germans), drink to excess, engage in casual trysts with foreigners (a concern that Gestapo and SS Security Service surveillance reports often expressed about young women on cruises), spend their money on kitschy souvenirs (the regime's strict currency regulations dampened the purchasing power of tourists in any case) or disregard the strict schedules of tour directors. Tourism, as KdF practised it, thus conformed to the regime's determination to maintain a modest, disciplined consumption. Its ability to keep the cost of tour packages low compared to commercial tourism by arranging lodgings in private accommodation and negotiating low rail and bus fares conveniently dovetailed with the repeated insistence of its spokesmen that workers did not need higher wages to enjoy an improved standard of living. Wage increases were unnecessary because workers could avail themselves of the 'cultural property' of the nation and enjoy the sun, surf and cruises at bargain basement rates (NSG, 1935a, 5–6; Recht zur Freude, 1934: 5–11; Starcke, 1936: 3–4).

As the historian Victoria de Grazia has argued recently, the competition between rival consumption regimes, which in turn signified alternative roads to modernity, shaped inter-war political conflicts in Western Europe, including Germany (De Grazia, 1998: 59–83). The first, the 'bourgeois' model, favoured small retail, limited distribution and class-defined hierarchies of taste. The second, or 'Fordist' regime championed the mass distribution of goods through assembly-line production and high wages, the projected outcome being the mitigation of class tensions by broadening access to market-based consumption. What we have seen thus far implies that Strength through Joy accorded more with Fordism than with bourgeois consumption. And indeed, KdF's desire to transform leisure travel into a mass entitlement has encouraged historians of tourism, most prominently Hasso Spode, to characterise KdF tourism as 'Fordist' or at least a 'Fordist variant' (Spode, 1997: 25–9). Although, as Spode acknowledges, the Nazi regime could not and would not raise wages, KdF otherwise appears as the very picture of rationalised, mass-produced leisure. Its trainloads of holidaymakers, 800–1000 per train, the contempt that well-heeled vacationers heaped on KdF tourists and its gargantuan resort complete with garages to protect the visible signs of the Nazi 'motorisation of the masses', Volkswagens (themselves indicative of Hitler's considerable admiration for Henry Ford) all offer further support for his argument. Nevertheless, the seeming weight of that evidence belies the difficulty in describing KdF as 'Fordist', for the regime's determination to suppress wages, even if at times unsuccessful, flouted the most fundamental plank of Fordism, that workers should earn enough to access commercial leisure and consumption directly.

Instead, KdF became a model of consumption all its own, one that to be sure borrowed from common discourses of tourism and the shared concerns of the international discussion on the leisure 'problem' but one that simultaneously promoted and reflected Nazism's radical nationalism, racism and expansionism. Above all, the Nazi regime's violent confrontation with the German Left, Europe's largest labour movement, defined Strength through Joy's possibilities. Although bitterly opposed to each other, the Socialists and Communists together had been Nazism's most serious competition for working-class supporters. In particular, the leftist network of social tourism, consumer cooperatives and recreational clubs contributed significantly to retarding Nazism's appropriation of working-class constituencies before 1933, despite its credible performance among working-class voters (Szejnmann, 1996: 189–216). KdF's subsequent profit from the confiscated assets of the Left, which included numerous recreational facilities and equipment, as well as the treasuries of the trade unions absorbed by the Labour Front, resulted directly from the regime's destruction of the independent unions, the Socialist and Communist parties and the Left's many subsidiary associations (Smelser, 1988: 149–79). Furthermore, the ideology of KdF tourism articulated the regime's solution to a society that it saw as consumed by social divisions and demoralised by defeat, namely the *Volksgemeinschaft*. Because of its determination to achieve 'community', which it explicitly contrasted with the Left's presumption of class conflict, KdF even distinguished itself, ironically enough, from its closest relative, the *Dopolavoro* ('After Work'). This was organised by vocation according to Fascist corporativist principles, while KdF defined itself as a mass organisation, a 'community' that effaced a prime cause of class distinction, one's occupation. However productivist in its own right, *Dopolavoro* had nothing comparable to the Beauty of Labour (NSG Kraft Durch Freude, 1939a: 7).

Nazism's insidious messages saturated KdF's tourism. Its domestic tours provided opportunities for travellers from one district (*Gau*) to appreciate the panoramic landscapes of others, while their housing and socialising – private lodgings and 'community evenings' with residents – encouraged tourists to 'get acquainted with' other regions of Germany. In that way, Germany's entrenched regionalism, which Nazism deemed nearly as corrosive as class divisions to national cohesion, would be overcome. Tours to East Prussia, which traversed through Polish territory, not only reminded participants of the injustices of Versailles but also that Germans had brought culture to the Slavs in their colonisation of the east during the Middle Ages. Eager to capitalise on the regime's expansionism, KdF quickly promoted tour packages to Austria and the Sudentenland after their annexation in 1938 (Auswärtiges Amt-Politisches Archive, R49245). KdF's cruises became means of reconnecting Germans living in 'colonies' abroad with their homeland, for expatriates served as tour guides in KdF's ports of call, and they took part in the festivities staged for passengers (Bundesarchiv Berlin-Lichterfeld, NS 22/781: 6). Moreover, the cruises featured regular propaganda broadcasts, swastika-draped morning ceremonies on board ship and staged rendezvous with German battle ships as a demonstration of the nation's military power (Liebscher, 1999: 61–72). Cruises to exotic ports of call, such as Tripoli in the Italian colony of Libya, which KdF's agreements with the Fascist *Dopolavoro* facilitated, underscored the 'otherness' of the local people and, as Daniela Liebscher has pointed out, promoted visions of vast spaces open to the gaze of the German 'master race' (*Herrenvolk)* (Bundesarchiv Berlin-Lichterfeld R58, No. 944: 195). Insisted Robert Ley, workers would come to appreciate racial differences only if they observed them first hand through tourism (Baranowski & Furlough, 2001, especially Part II). To be sure, KdF's struggle to popularise tourism found parallels in nations as politically diverse as the USA, Great Britain, the Soviet Union, Sweden and France, where central governments used tourism to strengthen national cohesion, encourage economic development and diminish social tensions (Keitz, 1997: 248–54; Spode, 1982). Nevertheless, Strength through Joy's debt to the ruthless suppression of the left and its willingness to conform its definition of the 'standard of living' to the Third Reich's drive for empire made it a uniquely Nazi nation-building project.

We should not confuse Strength through Joy's ambitions as to its social inclusiveness with its actual impact. The existing scholarship on KdF underscores its limited social bases, a conclusion my own research sustains. Despite the subventions that KdF received from the German Labour Front, the burden of purchasing vacation packages fell on the tourists themselves, including the many who deposited a portion of their wages or salaries in the Labour Front's bank. Moreover, regardless of the low cost of KdF tours, tourists had to factor into account the numerous extras not included in the package price. Even though more workers traveled during the 1930s than during the 1920s, only skilled, single workers, most of them male, or workers whose companies subsidised them – an intermittent rather than routine practice (Frese, 1991: 371–83) – had any hope of affording more than a short outing. Civil servants, teachers and white-collar workers, including many women, appeared disproportionately in the passenger or tour lists, namely the social constituency that had sustained the growth of Weimar tourism. Then too, Nazi party members showed an uncanny ability to secure the best accommodations on KdF trips, be they better rooms in pensions or cabins on board ship. The mounting evidence of KdF's inability to attract workers, particularly workers with families, at least partially motivated the construction of the resort at Prora. As Ley asserted defensively, working-class families would soon enjoy a week's seaside vacation for a mere 20 marks (Niedersächsisches Hauptstaatsarchiv, Hannover, VVP17, No. 2456). Finally, war preparations, not mass consumption, dominated the Third Reich and only post-war reconstruction, be it in West or East Germany, created the conditions for a genuine mass tourism; one that bore little resemblance to KdF. West German commercial tourism, which thrived with rapidly rising incomes, eliminated the need for KdF-style mediation between consumers and the market, however much KdF might have contributed to the fusion of consumerism and anticommunism, which the West German economic miracle so prominently featured. Unlike the Nazi regime, the German Democratic Republic largely eliminated the capitalist leisure and consumer marketplace and subsidised travel outright so that more workers could take advantage of it. The travel restrictions that the GDR imposed, which confined its citizens to the Soviet Bloc, departed significantly from KdF's show of exposing ordinary Germans to the most popular vacation destinations of the classes above them (Schildt, 1995: 180–202; Spode, 1999: 134–7).

To add to that note of caution comes yet another: because tourists are not passive recipients of the agendas of tourism promoters, we cannot assume that KdF tourists accepted its heavy-handed attempts to politicise its tourism. While frequently praising the comradeship that they witnessed, surveillance reports of the cruises underscored regionally defined tensions among passengers, a problem that KdF's method of tour organisation exacerbated. Guides transported 'participants', whom local promoters had signed up, by district or *Gau*. The segregation of participants by class, the product of snobbery or insecurity, belied the *Volksgemeinschaft* in miniature that KdF expected from its tourism (Baranowski, 2004: 165–75). Furthermore, KdF periodicals correctly discerned the individualist search for pleasure and self-fulfilment, one of the prime characteristics of consumer culture, in the behaviour of its tourists, who, if the SD's surveillance reports are accurate, chafed at KdF's demands for discipline, conformity and participation in political rituals. Heavy drinking, card playing and love making intermingled with adventure seeking and genuine curiosity suggests that German tourists took full advantage of the opportunity to break with their daily routine, the stated purpose of vacations. Ironically, KdF's own tour brochures could have aggravated the problem that its periodicals identified. Although the brochures proclaimed that the purpose of leisure was to provide recuperation in order to raise productivity, they increasingly resorted to the relaxed, tanned, youthful vacationers of commercial advertising, thus inadvertently catering to the hedonism that Strength through Joy usually deplored (for example NSG Kraft durch Freude, 1938).

Nevertheless, we cannot discount KdF's contribution to the remarkably durable popularity that the Nazi regime enjoyed until well into the war, however sceptically we approach its claims. The manner in which German cruise passengers compared their own standard of living with that in foreign destinations demands that we take seriously an important component of that popularity, which historians are just beginning to investigate: Nazism's sensitivity to the development of a modern consumer culture and the strategies it developed to tame it. In contrast to the now substantial literature for Britain, France and the USA, nations against which Nazi Germany frequently measured itself, the study of consumer culture for German history is in its infancy (Confino, 1997; *German History*, 2001). That German tourists could smugly deplore living conditions in North Africa while posing on camels for photographs goes without saying. Yet they even reacted negatively to the inhabitants of ideologically sympathetic states, notably Italy and Portugal, in ways that discomfited their tour directors. KdF tour leaders, not to mention their Portuguese or Italian hosts, strove to conceal the desperate poverty of Lisbon, Naples and Palermo and staged host and guest parties on board or on shore as expressions of solidarity. To little avail: German passengers frequently, and apparently freely, remarked on the hardship and squalor they observed, recoiling at the outstretched hands of begging children. If they occasionally praised Mussolini's or Salazar's determination to improve the lives of their citizens, they persisted in comparing local conditions to the 'high' standard of living in Germany and expressing their pride for that reason in being German (Bundesarchiv Berlin-Lichterfeld, R58, No. 949: 13–14; No. 950: 447–8). The attentiveness of such tourists to living standards could become downright chilling, as the remarks of participants on another cruise to Italy indicated. Noting the contrast between the squalor of Naples and Palermo and German 'cleanliness', they agreed that complainers should be forced to live in such conditions, which would still be superior to those in a concentration camp (Bundesarchiv Berlin-Lichterfeld R58, No. 950, 384). Thus, even when German tourists sometimes behaved contrary to KdF's intentions, their observations reveal KdF's relative success in devising a credible alternative to the prevailing options for increasing mass living standards, Fordism and socialism. As a modest vision of the 'good life' during a period when scarcity was more evident than prosperity – when consumer expectations were more subdued than those of the present – KdF helped to persuade the majority of Germans whom the terror did not directly affect that an improved economy, rising living standards and the regime's apparent commitment to social opportunity were what defined the Third Reich. As recent scholarship of the Spartan consumption of German housewives makes clear, even the explicitly anti-materialist premises of KdF might well have struck a deep chord, for scepticism toward the seemingly unrestrained mass consumption of the USA most certainly existed: a scepticism that coexisted uneasily with admiration (Reagin, 2001: 162–84).

The comments of German tourists are not surprising in light of the social constituency that populated KdF's longer trips, for the middle classes, in addition to being the primary market for tourist promoters, constituted National Socialism's most reliable support. Yet neither were working-class tourists immune to seeing Nazism's advantages despite the fears of KdF's office for Travel, Hiking and Vacations that the closet Marxists among them would spread their poison. 'Under Adolf Hitler we are all kaisers', one miner was said to have remarked after having been told during his cruise on the Sierra Cordoba through the Norwegian fjords that Kaiser Wilhelm had once enjoyed the same vista. Only praise could be heard, reported an SD agent from the small group of workers on board another cruise, this one with the steamship *Oceana*, in contrast to the carping of well-off passengers. Finally, having witnessed the standard of living in Portugal on a cruise to Madeira with the ship, *Der Deutsche*, some working-class passengers announced that they would not for anything change places with the Portuguese (Bundesarchiv Berlin-Lichterfeld, R58, No. 948: 60–1; No. 950: 86; for Austria, Bukey, 2000: 82–3, 86). Indeed, commented the author of a report of his cruise to the same destination in a KdF periodical, the Portuguese with whom he and his comrades came into contact could not believe that the Germans were workers because they appeared so well dressed. Only when the tourists showed their hands to their hosts did the latter become convinced (NSG, Kraft durch Freude, 1935c, 2–4).

The self-satisfaction among many Germans, workers included, was portentous enough before the war, for it erected the wall that segregated persecuted minorities, especially Jews, who among other disabilities they faced could not indulge in 'fairy-tale' trips, from the majority for whom at least a short trip was possible. As such, the impact of Strength through Joy complemented that of the radio, which like tourism signified the Reich's cautious sensitivity to consumer demand. Opting in most cases for light entertainment over propaganda, radio programmers catered to audiences for whom the horrors of the Third Reich remained peripheral (Pater, 1998: 146). In his diary entries from July 1936, Victor Klemperer, the Jewish professor of Romance languages from Dresden, contrasted his social marginalisation to the everyday experiences of Germans whom he knew but whose racial status protected them from sharing his predicament. Amidst comments regarding his and his wife's poverty, the result of his having lost his teaching post on racial grounds, he recorded the arrival of an Aryan acquaintance, on a KdF tour train. The friend regaled to Klemperer the details of her trip, particularly its low package price, describing too her voyage to Norway on a KdF ship. Concluded Klemperer bitterly, 'these KdF undertakings are prodigious circuses' (Klemperer, 1998: 178–9).

The degree to which tourism could reinforce the segregation of the regime's enemies from the 'normality' of everyday life emerges even more glaringly in two additional examples: the SD agents assigned to monitor tours, the personification of Nazism's intrusive surveillance who might have imposed the experience of repression on those who would otherwise have escaped it, felt able to accommodate themselves to the expectations of tourists. Although certainly not neglecting their main task, their reports devoted space to the quality of accommodations, food and train travel, not hesitating to recommend rectification if such services left something to be desired (Bundesarchiv Berlin-Lichterfeld, R58, No. 947: 127–8). Then there is the remarkable article in a KdF monthly on the trip of workers from the G. Franz'sche printing company to the town of Dachau. Combining business with pleasure, the outing commenced with a visit to a paper factory, followed by a tour of a castle garden and a museum of local folk art. Because the tour took place during the Oktoberfest, it concluded with food, drink and, of course, dancing. The notorious concentration camp went unmentioned. The Dachau of KdF tourists and the Dachau of the Nazi regime's political and racial victims would remain radically separate (NSG Kraft durch Freude, 1935b, 10–11).

In all likelihood, the war exploited and radicalised pre-war attitudes and practices. Although the tourism arising from the Wehrmacht's invasions and its relationship to KdF's troop entertainment programme deserves further study, the acquisition of *Lebensraum* unquestionably offered vast opportunities for realising personal ambitions and making concrete the imperial visions that KdF promoted: ambitions that extended beyond a European Reich to Africa and the high seas (Geyer, 1996: 134–64; Latzel, 1995: 447–59; and for Wehrmacht tourism in France Gordon, 1998: 616–38). A prime instrument of tourism, the camera, became crucial to deepening the racial stereotypes that justified the Third's Reich's draconian population policies, notably in Poland and the Soviet Union. Indeed, KdF played an important role in popularising the camera, for its tourist brochures and monthly magazines regularly sponsored contests, to which tourists submitted their snapshots of panoramic views and exotic locals (NSG Kraft durch Freude, 1939b). At minimum, the language of tourism had a way of creeping into the efforts of the Wehrmacht to maintain morale and thus the troops' willingness to fight. Photo albums, according to the Wehrmacht High Command, provided a perfect opportunity for soldiers to compose a souvenir of their 'special war experiences' (Bjundesarchiv/Militärarchiv Freiburg, W6/440; Abbott, 1999). That those 'experiences' would become more horrifying than pleasant for German soldiers (not to mention their victims) as the war progressed does not diminish the value of suggesting that *Kraft durch Freude* helped to link the *Volksgemeinschaft* and *Lebensraum*. Or, following Michael Geyer's provocative suggestion, it helped to tie the satisfaction of German consumer desires to war, conquest and genocide (Geyer, 1997: 691–4).

As its own, characteristically Nazi, mode of consumption, KdF promoted a restrained version of the 'good life', the less conspicuous consumption of modest gratification. The future 'good life', especially for workers, would become permanent only when the regime's armies had secured *Lebensraum* and only when the military and the SS had completed the racial revamping of Europe, transferring populations to benefit German settlers, transforming *Untermenschen* into a cheap labour force toiling for their German overlords and eliminating those like the Jews, whose 'otherness' was so complete as to deny them a place in the New Order at all. For all of Hitler's undeniable fascination with Fordism, he had concluded during the 1920s that sufficient 'living space' had provided the basis of American prosperity (living space that resulted from the expulsion and killing of indigenous peoples) for only then could mass production and mass consumption have become realities (Gassert, 1997: 87–103; Zitelmann, 1989: 306–78). Once Germany had achieved the space that America possessed, the plans for single-family homes, complete with gardens and Volkswagens, social insurance benefits, generous vacations and more tourism, would be implemented. Contrary to Benjamin Dawson's rose-coloured vision of the Third Reich, bettering mass living standards through Nazism would not come to pass through the regime's participation in international agreements on social policy. Even the interim solution, Strength through Joy, which might have seemed benign to appeasers such as Dawson, remained inescapably wedded to war and empire.

References

Abbott, S. (trans.) (1999) *The German Army and Genocide: Crimes against War Prisoners, Jews, and Other Civilians, 1939–1944*. New York: New Press.

Auswartiges Amt-Politisches Archive (AA-PA), Bonn, R49245, German Legation in Lisbon to Foreign Ministry, Berlin, 14 June 1938.

Baranowski, S. (2004) *Strength through Joy: Consumerism and Mass Tourism in the Third Reich*. Cambridge: Cambridge University Press.

Baranowski, S. and Furlough, E. (eds) (2001) *Being Elsewhere: Tourism, Consumer Culture and Identity in Modern Europe and North America*. Ann Arbor and London: University of Michigan Press.

Berghoff, H. (1996) Konsumerguterindustrie im Nazionalismus: Marketing im Spannungsfeld von Profit-und Regimeinteressen. *Archiv fur Sozialgeschichte* 36, 293–322.

Berghoff, H. (2001) Enticement and deprivation: The regulation of consumption in pre-war Nazi Germany. In M. Daunton and M. Hilton (eds) *The Politics of Consumption: Material Culture and Citizenship in Europe and North America* (pp. 165–84). Oxford and New York: Berg.

Bukey, E.B. (2000) *Hitler's Austria: Popular Sentiment in the Nazi Era 1938–1945*. Chapel Hill and London: University of North Carolina Press.

Bundesarchiv Berlin-Lichterfeld R4311/546a. Dawson to the Chancellor and Führer of the German Reich, 24 June 1935; German Embassy, London to German Foreign Ministry, 25 July 1935.

Bundesarchiv Berlin-Lichterfeld R58. Nos. 944, 947–50.

Bundesarchiv Berlin-Lichterfeld NS22/781.

Bundesarchiv/Militärarchiv Freiburg, W6/440.

Confino, A. (1997) Consumer culture is in need of attention: German cultural studies and the commercialization of the past. In S. Denham, I. Kacandes and J. Petropoulos (eds) *A User's Guide to German Cultural Studies* (pp. 181–8). Ann Arbor: University of Michigan Press.

Confino, A. and Koshar, R. (2001) Régimes of consumer culture: New narratives in twentieth-century German history. *German History* 19 (2), 135–61.

Cross, G. (1993) *Time and Money: The Making of Consumer Culture*. London and New York: Routledge.

De Grazia, V. (1981) *The Culture of Consent: Mass Organization of Leisure in Fascist Italy*. Cambridge: Cambridge University Press.

De Grazia, V. (1998) Changing consumption regimes in Europe, 1930–1970. Comparative perspectives on the distribution problem. In S. Strasser, C. McGovern and M. Judt (eds) *Getting and Spending: European and American Consumer Societies in the Twentieth Century* (pp. 59–83). Cambridge: Cambridge University Press.

Dopolavoro und Kraft durch Freude (1936) *Arbeitertum: Blatter für Theorie und Praxis der Nazionalsocialistische Betreibszellen Organisation* 5 (1 February), No. 21.

Eine nachdenkliche Geschichte (1937) *Schönheit der Arbeit* 2 (Nov. 7), 277–82.

Essen und Essen ist Zweierlei (1938) *Schönheit der Arbeit* 2 (1), 446–50.

Frese, M. (1991) *Betriebspolitik im 'Dritten Reich': Deutsche Arbeitsfront, Unternehmer und Staatsbürokratie in der westdeutschen Grossindustrie, 1933–1939*. Paderborn: Ferdinand Schoningh.

Fritzsche, P. (1998) *Germans into Nazis*. Cambridge, MA: Harvard University Press.

Frohmann, B. (1976) Reisen mit 'Kraft durch Freude'. Eine Darstellung der KdF-Reisen unter besonderer Berücksichtigung der Auslandsfahrten. MA thesis, Karlsruhe University.

Gassert, P. (1997) *Amerika im Dritten Reich: Ideologie, Propaganda und Volksmeinung 1933–1945*. Stuttgart: Franz Steiner.

German History (2001) Special issue on consumerism in Germany 19 (2).

Geyer, M. (1996) Reisen in der UdSSR 1933–1945. In R. Bessel (ed.) *Fascist Italy and Nazi Germany: Comparisons and Contrasts* (pp. 134–64). Cambridge: Cambridge University Press.

Geyer, M. (1997) Germany, or the twentieth century as history. *South Atlantic Quarterly* 94, 691–4.

Gordon, B. (1998) War and tourism: Paris in World War II. *Annals of Tourism Research* 25 (3), 616–38.

Hennig, C. (1999) *Reiselust: Touristen, Tourismus und Urlaubskultur*. Frankfurt am Main: Suhrkamp Taschenbuch.

International Labour Office (1939) Studies and Reports, Series G (Housing and Welfare), No. 5, *Facilities for the Use of Workers' Leisure During Holidays*. Geneva: International Labour Office.

International Olympic Committee (1994) *The International Olympic Committee – One Hundred Years. The Idea – The Presidents – The Achievements*, Vol. 1. *The Presidency of Henri de Baillet-Latour (1925–1942)*. Lausanne: International Olympic Committee.

Kahl, W. (1940) *Der deutsche Arbeiter reist!* Berlin: Deutscher Verlag.

Keitz, C. (1997) *Reisen als Leitbild: Die Entstehung des modernen Massentourismus in Deutschland*. Munich: DTV.

Klemperer, V. (1998) *I Will Bear Witness: A Diary of the Nazi Years, 1933–1941* (trans. M. Chalmers). New York: Random House.

Koshar, R. (1998) 'What ought to be seen': Tourists' guidebooks and national identities in modern Germany and Europe. *Journal of Contemporary History* 33 (3), 323–40.

Koshar, R. (2000) *German Travel Cultures*. Oxford and New York: Berg.

Landeshauptarchiv Magdeburg (LM) (1934–43) Ebenhahn, Gaureferent des Amtes Schönheit der Arbeit am sämtliche Herrn Landrate in Gau-Magdeburg-Anhalt, 12 May 1936, Oberprasidium des Provinz Sachsen-Magdeburg 25, No. 68, NS-Gemeinschaft 'Kraft durch Freude.

Latzel, K. (1995) Tourism und Gewalt: Kriegswahrnehmungen in Feldpostbriefen. In H. Heer and K. Naumann (eds) *Vernichtungskrieg: Verbrechen der Wehrmacht 1941–1944* (pp. 447–58). Hamburg: Hamburger Ed.

Ley, R. (1935) Die Gründung der NS-Gemeinschaft 'Kraft durch Freude'. In R. Ley, *Durchbuch der sozialen Ehre. Reden und Gedanken für das schaffende Deutschland.* Berlin: Mehden.

Liebscher, D. (1999) Mit KdF 'die Welt erschliessen'. Der Beitrag der KdF-Reisen zur Aussenpolitik der Deutschen Arbeitsfront 1934–1939. *Zeitschrift für Sozialgeschichte des 20. und 21. Jarhhunderts* 12 (1), 42–71.

Mason, T. (1976) *Sozialpolitik im Dritten Reich: Arbeiterklasse und Volksgemeinschaft.* Opladen: Westdeutscher Verlag.

Mason, T. (1993) *Social Policy in the Third Reich: The Working Class and the 'National Community'* (translated by J. Broadwin, ed. Jane Caplan). Providence, R1, Berg.

Mommsen, H. and Grieger, M. (1996) *Das Volkswagenswerk und seine Arbeiter im Dritten Reich*. Dusseldorf: Econ Verlag.

Niedersachsisches Hauptstaatsarchiv, Hannover (1937) KdF-Bad auf Rugen wird Wirklichkeit: Freien-Eldorado der 20.000-Fernheizwerk und Wolkan-Restaurant. VVP 17, No. 2456 (22 September).

Nolan, M. (1994) *Visions of Modernity: American Business and the Modernization of Germany*. New York: Oxford University Press.

NSG Kraft durch Freude, Gau Pommern (1934) *Monatsprogramm*. No. 1 (1 December).

NSG Kraft Durch Freude, Gau München-Oberbayern (1935b) In herbstliche Dachau mit der Betriebsgemeinschaft G. Frans'sche Bundruckerei. *Kraft Durch Freude* (Nov.), 10–11.

NSG Kraft durch Freude, Gau Mecklenburg-Lubeck (1935a) Der Weg zur Gemeinschaft. *Kraft durch Freude* 4 (Apr.), 5–6.

NSG Kraft durch Freude, Gau Sachsen (1935c) *Monatsprogramm* (May), 2–4.

NSG Kraft durch Freude, Gau Sachsen (1936) *Monatsprogramm* (May), 25–7.

NSG Kraft Durch Freude, Gau Oberdonau (1938) Dein Urlaub 1939 mit Kraft durch Freude. Berlin.

NSG Kraft durch Freude, Gau Halle-Merseburg (1939a) *Jahresfahrtenbuch 1939.*

NSF Kraft durch Freude, Gau Steiermark (1939b) Wer tut mit am grossen KdF-Foto-Wettbewerb? In *Mit Kraft Durch Freude in den Urlaub. Sommerprogramm 1939*.

NSG Kraft durch Freude, Reichsamt Reisen, Wandern und Urlaub (1939c) *KdF-Schiff Robert Ley*. Berlin: Die Deutsche Arbeitsfront.

NSG Kraft durch Freude, Gau Köln-Aachen (1939d) Liebe in Afrika. Ein wahres KdF Erlebnis erzhalt von Heinz Magka. *Kraft durch Freude* 4 (3), 4–6.

Overy, R. (1994) Guns or butter? Living standards, finance and labour in Germany, 1939–1942. In R. Overy (ed.) *War and Economy in the Third Reich*. Oxford: Oxford University Press.

Pater, Monika (1998) Rundfunkangebote. In I. Marssolek and A. von Saldern (eds) *Zuhoren und Gehortwerden I: Radio im Nazionalsozialismus: Zwischen Lenkung und Alelkung*. Tubingen: Edition Diskord.

Rabinbach, A. (1979) The aesthetics of production in the Third Reich. In G. Mosse (ed.) *International Fascism: New Thoughts and Approaches* (pp. 189–222). London and Beverly Hills: Sage.

Reagin, N. (2001) *Marktordnung* and autarkic housekeeping: Housewives and private consumption under the Four-Year Plan, 1936–1939. *German History* 19 (2), 162–84.

Recht zur Freude. Deutsche Arbeiter fahren zur See (1934) *Arbeitertum* 4 (5), 5–11.

Reichel, P. (1993) *Das schöne Schein des Dritten Reich: Faszination und Gewalt des Faschismus*. Frankfurt am Main: Fisher Taschenbuch.

Reichsamtsleitung Kraft durch Freude (1938) *Unter dem Sonnenrad. Ein Buch von Kraft durch Freude*. Berlin: Verlag der Deutsche Arbeitsfront.

Rogers, D.T. (1998) *Atlantic Crossings: Social Politics in a Progressive Age*. Cambridge, MA: Belknap Press of Harvard University.

Rostock, J. and Zadnièek, F. (1995) *Paradiesruinen: Das KdF-Seebad der Zwanzigtausend auf Rugen*. Berlin: Ch. Links.

Schildt, A. (1995) *Moderne Zeiten: Freizeit, Massenmedium und 'Zeitgeist' in der Bundesrepublik der 50er Jahre*. Hamburg: Has Christians.

Smelser, R. (1988) *Robert Ley: Hitler's Labor Front Leader*. Oxford, New York and Hamburg: Berg).

Spode, H. (1980) 'Der deutsche Arbeiter reist': Massentourismus im Dritten Reich. In G. Huck (ed.) *Sozialgeschichte der Freizeit. Untersuchungen zum Wandel der Alltagskultur in Deutschland*. Wuppertal: Peter Hammer.

Spode, H. (1982) Arbeiterlaub im Dritten Reich. In C. Sachse (ed.) *Angst, Belohnung, Zucht und Ordnung: Herschaftsmechanismen im Nazionalsozialismus*. Opladen: Westdeutscher Verlag.

Spode, H. (1997) Ein Seebad fur zwanzigtausend Volksgenossen: Zur Grammatik und Geschichte des fordistischen Urlaubs. In P.J. Brenner (ed.) *Reisekultur in Deutschland: Von der Weimarer Republik zum 'Dritten Reich'* (pp. 7–47). Tubingen: Max Niemeyer.

Spode, H. (1999) Der Tourist. In U. Frevert and H-G. Haupt (eds) *Der Mensch des 20. Jahrhundert*. Frankfurt am Main and Chicago: Campus.

Starcke, G. (1936) Kraft durch Freude hebt den Lebensstandard unseres Volkes. *Arbeitertum* 5 (15 February, 22), 3–4.

Szejnmann, C-C. (1996) The rise of the Nazi Party in the working-class milieu of Saxony. In C. Fischer (ed.) *The Rise of National Socialism and the Working Classes in Weimar Germany* (pp. 189–216). Providence, RI: Berghahn.

Von Huebbenet, A. (1939) *Die NS-Gemeinschaft 'Kraft durch Freude'. Aufbau und Arbeit*. Berlin: Junker und Dunnhaupt.

Weiss, H. (1993) Ideologie der Freizeit im Dritten Reich: die NS-Gemeinschaft 'Kraft durch Freude'. *Archiv fur Sozialgeschichte* 33.

Wilhelm Gustloff, das Bild eines Schiffes (1938) *Schönheit der Arbeit* 3 (Jul. 3), 109–23.

Zitelmann, R. (1989) *Hitler: Selbstverständnis eines Revolutionäres: Zweite, uberarbeitete und ergäntze Auflage*. Stuttgart: Klett-Cotta.

Chapter 8

'Travel in Merry Germany': Tourism in the Third Reich

KRISTIN SEMMENS

Introduction

Tourism has remained a relatively unexplored topic for historians of Nazi Germany. While research into the *Kraft durch Freude* (KdF, Strength through Joy) holidays continues, the practices of commercial tourism, the contours of its culture and its organisational structure have attracted considerably less attention. In many ways, the past neglect of this subject is understandable. Tourism sits uncomfortably alongside persecution, terror and genocide, the defining hallmarks of the Nazi regime. In the context of a murderous dictatorship, tourism indeed seems a 'soft topic', one that threatens to ignore more fundamental historical problems (Confino, 1999). Yet such an assessment is misguided. As many historians have come to acknowledge, what once appeared almost trivial or trifling can actually reveal a great deal about the past. Moreover, if historians have considered tourism to be a soft topic, the Nazi regime certainly did not. It saw tourism as an important branch of the German economy, which demanded support and regulation by the state. More significantly, tourism offered a means to advance the regime's political agenda, for it served the creation and unification of a racially purified, unswervingly loyal and deeply patriotic *Volksgemeinschaft* (national community). The regime, therefore, embarked upon a thorough and effective coordination of all German tourism organisations. Soon it enjoyed unchallenged authority over leisure travel by Germans within Germany.

This chapter is drawn from my doctoral dissertation, which attempts an inclusive foray into the world of domestic commercial tourism under the swastika through its analysis of three very different tourist destinations: Berlin, Weimar and the Black Forest (Semmens, 2002). By providing a reconstruction of that world, this larger project seeks to enrich what is to date a relatively meagre historiography. At the same time, it employs tourism as a prism through which to view and shed new light on larger issues in Third Reich history. These include the Nazi regime's politicisation of cultural practices, its impact on daily life, the nature of its authority, the role of popular demand and the modernity of Nazism itself. My study thus confirms the intimate connection between scholarly research into tourism and the most fundamental problems of the Nazi dictatorship.

The present chapter limits its discussion, however, to three interconnected aspects of that larger work. It begins with a brief overview of the meaning of leisure travel in Nazi Germany. Here I outline the kinds of ideological and political capital invested by the Hitler state in the practices and promotion of tourism. The discussion then turns to the Nazi regime's coordination (*Gleichschaltung*) of German tourism, in order to establish the degree and nature of its control within this sphere. Finally, I assess the effects of these measures on the tourist experience itself by examining two distinct, yet at times overlapping commercial tourist cultures in the Third Reich, the Nazi and the 'normal'.

The Nazi Meaning of Tourism

Modern tourism has always been susceptible to political instrumentalisation, even though it is an activity predicated upon the search for relaxation, pleasure and entertainment. Tourism has been used, for example, to cultivate nationalist sentiment amongst Germans in the Habsburg Empire, to uphold the legitimacy of Ferdinand Marcos' 'New Society' in the Philippines and to highlight Palestinian suffering in Israeli-occupied Hebron (Clarke, 2000; Judson, 2002; Richter, 1980). In inter-war Europe, fascist and communist regimes alike viewed tourism as a means to advance their respective ideological agendas. The national organisation of leisure thus became a priority; the 'problem of pleasure' was taken very seriously indeed (Jameson, 1983). In Nazi Germany, pleasure travel soon joined the list of things allegedly revolutionised by National Socialism. But why was tourism important to the Nazis? What political role was it expected to play?

First and foremost, leisure travel served the physical rejuvenation of the *Volk* and the restoration of its capability to work, thereby strengthening the German people for coming struggles. Accordingly, KdF holidays and commercial vacations alike prepared for future mass mobilisation. At the same time, however, leisure travel allegedly served the avoidance of war. Accordingly, within the field of foreign policy, international tourism had a special role to play. Heralded as 'peace work in the purest sense', its task under Hitler was to convey the truth about the new Germany. 'Come to

Germany and see for yourself', the regime now urged its foreign visitors (Archiv für Tourismus, 1934: 26).

Of course, nothing was further from the true goals of Nazism than 'peace and understanding between the peoples', the supposed reward of international tourism according to Propaganda Minister Joseph Goebbels (Goebbels, in *Der Fremdenverkehr*, 1936a: 1). In contrast, the political purposes of *domestic* tourism were openly and bluntly declared: an increase in nationalist sentiment and greater unity within the 'national community'. Firsthand encounters with the 'German lands', the propagandists maintained, 'deepen[ed] the love and the understanding of the German people for the landscape, the history and the culture of their Fatherland' (Heinrich Lammers, in *Der Fremdenverkehr*, 1936: 1). Sightseeing, they claimed, fomented German patriotism. Domestic tourism also decreased regionalist, religious and class differences by bringing people together from all over the country. It allowed Germany's disparate 'tribes' (*Stämme*), the propagandists asserted, to 'get to know, understand and treasure each other and so become a united German people'; at the same time, the *Volk* was made aware of its 'racial uniqueness' through the experience of being a tourist (*Der Fremdenverkehr*, 1936b: 5; Bundesarchiv Berlin-Lichterfelde, NS5 VI/19470). Domestic tourism was clearly an important political factor for the Nazis. Soon after their assumption of power, therefore, they began to intervene extensively in order to encourage, steer and control it.

The Nazi *Gleichschaltung* of German Tourism

Three key points emerge when we examine the *Gleichschaltung* (coordination) process in the context of tourism. First, the Nazi regime's measures met with a great deal of consent amongst Germany's tourism officials, since they appeared to fulfil several of their pre-1933 demands. In general, the ailing German tourism industry, battered and bruised by the economic crises of the early 1930s, viewed Hitler as a long-awaited physician, capable of curing its ills. Many individuals were therefore prepared to accept a loss of autonomy in return for the promised simplification, state protection and professionalisation of their industry. Second, the Nazis' synchronisation of German tourism was in no way superficial or cosmetic. The organisational structure of tourism looked very different under Hitler. Real changes occurred, which affected the daily practices of tourism organisation and promotion from the national to the local level. Third, *Gleichschaltung* here was not incomplete and uneven, as it has been described in other spheres. The picture that emerges of the Nazi regime at work in the tourist sector is thus admittedly at odds with the usual image of the internally chaotic nature of the structure of governance in the Third Reich (Caplan, 1978: 234; Kershaw, 2000: 74–6). In fact, my work suggests that the implementation of Nazi tourism policy was both extremely thorough and remarkably effective.

Rather than recounting each and every stage of the coordination process, the following pages focus on those measures that had the greatest impact upon the organisation and promotion of German commercial tourism. Local tourism societies and organisations were the first to be affected. As with German associational life as a whole, at least 51% of their executive committee members now had to belong to the NSDAP. Nor was the tourism industry exempt from the processes of 'de-Jewification' (*Entjudung*), since, the tourism journal *Der Fremdenverkehr* explained, the 'Jewish question' also needed resolution in the sphere of tourism (*Der Fremdenverkehr*, 1936c: 5). Racially unacceptable figures soon disappeared, as did those with questionable political affiliations. Former chairmen and managing directors stepped down or were 'voted' out of office. Sometimes this meant that unskilled Nazis with little or no tourism experience took their place. More often, however, the 'new' committees looked remarkably similar to their predecessors.

As Germany's tourism officials hurried to align themselves with the regime, the *Gleichschaltung* process continued. On 23 June 1933, the regime passed the Law for the Reich Committee for Tourism (*Gesetz über den Reichsausschuß für Fremdenverkehr*), which established a national body responsible for all tourism matters within the Ministry of Propaganda. Joseph Goebbels became its president, with Hermann Esser as its vice-president. The members of the Reich Committee fell into three categories: representatives of various Reich Ministries, representatives of the state governments and representatives of other groups with direct interests in the promotion of tourism, such as Lufthansa and various hotel and restaurant associations. A later amendment added *Kraft durch Freude* to the list.

The Nazis had not created something entirely new with the Law for the Reich Committee for Tourism but they had made some significant changes. First, by placing tourism under the authority of the Propaganda Ministry, the regime institutionalised its conception of leisure travel as an ideological matter and not merely an economic or transportation one. Contemporary commentary certainly stressed this shift in emphasis (*Weimarische Zeitung*, 1933). Second, the Reich Committee now gained a legal foundation. It became a Reich Authority (*Reichsbehörde*) and, as such, gained substantial new powers over its members. Third, the Nazis' first tourism law created 24 state tourism associations (*Landesverkehrsverbände*). As Germany's final arbiter in all touristic matters, the Reich Committee both oversaw and directed their activities. At this stage, membership in the state tourism associations remained voluntary. Later, such potential independence and autonomy – anathema to the Hitler dictatorship – would have to be eradicated.

The establishment of the Reich Committee for Tourism was an important first step in the National Socialist *Gleichschaltung* campaign. However, the regime had not yet established its full authority over Germany's tourism organisations. Its second tourism law, introduced on 23 March 1936, greatly intensified the Nazification process, particularly in the sphere of tourism promotion and publicity. The Law for the Reich Tourism Association (*Gesetz über den Reichsfremdenverkehrsverband*) had two important consequences. It altered the legal status of the existing association, giving it sweeping new powers, and it created the tourism communities (*Fremdenverkehrsgemeinde*). In theory, the new legal designation – the Association became a corporate body of public law – did not imply 'total state control' but rather 'special supervision by the state' (Thuringisches Hauptstaatsarchiv, 1936a). In reality, of course, total state control was indeed the aim. Likewise, on paper, the Association did not gain the status of a Reich Authority like the Reich Committee for Tourism, of which it remained a member. Yet the legal differences, noted one Berlin lawyer, were essentially 'meaningless' in terms of the Association's actual ability to enforce its directives (Vom Berg, 1939: 32). Even more significant was the Reich Tourism Association's newfound ability to 'regulate downward' into the most basic 'communal cells', the newly established tourism communities (*Kölnische Zeitung*, 1936). The Nazis' second tourism law defined a tourism community as any community in which the annual number of overnight stays regularly exceeded one quarter of the number of inhabitants or any community that had a high rate of excursion traffic. In 1936, there were 24 state tourism associations and approximately 6000 tourism communities. After the Austrian *Anschluß*, those numbers rose to 30 and 8000 respectively. An officially proclaimed tourism community had to join the appropriate state tourism association and pay annual financial contributions. In turn, that association oversaw all its activities and was responsible for enforcing the decrees and advertising guidelines of the Reich Committee for Tourism and the Reich Tourism Association. Nazi propaganda still stressed the purported autonomy of the tourism communities but real local self-governance had become a thing of the past (Thüringisches Hauptstaatsarchiv Weimar, 1936b; von Heilingbrunner, 1938: 8). Likewise, although a great deal of propaganda was devoted to the supposed independence of the state tourism associations, the limited autonomy they had hitherto enjoyed now disappeared (von Heilingbrunner, 1936: 4). Yet many within the industry still welcomed the Nazis' latest move, especially as visitor numbers continued to rise: the Nazis did actually appear to be good for German tourism.

The Reich Tourism Association Law had radically increased and broadened the regime's control over leisure travel in Germany. In fact, it is difficult to overstate the power that the Nazi state now wielded over German tourism. Its authority was not just enshrined on paper but made itself felt at a practical level. Day-to-day aspects of tourism work were all potentially affected. The Reich Tourism Association named the chairmen of the state tourism associations, as well as their managing directors; it set their rates for annual financial contributions and approved their budgets; it authorised the creation of any sub-committees. It also threatened any violations of its orders with a 1000 RM fine. On the local level, all tourism communities now had to subscribe to *Der Fremdenverkehr*, Nazi Germany's official tourism journal. They had to inform the Reich Tourism Association of all conferences and congresses taking place, any overseas travel by their directors and the names of new top-level employees. They required official authorisation for the publication of a *Fremdenblatt* (tourist newspaper), which the regime regularly denied. They had to send in copies of all official souvenirs, brochures, guidebooks and posters for approval. Tourism societies naturally continued to advise tourists, organise excursions and arrange guided tours. However, the regime was poised to intervene at any moment, particularly as it was kept abreast of all activity through the constant stream of information it demanded. From 1936 onwards, then, it makes sense to speak of a truly totalitarian politics of tourism. But what did the *Gleichschaltung* process mean for German tourists themselves? Did tourism under the swastika look any different to them? To answer such questions, we must take a closer look at the tourist cultures of Nazi Germany.

Tourist Cultures in the Third Reich

Tourism is an historically specific form of travel: it is travel for pleasure, which takes place in leisure time. If tourism is thus the general activity at issue, then the term 'tourist culture' can be used to indicate the wider machinery that promotes, codifies and facilitates that activity. The analysis of any tourist culture in the past should include an examination of the travel infrastructure at that time, the varieties of contemporary travel literature on offer and the 'travel ideology' of the day, best defined as 'reflections about travel, its sense and its function in society' (Brenner, 1997: 2). Two distinct commercial tourist cultures existed under the swastika: the Nazi and the 'normal'. They shared an ideological basis and relied upon similar modes of transportation, accommodation and marketing. Yet there were significant differences in the types of attractions they promoted and the language they employed in their literature. While each tourist culture possessed additional distinguishing characteristics, I focus here on the differences between the key texts they both used: tourist brochures and travel guide-books.

Nazi Tourist Culture

An explicitly Nazified tourist culture emerged soon after the Nazi takeover of power. Its literature promoted new sights and attractions deemed 'worthy of seeing' (*sehenswürdig*), which were explicitly connected to the Nazi regime in some way. In turn, these were encoded within a distinctly politicised discourse that imbued them with the ideas of National Socialism. Through its extensive rebuilding programme, the Nazi regime literally created new sightseeing attractions in cities like Berlin and Weimar. Most of these buildings – such as Berlin's Reich Chancellery and the Gauforum in Weimar – were not conceived primarily as tourist attractions but they were soon transformed into them by the tourism industry. They were quite literally the 'star' attractions at certain destinations. For example, a 1941 Grieben guide to the German capital gave the Reich Chancellery its highest rating: three stars (***). While traditional tourist sites like the Brandenburg Gate or the Goethe House were naturally not ignored, the literature of this thoroughly Nazified tourist culture created a clear hierarchy of the most valuable sights in particular cities. The texts also depicted these new buildings as symbols of the power and success of the Nazi regime itself.

The architectural triumphs of the Third Reich were physical new constructions. They did not actually need descriptions in guide-books or brochures for tourists to notice them, although their meaning was reinforced by these texts. In contrast, the so-called sites of Nazi 'martyrdom' were transformed into new sightseeing attractions by the tourist literature itself. Formerly meaningless locations, invisible on the tourist landscape, were imbued with ideological value and were consequently turned into something worth seeing. One example of such Nazified tourist literature was a guide published by two SA members, *We Ramble through National Socialist Berlin: A Guide to the Sites of Memory of the Struggle for the Reich Capital* (von Engelbrechten & Volz, 1937). The guide offered a 22-page history of the SA and the NSDAP in Berlin, included a chronological table of key events beginning in 1920 and ending in 1936, and even provided election results for the years 1921 to 1933. This background information was followed by detailed descriptions of the individual sites – monuments, graves, houses, restaurants and pubs – sorted by the year in which important events had taken place there. The sites of street battles, mass meetings and murder became the attractions of this tour.

The SA guidebook was, however, an exceptional text. There was no similar guide to Weimar, a city in which Nazi tourist culture also found roots, or, as far as current research reveals, for any other German city. It is not the hyper-Nazified *Wir wandern*, therefore, that one should regard as the emblematic text of Nazi tourist culture but rather guides like the Berlin Tourism Society's *Berlin A–Z* (Berliner Verkehrsverein, 1935). *Berlin A–Z* differed from the SA guide in many ways. The latter offered no practical travel, restaurant or hotel information, although the opening times of various museums were given. Thus it was not, as Rudy Koshar claims, a 'true hybrid' (Koshar, 2000b: 138). In contrast, *A–Z* did represent a truly hybridised form of brochure, which incorporated new Nazi sights into the more 'normal' discourse of tourism. In and amongst information about banks, museums and hotels, a separate section was devoted to 'The Resting Places of SA Men Fallen in Berlin'. This conflation of the ideological with the practical was a common motif of politicised tourist literature under Hitler.

After 1933, references to the Nazi cult of the fallen appeared in a variety of touristic material about the capital. Horst Wessel, supposedly murdered by Communists, and the much-lauded composer of the Nazi anthem, *Die Fahne hoch*, remained the most frequently named 'martyr': most brochures and guides made at least a brief allusion to sites associated with him (for example, Baedeker, 1936: 6; Berliner Verkehrsgemeinschaft, n.d.: 25; Reichsbahnzentrale für den deutschen Reiseverkehr, 1936: 19; Woerls Reisehandbücher, 1938: 92). This commemoration of Nazi heroes found its place in tourist literature about Weimar as well. Plaques honouring the city's 'greats' included one to Hans Maikowski, erected at the house where he had lived in 1932. According to the 1943 edition of the Woerl guide to Weimar, Maikowski, a *Sturmführer* of the SA, was 'persecuted in the period of the struggle for Germany … [and] was murdered in Berlin on the day of national renewal (30 January 1933)' (Woerls Reisehandbücher, 1943: 25). His legend thus lived on in tourist propaganda.

Nazi tourist culture was based primarily on entirely new attractions and new historical interpretations. That is, it was engaged largely in making additions to the sightseeing canon. At the same time, however, it depended upon erasure, obliteration and eradication. By their silences and omissions, guidebooks and brochures deemed some attractions 'unworthy' after 1933. Other sites therefore disappeared from the tourist gaze, symbolically if not always physically. The process did not only take place within the pages of the tourist material itself. Some pre-existing attractions underwent actual material alterations after 1933 that were subsequently reflected in the texts about them. In Weimar, for example, the plaque commemorating the 1919 National Assembly was removed from the National Theatre in 1933. After this physical obliteration, all references to the event it had once memorialised were similarly struck from Weimar brochures and guides. In Berlin, as elsewhere, the process of memory distortion took place through the renaming of streets and squares. The Nazi regime wanted to bury the capital's ignominious democratic past, which had left its traces on the city map, with new names connected to the regime. Thus began the ritual of re-naming so characteristic of Germany's 20th century. The mainly working-class district of Friedrichshain was transformed into Horst-Wessel-Stadt. Stresemannstraße was re-christened Saarlandstraße and the Platz der Republik became Königsplatz. Hermann-Göring-Straße took the place of Friedrich-Ebert-Straße. The capital also honoured the Nazi movement's 'martyrs', such as Herbert Norkus (a member of the Hitler Youth allegedly murdered by Communists in Berlin in 1932), through re-named streets. Not surprisingly, by 1936, Berlin's synagogues had also disappeared from most tourist maps.

That an explicitly politicised tourist culture emerged in Hitler's Germany is hardly surprising. What is perhaps less so is that its contours were not dictated from above. The Reich Committee for Tourism and Reich Tourism Association issued vague commands that tourist literature be 'more German' or in the 'National Socialist spirit' but explicit interpretations of what this actually entailed were not provided. Thus, while an overtly ideological tourist culture, which in large part depended on Nazified tourist literature, did emerge after 1933, actual guidelines dictating this transformation – such as the inclusion of NSDAP-related attractions – were exceedingly rare. Yet, as we have seen, this in no way hindered the Nazification of tourist material about Berlin and Weimar, which, ultimately, proved very popular amongst the German travelling public.

After 1933, then, a very different kind of tourist experience was available in Germany. It was not, however, the result of any 'subterfuge' on the Nazis' part (Koshar, 2000b: 158). Its politicised features were never subtle or understated. The ideological message was explicit. Within this

Nazi tourist culture, new sights became the highlights of visits to particular cities. Memorials to the Nazi 'martyrs' appeared at times amongst the traditional German memory sites on the tourist's itinerary. Some brochures incorporated tourist information within a newly ideologised framework. At the same time, tourist literature demonised or fell silent about Germany's democratic past. Yet Nazi tourist culture was not simply the result of 'a process of agglutination', whereby Nazi symbols were added to the 'pre-existing symbolic landscape', while others were taken away (Koshar, 2000a: 71). These additions and omissions represented more than merely superficial alterations to a previous tourist culture. They formed the basis of a new, distinct tourist culture. While these changes admittedly dealt mostly with the *look* of things, the introduction of new photographs in a brochure or revised content in a guidebook actually affected the very core of the tourist experience, for tourism is a practice based essentially on seeing. Nazi tourist culture thus demanded a new way of seeing specific German destinations.

Yet this overtly Nazified variant was by no means the only or even the predominant tourist culture in the Third Reich. It was limited to specific locales and coalesced only around particular sights, events and experiences. Predictably, it took hold in places with strong links to the Nazi Party, like Munich and Nuremberg: Munich was promoted as the 'Capital of the Movement' while Nuremberg was marketed as the 'City of the Party Rally'. However, a distinctly Nazified tourist culture also surfaced at contested sites, where the Republican past had to be obliterated and the future reinvented, such as Berlin and Weimar.

Nazi tourist culture appears to have been genuinely popular. The German public displayed a very real fascination with the Nazis' new structures, their history of struggle and their mass spectacles. Nazi tourist culture thus became another venue in which Germans could learn more about, express approval of, and perhaps even pay homage to, the Hitler dictatorship. Choosing a particular tourist experience – be it a visit to the Reich Chancellery or the Horst Wessel Museum – represented a conscious choice to enter a public sphere in which the doctrine of Nazism was acclaimed, for tourists did have an alternative. Other, more numerous destinations were promoted in material where references to Nazi martyrs and the 'new' Germany were the exception rather than the rule.

'Normal' Tourist Culture

The omnipresent swastika perfectly symbolised the 'insatiable, invasive character' of National Socialism (Burleigh, 2000: 14). It was everywhere – on flags, banners, badges, uniforms, buildings, monuments, letterhead and stamps. For German tourists, however, the swastika, along with other key signs and signifiers of the Hitler dictatorship, was never so ubiquitous. Certainly, in the distinct, blatantly politicised tourist culture characteristic of cities like Berlin, it took pride of place. There, the swastika typified an explicit ideologisation of the tourist landscape. Yet, at the same time, the swastika was absent from many other common tourist experiences. In the Third Reich, a seemingly 'normal' tourist culture persisted, which lacked the distinguishing characteristics of its Nazified counterpart. It was based on traditional sightseeing attractions, rather than newly constructed buildings or recently invented sites of Nazi martyrdom. Unlike Nazi tourist culture, which centred on historical rupture, it promoted a vision of timelessness by focusing on seamless, unbroken continuities with the past. Its language was also surprisingly a-political: references to the Nazi movement's leaders, anniversaries and ideological tenets were infrequent.

When visitors journeyed to areas like the Black Forest, they discovered a tourist culture apparently free from Nazi influence, whose literature was also surprisingly swastika-free. As a result, tourist material for the Black Forest bore a strong resemblance to the material of the 1920s. There are, of course, the obvious clues the historian can use to distinguish between them: the photographs of the local town hall flying a Nazi flag, for example, or the presence of Adolf-Hitler-Straße on the map. The argument is not, of course, that swastikas were missing from Black Forest tourist literature entirely. Brochures, guides and advertisements naturally included images of buildings, swimming pools or special events in which Nazi symbols were present. Yet even these scenes, essentially everyday images in the Third Reich, were infrequent when compared to material about Berlin and Weimar. In the Schwarzwald, the visual images invoked tended instead toward depictions of natural beauty devoid of human influence or of 'natives' in traditional costume. In any case, touristic Nazification – here defined as the process by which tourist material or tourist experiences were imbued with National Socialist values and meaning – involved more than depictions of everyday scenes. It required an overt contextualisation, a broader referential framework and a more explicit incorporation into a larger political agenda. Context was crucial. One of the most obvious ways in which tourist material was Nazified was through direct references to National Socialism in the text. A guide to the state of Thuringia, for example, opened with a quote from Adolf Hitler, while Berlin's brochures often charted the city's history from the Nazis' assumption of power. In the Black Forest, in contrast, few brochures and guidebooks made such references and most historical chronologies of either individual towns or the region as a whole ended long before 1933 (see, for example, Stadtarchiv Freiburg, 1938: 21).

How should we explain the absence of Nazified tourist literature in this region? Clearly, it was not the result of any lack of interest in Black Forest tourism on the part of the Nazi regime. The Nazis saw tourism everywhere in Germany and later, in the countries they occupied, as a matter of great economic, cultural and political significance. The Black Forest was no exception. In fact, tourism in Baden-Baden, a real jewel in the Black Forest crown, was considered a matter of such national importance that the Baden Minister of the Interior served as chairman of the local tourism authority. Furthermore, this absence did not stem from the dictatorship's inability to enforce certain touristic norms on the region. The Black Forest's tourism organisations were thoroughly coordinated and their literature had to be inspected and approved. Here, as elsewhere, the Nazi regime acted swiftly when it felt specific directives had been contravened. Simply put, the mechanisms were in place for the Nazi regime to do with Black Forest tourism – its organisation, its promotion, its personnel and its literature – what it wished. It was not too weak to impose more overt forms of Nazification. Finally, the missing swastika in Black Forest tourist literature did not indicate a lack of Nazi sentiment. The region was hardly a hotbed of resistance to Hitler, although its many Catholic communities may not have been among his staunchest supporters. Since official guidelines rarely dictated ideologised content or images, the vast majority of local tourism officials and promoters were not standing up to, or voicing their disapproval of, the regime when they failed to include references to the Nazi movement beyond the obligatory 'Hitler Street' on the map. We must therefore look elsewhere to explain the absent swastika.

At the most basic level, the Black Forest lacked touristic elements that were easily incorporated within the Nazi worldview. It lacked Nazi 'martyrs', it lacked sites associated with key Nazi events, it lacked massive building projects and it lacked the contested status of Berlin and Weimar. While the absence of an obvious link to Nazi ideology did not always stop the regime from finding, inventing or applying one, the ideologisation process was greatly facilitated by more effortless connections to Nazi values. Additionally, there was a much less pressing need for Black Forest tourist literature to be 'reclaimed' after 1933, since the Weimar Republic had left far fewer traces there than it had in Berlin or Weimar. Few towns in the Black Forest had such clear links to Germany's first democracy; as a result, the tourism publicity of the 1920s made few explicit references to it. Moreover, Black Forest material had always stressed historical continuity and remoteness from the political present, which further explains the lack of touristic ideologisation in tune with democratic values after the First World War. Apart from photographs bearing Republican flags or maps with re-named streets, there was relatively little that tourism officials had to eliminate or replace with allusions to Nazism once Hitler was in power.

The Black Forest also offered an entirely different kind of tourist experience than did Berlin or Weimar. It promoted different kinds of attractions and defined different sights as 'worthy of seeing'. Rather than visit the Reich Chancellery, tourists attended a peasant wedding in Neustadt or went skiing on the Feldberg. Instead of touring Goethe's house or the Gauforum, visitors rented boats on Lake Titisee or observed craftsmen making 'authentic' cuckoo clocks. The Black Forest's timeless, rural landscapes and its inhabitants' traditional lifestyle seemed to offer an escape from the present. Local tourism officials recognised what tourists were after and therefore promoted the region's ancient customs, buildings and dress alongside the natural attractions in countless brochures, guides, advertisements and postcards. The presence of swastikas or ideological discourse would thus in many ways have been entirely out of place; it would have disturbed the Black Forest's tourist aesthetic.

It could be argued, of course, that the German landscape and the depiction of local peasants and farmers potentially lent themselves to Nazism's myth of 'blood and soil'. However, the promotion of Germany's 'authentic' *Volk* traditions in tourist literature under Hitler was by no means unique. The overarching framework stressing rootedness, community and historical continuity pre-dated the Nazi regime (Stadtarchiv Freiburg, 1932). While they certainly accorded with Nazi ideals after 1933, such themes therefore rarely marked a conscious, new advertising strategy on the part of local tourism officials, eager to align their offerings with the goals of the regime. The evocation of local traditions succeeded the Nazi regime as well. Today the costumes, houses and festivals of the Black Forest, along with its 'rugged and romantic' landscape, still draw tourists, who, according to one souvenir picture book, desire an 'escape … from modern life' (Teklenborg, 1996: 3). In Berlin and Weimar, where buildings associated with the new regime appeared, where sites of struggle and martyrdom were numerous and where traces of the Republican past needed to be demonised or totally obliterated, the Nazification of tourist culture seemed almost inevitable. In contrast, destinations like the Black Forest offered less fertile ground for Nazi tourist culture to take root.

Yet these admittedly significant distinctions do little to explain the seemingly paradoxical nature of tourism publicity and practices in the

Third Reich. Every aspect of tourism under Hitler was to serve the Nazis' ideological aims but guidelines and directives for tourist literature did not uniformly enforce the addition of Nazi-centric images and text. Given the great degree of control the Nazi regime enjoyed over all facets of tourist culture in Germany, how are we to explain its 'stunning normality' at certain times and in specific locations? (Koshar, 2000b: 127).

Rudy Koshar maintains that, with regard to travel guide-books and many tourist practices, 'Nazism's totalitarian impulse may have come up against a certain immutability' (Koshar, 2000b: 158). He rightly discerns that a number of German leisure travel 'conventions', which preceded the Nazi assumption of power, endured under Hitler. Clearly, there was a great deal of continuity. Yet the persistence of an apparently 'normal' tourist culture in the Third Reich did not denote some kind of touristic triumph over Nazism and its totalising ambitions. The Nazis not only tolerated a non-Nazified German tourist culture, they also actively promoted it. This conscious cultivation of continuity – the absence of the swastika in short – was in tune with the Nazis' propaganda strategy as a whole. The Nazis recognised the value of those enterprises that appeared in an a-political guise. But the illusion of normality and historical continuity they created was, in fact, cultivated by the regime itself. In other words, the Nazis actually permitted and even promoted certain touristic continuities and omissions: this was the state's own promotion of a superficially 'state-free' sphere. In sum, although it maintained the power to intervene, coerce and compel, the Nazi regime sanctioned much of what German tourists expected and wanted. In Berlin, visitors anticipated, and presumably often desired, an overtly politicised reading of the capital. Elsewhere, in places like the Black Forest, however, they sought what looked like an escape from the Nazi everyday.

In addition to the Nazi regime's attitude toward effective propaganda, the endurance of a seemingly 'normal' tourist culture under Hitler revealed something else about the Hitler dictatorship. Historians now recognise that the Nazis were, despite their unquestioned authority and their willingness to resort to terror and coercion, quite sensitive to public opinion. They were also aware of, and, on occasion, ready to adapt to, consumer demand in order to promote consumer satisfaction. The notion of a totalitarian state being preoccupied with pleasing its 'customers' might appear somewhat incongruous. But in reality, it simply underscores the inherent duality of the Third Reich. Recent historiography has begun to acknowledge that the murderous Nazi regime was simultaneously a 'regime of consumer culture' (Confino & Koshar, 2001: 135–61). While their total claim on German society lay unchallenged, the Nazis regularly responded to the travelling public's desires. The continued existence of a tourist culture in which overtly ideological rhetoric, Nazi symbols and other politicised changes to tourist praxis were largely absent must be seen in this context. Clearly, the customer was not always right in the Third Reich but the regime could not simply discount his or her preferences, which were, after all, still articulated within the larger political context of Nazi hegemony. The regime 'appreciated the importance of consumer satisfaction' and, for many tourists, satisfaction came with the consumption of superficially 'normal' travel experiences (Confino & Koshar, 2001: 148). Yet we must continually speak of a *seemingly* 'normal' tourist culture, because in truth so much had changed. The Nazi regime had thoroughly coordinated Germany's tourism organisations and enjoyed extensive control over German tourism publicity. 'Normal' was clearly a relative concept.

Conclusion: Holidays and Horror

Peter Monteath writes of the difficulties in researching a 'superficially benign aspect of the Nazi regime' like tourism (Monteath, 2000: 35). Yet it is easy to diagnose the most malignant aspects of Nazism – its racial hatreds, its nationalist chauvinism and its exterminatory politics – even here. From 1933 onwards, tourism was securely yoked to the broader National Socialist campaign, as the following cases reveal. In May 1936, *Das Reisebüro*, the official journal of the German travel agency industry, printed a letter it had recently received from the Thuringia State Tourism Association. Its subject was the 'idyllic destination' of Judenbach, a town high in the Thuringian hills. Despite its name, the letter continued, Jews (*Juden*) had never resided there. The place 'had only its name in common with the non-Aryan race'. This information, the letter concluded hopefully, would surely clear up any potential 'misunderstandings' for future German tourists to the area (*Das Reisebüro*, 1936). Months later, Elsa Cobler, whose Jewish husband had converted to Christianity in 1933, was prohibited from building a holiday home in the Black Forest resort town of Hinterzarten. The 'creation of a Jewish colony', it was alleged, would be damaging to tourism in the area, since many leading Nazis vacationed there (Kreisarchiv Breisgau-Hochschwarzwald, B1–1–1554). That same year, a German boy took an automobile trip through Germany with his parents. In his memoir, he narrated his adventure:

> It was a whirlwind tour … I was in charge of
> choosing postcards and small albums of local
> sights to serve as souvenirs. … From Berlin we headed

> southwest through Wittenberg, indelibly linked to Martin Luther …, then on to Leipzig … Then Weimar, the city of Goethe and Schiller, and of the Weimar Republic. … We kept up this breathtaking pace … [through] all these little towns, castles, museums, romantic forests. … We turned westward … and admired picture-postcard villages. On the tenth day we were back home, and the last entry in my photo album has one name in letters far larger than any others: BERLIN (Gay, 1998: 74–6).

His account embodies many elements characteristic of the modern tourist experience: the speed of automobile travel, an appreciation for natural beauty and national history and the purchase of souvenirs and postcards. For the Jewish historian Peter Gay, however, this journey also marked a 'final farewell to Germany'. He was eventually able to leave the country in 1939. In and amongst his descriptions of picturesque villages and spectacular scenery, the reality of the Third Reich intrudes. 'As we drove toward a hamlet called Hahn', he recalls, 'we were confronted with a large hand-lettered poster proclaiming to anyone who cared to know that Hahn was, and would remain, "clean" of Jews – *Hahn ist und bleibt judenrein*' (Gay, 1998: 76).

In Nazi Germany, tourism not only provided a platform for further racial exclusion. According to the regime, it also had an inherently racist objective to fulfil: the unification of an Aryan-only *Volksgemeinschaft*. An overtly Nazified tourist culture explicitly proclaimed the Nazis' racist, nationalist and imperialist aims, while, at the same time, a seemingly 'normal' tourist culture effectively masked them. 'Travel in Merry Germany', the Reich Tourism Association's slogan for 1937, perfectly exemplified how tourism was used both to celebrate the Nazis' 'achievements' and obscure the horrors of a murderous regime. Until recently, the touristic turn in Third Reich historiography was hindered by a perceived dissonance between holidays and horror, vacations and violence, tourism and terror. However, as this chapter has shown, these were never completely separate phenomena but, instead, became intertwined after 1933. Tourism under Hitler was thus never peripheral to the Nazi campaign. It was part of it.

References

Archiv für Tourismus (1934) *Tätigkeitsbericht der Reichsbahnzentrale fur den Deutsche Reiseverkehr* (p. 26). Berlin: Archiv für Tourismus.

Baedeker, K. (1936) *Berlin und Potsdam* (21st edn.). Leipzig: Baedeker.

Berliner Verkehrsgemeinschaft (n.d.) *Fuhrer fur die Besichtigungs-Rundfahrten mit der Berliner Verkehrsgemeinschaft*. Berlin: Berliner Verkehrsgemeinschaft.

Berliner Verkehrsverein (1935) *Berlin von A–Z. Amtlicher* Fuhrer. Berlin.
Brenner, P.J. (1997) Einleitung. In P.J. Brenner (ed.) *Reisekultur in Deutschland: Von der Weimarer Republik zum 'Dritten Reich'*. Tubingen: Max Niemeyer.
Bundesarchiv Berlin-Lichterfelde, NS5 VI/19470. Reisen und wandern uberwindet den Partikularismus, *Deutsche Arbeits Frant* (*DAF*), 8 August 1939.
Burleigh, M. (2000) *The Third Reich: a New History*. London: Pan Macmillan.
Caplan, J. (1978) Bureaucracy, politics and the National Socialist state. In P. Stachura (ed.) *The Shaping of the Nazi State*. London: Croom Helm.
Clarke, R. (2000) Self-presentation in a contested city: Palestinian and Israeli political tourism in Hebron. *Anthropology Today* 16 (5), 12–18.
Confino, A. (1999) Review of *Reisen als Leitbild: Die Entstehung des modernen Massentourismus* by Christine Keitz and *Reiselust: Touristen, Tourismus und Urlaubskultur* by Christoph Hennig. *German History* 17 (3), 438–9.
Confino, A. and Koshar, R. (2001) Regimes of consumer culture: new narratives in twentieth-century German history. *German History* 19 (2), 135–61.
Das Reiseburo (1936) An die deutschen Reiseburos! 9 (9/10), 1–15 May.
Der Fremdenverkehr (1936a) Vol. 1 (2 May, 1), 1.
Der Fremdenverkehr (1936b) Vol. 1 (30 May, 5), 5.
Der Fremdenverkehr (1936c) Funf Minuten Schulung Vol. 1 (May, 2), 5.
Gay, P. (1998) *My German Question*. London: Yale University Press.
Jameson, F. (1983) Pleasure: A political issue. In F. Jameson (ed.) *Formations of Pleasure*. London: Routledge.
Judson, P. (2002) 'Every German visitor has a *volkisch* obligation he must fulfil'. Nationalist tourism in the Austrian Empire, 1880–1918. In R. Koshar (ed.) *Histories of Leisure*. London: Berg.
Kershaw, I. (2000) *The Nazi Dictatorship* (4th edn). London: Arnold.
Kolnische Zeitung (1936) Der Reichs fremdenverkehrsverband. Das Reichgesetz, 3 April.
Koshar, R. (2000a) *From Monuments to Traces: Artifacts of German Memory, 1870–1990*. Berkeley, CA: University of California Press.
Koshar, R. (2000b) *German Travel Cultures*. Oxford: Berg.
Kreisarchiv Breisgau-Hochschwarzwald (1936) B1–1–1554, Bezirksamt Neustadt to Baden's Ministry of the Interior, 29 September 1936.
Monteath, P. (2000) Swastikas by the seaside. *History Today* 50 (5), 31–5.
Reichsbahnzentrale fur den deutschen Reiseverkehr (1936) *Berlin, Potsdam und Mark Brandenburg* (17th edn). Berlin: *Reichsbahnzentrale fur den deutschen Reiseverkehr.*
Richter, L. (1980) The political uses of tourism: A Philippine case study. *The Journal of Developing Areas* 14 (1), 237–57.
Semmens, K. (2002) Domestic tourism in the Third Reich. PhD thesis, University of Cambridge.
Stadtarchiv Freiburg (n.d.) Dve 2159. Freiburg: Städtisches Verkehrsamt. *Waldschut am Hochrhein – Fuhrer durch die Stadt und Umgebung*.
Stadtarchiv Freiburg (1932) C4/XVI/21/2. Reichsbahnzentrale fur den deutschen Reiseverkehr, *Deutschland – Trachten und Gestalen*.
Stadtarchiv Freiburg (1938) Fuhrerdurch die Schwartzwald hauptstadt. Dwb 270. Freiburg: Städtisches Verkehrsant.
Teklenborg, Bert (1996) *Reisetour durch den Schwartzwald*. 5th edn., Bad Mustereifel: Ziethon-Panorama.

Thuringisches Hauptstaatsarchiv Weimar (1936a) Rechtliche Gedanken zur Neuordnung im Fremdenverkehrswesen. *Thüringer Hotel-Nachrichten* 17 (23 April 1936). Thüringisches Hauptstaatsarchiv Weimar, Thüringisches Wirtschaftsministerium, 5006, Thuringischer Gemeindetag, 453.

Thuringisches Hauptsaatsarchiv Weimar (1936b) *Nachrichtendienst das Deutscher Gemeinindetags*, 21 April 1936.

Vom Berg, C. (1939) *Das deutsche Fremdenverkehrsrecht*. Berlin.

Von Engelbrechten, J.K. and Volz, H. (1937) *Wir wandern durch das nationalsozialistische Berlin: Ein Fuhrer durch die Gedenskatten des Kamfes um die Reichshauptstadt*. Munich: Zentral verlag der NSDAP.

Von Heilingbrunner, R. (1936) Uber die Selbstandigkeit der Landesfremdenverkehrsverbande. *Der Fremdenverkehr* 1 (2 May, 1).

Von Heilingbrunner, R. (1938) Die Organisation des deutschen Fremdenverkehrs. *Jahrbuch des deutschen Fremdenverkehrs*.

Weimarische Zeitung (1933) Das Fremdenverkehrswesen (19 July).

Woerls Reisehandbücher (1938) *Illustrierter Fuhrer durch die Reichshauptstadt Berlin und Umgebung mit Einschluss von Potsdam* (20th edn). Leipzig: Woerls.

Woerls Reisehandbücher (1943) *Illustrierter Fuhrer durch Weimar und Umgebung* (19th edn). Leipzig: Woerls.

Chapter 9

Coffee, Klimt and Climbing: Constructing an Austrian National Identity in Tourist Literature, 1918–38

CORINNA M. PENISTON-BIRD

In his essay on Austrian national identity between 1918 and 1938, the historian Kurt Skalnik stated with regret that, despite extensive research, he had been been unable to find any evidence of a positive stance being taken towards the First Republic (Skalnik, 1983: 14). This view is not unique: the inter-war period is a period in which Austrians are credited with little commitment to their national identity, particularly in terms of the independent nation state (Bruckmüller, 1984; Pelincka, 1979; Stourzh, 1990). There is one area, however, in which the Austrian nation was always presented in the best possible light – that of the tourist industry. In the tourist literature, evaluations of space were articulated, emotional attachments were expressed and a relationship between people and the territory they inhabit was made explicit. In a contemporary definition, the Swiss professors Hunziker and Krapf defined the tourist industry as 'the sum of the phenomena and relationships arising from the travel and stay of non-residents'. The term non-residents covers both domestic and foreign tourism (Burkart & Medlik, 1981: 41). A sense of place and a sense of collective identity are both a prerequisite and a consequence of tourism. The title of this chapter, with its reference to cuisine, art and alps, offers a brief snapshot of the way in which Austria was packaged for consumption as the location of exquisite culinary experiences, cultural wealth and exciting sporting activities, all in stunning surroundings inhabited by a friendly people. Tourist publications reveal that the tourist trade was one of the few areas in which Austria's post-war situation was turned to her own advantage and where Austrian national identity was endowed with a sense of value and pride. However simplified, selective or superficial, the

---

This paper is dedicated to the memory of Theresa Näglein.

assessment of the physical aspects of a nation and of the nature of its identity is a requirement of the tourist trade. The specificity of this case study should not mask the broader implications of this investigation for the relationship between tourism and national identity, as is made explicit later.

The inter-war period in Austria is a fertile period for investigating the relationship between tourism and national identity, because both had to develop simultaneously in a time of political, economic and geographical dislocation. Between 1918 and 1938, Austria had to adapt to its post-imperial existence as a nation state. Perceptions of its identity were over-shadowed by political agendas and doubts surrounding the country's viability. In 1918, Austria was, in the words of the French prime minister Georges Clemenceau, the country that was 'left over' (*'ce qui reste'*) when the Succession States broke away from the defeated Habsburg Empire. As the British journalist G.E.R. Gedye commented, 'The new state of Austria … was simply the residue, the dregs and lees of Empire, the part which nobody thought worth while absorbing, just the huge city of Vienna and the bare bones of the Alps' (Gedye, 1928: 302). In the Treaty of St Germain (1919), an empire of 676,000 km^2 was reduced to an area of 110,000 km^2. Of its surface 62% was taken up by the Alps. The Austrian residue of the Empire consisted of two distinct areas: the huge industrial and multi-cultural city of Vienna in the east, where a third of the population resided; and the predominantly agrarian west, with individual manufacturing islands such as Graz. The satirist Karl Kraus called these the 'two Austrias' and they were equally divided by politics, since the rift between 'red' Vienna and the provinces further destabilised the country. Throughout the inter-war period, debates continued on the coherence of this residue, over whether the new landlocked Austria was economically viable and what alternative form of existence Austria should seek, such as union *(Anschluß)* with Germany or the resurrection of Austria's supra-national mission in Europe through a Danubian Federation, a revised revival of the Empire (Peniston-Bird, 1997).

The tourist industry, however, provides a unique area in which Austrian national identity was consistently approved. The disadvantages reviled elsewhere were here transformed into assets. The incoherent mass of valleys and mountains, for example, was presented as a major attraction, the 'bare bones of the alps', as ideal for both sporting activities and convalescent homes. Similarly, the disparate provinces represented not lack of cohesion but glorious diversity. As an article on Austria's land-scapes in the tourist magazine *Österreichs illustrierte Fremdenverkehrs und Reise Zeitung* put it:

> Opposites of cultures, of landscapes, impact upon one another here, [and] are reconciled ... Grillparzer's words, that to understand the essence of Austria one must look at the country from the Kahlenberg, are not entirely true. One should stand on the Großglockner ... so that the horizon extends almost to the boundaries of the whole state. In this wide area opposites and contradictory cultures are reconciled into a single melody. And this melody is the undefinably Austrian. (Reinalter, 1933: 6)

The musical analogy is no coincidence – Austrian identity was not only associated with but described through its music. The inspiration which Austria's geography provided to great composers, and artists, was drawn upon to provide conclusive evidence of the value of the landscape. The extract further refers to the Austrian mission of reconciliation, quotes an Austrian dramatist, identifies two symbols of Austria and speaks with pride of the landscape (and, by implication, the infrastructure); five component parts of Austrian national identity identified in as many sentences. The emphasis on diversity and harmony conveys two messages simultaneously, implying both a wide variety of attractions and a coherent brand: the best of both worlds. Individual features had competitors in other countries – the Swiss also had Alps, the French could also promote a culturally vibrant capital, and the Germans also laid claim to great classical composers; but Austria could offer a unique blend. Complementary paradoxes typified descriptions of Austria, which was represented as both diverse and coherent, rural and industrial, traditional and modern, unique and familiar. This version of Austrian identity could encompass, even thrive on, difference without sacrificing unity.

Travel to and within Austria had long roots, traceable at least as far back as trade and pilgrimage in the Middle Ages (Bernecker, 1968; Puchinger, n.d.). From 1840 until the First World War, the tourist trade grew on average between 2 and 5% per year (Arnold, 1978). The first tourist organisation was founded in 1879 in Styria and the other provinces swiftly followed suit. Close links between hiking and tourism had existed from the outset of the Austrian tourist industry. The first Austrian *Alpenverein* was founded in 1862 and many followed. These organisations took on the task of providing paths and erecting mountain shelters. The first tourist organisation was linked with an alpine organisation: under the auspices of the Styrian *Gebirgsverein* a tourism section was formed which set itself the task of fostering and supporting all undertakings aimed at increasing visitors. In the three years after 1879, over 100 municipalities set up local tourist organisations. Tourism received much impetus from the expansion of the railway network, the popularity of health spas and the development of alpine sports. However, the First World War interrupted the development of the international tourist industry across Europe and the post-war years were not auspicious for tourism. Fluid borders, boundary disputes, coal and food shortages and the collapse of transport systems did nothing to encourage travel. Austria remained vulnerable throughout the inter-war period to rumours of conditions inconvenient or perilous to tourists. The industry was also hampered by organisational problems, including passport and customs difficulties, the supplemental charges on overnight stays levied by the municipal governments and the need to meet international standards in pricing and services.

Nonetheless, provided that such problems could be addressed, the tourist industry had certain factors in its favour. Austria could exploit its location at the centre of Europe and at the crossing of traditional travel routes between east and west, and north and south. It could also offer scenic variety, the city of Vienna and a longstanding tradition of culture and trade. With an active approach to the promotion of the four determinants for success – accessibility, attractions, facilities and organisation – the tourist industry had great potential (Burkart & Medlik, 1981: 46). The organisational framework of the industry was complex, with institutions at both provincial and national level. Under the monarchy, a state department, the *Reichsstelle für den Fremdenverkehr* within the *Ministry für öffentliche Arbeiten* (Ministry for Public Affairs) had been established. In the First Republic, the provinces retained their responsibilities for tourism, forming *Landesfremdenverkehrsämter* despite the founding of the Ministry for Trade and Transport in October 1923, which examined matters relevant to motor transport, roads and rail, and thereby to tourism also. There were *Landesverkehrsämter* in every province except Vienna, where there was a *Fremdenverkehrskommission der Bundesländer Wien und Niederösterreich*. The Ministry, which published *Österreichische Reise und Verkehrs Nachrichten*, acted as a federal body. Though under-funded, its role was not insignificant, particularly in terms of organising links abroad. Federal Minister Dr Hans Schuerff brought together provincial representatives of the tourist trade in August 1923, with the formation of the *Ausschuß für Fremdenverkehrs-angelegenheiten*. This met three times a year and largely served as an advisory body. It included representatives of provincial government and tourist organisations, of federal ministries and representatives of transport, boards of trade, hotel and publican associations, of spas and health resorts, of farmers, the *ÖAMTC* (a motoring organisation), the Press and other economic associations interested in tourism. In 1922 the *Österreichische Verkehrswerbungs Ges.m.b.H.* was formed with representatives of the

Österreichische Bundes Bahn (ÖBB: the federal railway and a dominant force in Austrian tourism), the *Erste Donau Dampfschiffahrts-Gesellschaft* (DDSG: the Danube Steam Ship Company), the municipality of Vienna, and the *Österreichische Verkehrsbüro*. It was renamed and restructured in 1923 and 1933. The most significant change came on 1 June 1933 when the *Staatssekretariat für Arbeitsbeschaffung und Fremdenverkehr* was formed in the ministry of trade and industry. This was the first state organisation to hold responsibility for national tourism in Austria, and for national advertising (with a budget of one million schillings). The constitution of 1 May 1934 declared promotion of provincial tourism, and coordination between local tourist organisations, to be the responsibility of the relevant provincial capital. The constitution also stipulated that the fostering of the tourist trade, in so far as it related to the entire federal area, was a matter for the Federal Government (Article 34, No. 9). The most centralised the industry became was through the resultant *Österreichischen Verkehrswerbung; Werbedienst des Bundesministeriums für Handel und Verkehr* (decreed 9 October, 1934), a consequence of the recognition that increasingly threatening developments would have a negative impact on Austrian tourism unless the state could exercise some control over the industry, a view that accorded with the authoritarian principles of the Corporate State (Otruba, 1978). The *Verkehrswerbung* was dissolved after the *Anschluß* in 1938.

Tourist propaganda was disseminated through advertising agencies and travel offices, through newspapers, magazines, pamphlets and trade fairs. This chapter draws upon a wide range of sources to examine provincial, federal and private representations of Austria. Traditional tourist publications can be divided into two types: those designed to provide information for people involved in the tourist trade; and those aimed at the potential tourist. The latter included articles about particular areas of interest and book reviews, as well as providing information on subjects such as local customs, tipping, transport conditions or organised tours. The former provided statistics; discussed advertising methods; debated the impact of state policies; and lobbied for improved road markings, better prices on railways, better telephone connections between the provinces and Vienna and less restrictive visa laws. The growth in forms of media also aided the industry: radio also played a role in promoting Austrian tourism, for example through the transmission of the Salzburger Festspiele in 1925 or the Beethoven Festival on 26 March 1927, to Germany, Czechoslovakia and Yugoslavia. Suggested by the actor, director and theatre manager Max Reinhardt (Max Goldmann) in 1906, the *Festspiele* were first held in 1920. Operetta was considered an ambassador for Austria: Fritz Rodeck argued that Viennese operetta had no foreign competitors, and had developed 'into an article for export of such tremendous commercial significance that the layman cannot possibly estimate its magnitude'. Austrian cinema fell into a similar category (Rodeck, 1927). The latter could be aimed at both foreign and domestic audiences, although the indigenous population was also wooed with documentary films such as *Mit dem Postkraftwagen durch Österreichs Alpenwelt* ('Through Austria's alpine world in a postal bus'.) In 1931, there were 250 postal bus routes covering 8500 km. The genre films known as *Wien Film* played an important rôle in promoting Austria at home and abroad, especially after the imposition of the 1000 mark tax (see later). Films such as *Carnival in Vienna* (1935); *Vienna – Home of Waltzes* (1936) or *How a Frenchman Perceived Vienna* (1937) used a glorified capital as their backdrop.

The complex relationship between provincial and national tourism parallels the relationship between provincial and national identity. Provincial identities were well established by 1918 but the problems of the First Republic highlight the two difficulties in expanding that identity to a national level: the difficulties of securing loyalty to the artificial creation of the centralised state, and of expanding individuals' ties of loyalty from their immediate surroundings to the nation. The rôle of the individual provinces in the development of Austrian national identity remains under-researched (Jambor, 1971; Bowman, 1995). However, provincial identity could serve either to hinder (through separatism) or to foster (by providing a basis for) the development of an Austrian national identity. Differences could be glossed over in tourist publications, where a component might represent the whole. For example, Austria's different provincial identities were reflected in a broad variety of *Trachten* clothing (regional costume) which also represented a regional and rural identity standing firm against an industrialised urban identity. However, posters such as *Österreich ladet ein* (Austria invites you) used an individual in *Trachten,* in this case, a woman in a *Dirndl* standing against a lake framed by mountains, to symbolise the whole country and its inhabitants.[1] Tourism could also be seen as providing a vital impetus to the welding of the disparate into the unified. In these cases, the tensions between regional identities, and between the region and the collective, were addressed more overtly. In his publication entitled *Fremdenverkehr unsere Stärke* (Tourism our Strength), Hans von Hortenau addressed the tensions between the capital and the rest of the country:

> As far as we Austrians are concerned, the feeling of togetherness, which is founded on our historical development and tradition, could be deepened and extended by a mutual understanding between

> Vienna and particularly our inhabitants of the Alpine provinces. Despite passionate, sacrificial love for our common *Vaterland*, it is occasionally erroneously supposed by some Viennese that the simple, direct way of thought and the simple, modest way of life of the provincial is backward, while the cheerful disposition and the life-affirming gaiety of the Viennese is perceived as frivolity by the provincial. Many disturbances of the peaceful development, so vital for our country, could have been avoided in the last few years if there had been an expansion of mutual appreciation between the capital and the provinces ... Travelling is an ideal means of deepening such mutual understanding. (Von Hortenau, 1937)

Hortenau's solution for the conflict between a 'traditional rural' life and the perception of a decadent city was contact through travel. According to tourist propaganda, city dwellers could find their roots, peace and health in the country; conversely, rural travellers would find education, enlightenment and modernity though their travels.

The divide was not only between centre and periphery, however, but also between composite parts and the whole. In an article written in 1927, the *Landeshauptvertreter* of the Burgenland, Ludwig Leer, argued that the Peace Treaties, which had otherwise placed millions under foreign rule, had freed 300,000 Germans from Magyar rule in the Burgenland. This population needed to form ties with the other Austrian provinces. Leer saw in travel the foundation for a 'spiritual taking possession' which would complete the political union:

> For in no other country has tourism the political, yes, patriotic mission that it has for us. Only tourism can spin the thousands of threads, which connect us with the way of thinking and feeling of the Austrian. (Leer, 1927: 53)

Contact between provinces was dependent upon geographical location and national infrastructure. Easy travel was important to all types of tourist but improved internal communications had a particularly important function to fulfil in Austria. The provinces of the Tyrol and the Burgenland had poor links with the rest of Austria. As the Landeshauptmann of the Burgenland, Josef Rauhofer, wrote of his province's *Anschluß* with the rest of Austria:

> the primary concern was and is the question of infra-structure, for the question of whether the province is permanently connected with the western economic and cultural areas, or whether it remains forever in a Cinderella rôle, depends upon the solution to this issue. (Rauhofer, n.d.)

East Tyrol had a similar problem. Following the Treaty of St Germain, East Tyrol no longer had a land-link to North Tyrol until the construction of the Großglockner-Hochalpenstrasse in 1935, which cost 25.8 million schillings to build. It also helped Austria to build up its rôle as a link between northern and southern Europe. By 20 October 1935, the road had been used by 130,600 people, in 19,300 cars and 4200 buses, on 5500 motorbikes and 4300 bicycles. A third of all vehicles were foreign. As these were toll-paying travellers, the pass is an example of tourism's importance for recouping the financial outlay of infrastructural improvements. The pass was promoted in the film *Singende Jugend* (*Singing Youth*, 1936) which tells the tale of a poor provincial lad with a beautiful voice but an evil step-father, who succeeds in joining the *Wiener Sängerknaben*. The action takes place against the background of the mountainous scenery of the Groß Glockner and East Tyrol, and promoted three tourist attractions at once – the modern infrastructure, the mountains and the Vienna Boys' Choir, which had been revived in 1924 by Josef Schnitt, director of the Hofburg orchestra. Between 1921 and 1937, the Austrian road network grew from 27,000 km to 86,000 km, figures which reflect a recognition of the importance of the motoring tourist but which also helped to create a national infrastructure, incoherent after the dissolution of the monarchy. The role of roads in linking provinces should not be overemphasised: initially cars drove on the right-hand side of the road in the west, and on the left in the east, and tourism publications repeatedly commented on the poor road surfaces. The rail and air networks were similarly expanding: by 1936 the rail network had expanded from 5844 to c. 7400 km of track (Brieger, 1936; Solvis, 1933).

There is an interesting emphasis on transport methods in Austrian tourist publications. Posters, for example, suggested a complementary relationship between the landscape and the modern transport that allowed its consumption, such as cable cars, trams, automobiles and trains. The first cable car, the *Zugspitzenseilbahn,* was opened in 1926, followed in 1928 by the *Hahnenkammseilbahn* in Kitzbuhl, the *Patscherkofelseilbahn* in Igls and the *Nordkettenseilbahn* in Innsbruck. In the poster *Ferien in Österreich* a cable car climbs on the diagonal in front of an imposing mountain vista, rising past a steep incline: human ingenuity and technical achievement presented in juxtaposition with natural, awe-inspiring scenery, conquered and unconquerable. The emphasis on modern transport methods within Austria highlights one of the fundamental paradoxes in Austrian tourist literature: the representation of Austria as deeply traditional, historical, and eternal, and simultaneously as modern and forward-looking. The contradiction is not, however, surprising, given the fundamental role of the transport organisations in promoting Austrian tourism. A guide published by the Austrian Federal Railways (ÖBB), for example, informed the traveller:

> He who is interested in the general aspect of the country may, without even having to quit the broader highways of traffic, enjoy the varied beauty of truly magnificent scenery. From the window of a railway-car he may view the splendour of high mountains ... from the safe cabin of a cable railway he may let his eye roam over low-lying forests ... from a deck-chair on board a Danube steamer he may gaze at the ruined castles which, ever since the days of the Nibelungs, have been the wardens of Europe's greatest natural highway.

This not only describes a holiday for those too lethargic to bother to set foot on the land itself, it also suggests that in Austria the old could blend seamlessly with the new: technical progress and rural historical sites complementing each other. This blend was particularly evident in representations of the capital city which represented both the past and the future, tradition and progress. Cicely Hamilton found in her travels in the early 1930s that the cult of old Vienna was particularly popular: postcards and prints, for example, depicted scenes from the Biedermeier period to Franz Joseph's day (Hamilton, 1935). However, the capital city was also sold as a cosmopolitan forward-looking city with future-oriented trade-fairs, exciting, even decadent, night life, and a huge range of cultural opportunities. One poster made this explicit in its caption and image: against a backdrop of the city represented by a horizon of churches and St Stephen's Cathedral set against belching industrial chimneys and workers' housing, the slogan reads 'Vienna and the Viennese: the old and the new Vienna'.

At whom was this blend directed? There was some disagreement in the First Republic about the economic consequences of domestic tourism, as questions were raised as to whether it generated income or merely redistributed it. However, domestic tourism had the advantage over foreign tourism that it was less dependent on foreign political situations and provided a rare area over which Austrians could exercise some control. As was argued in *Fremdenverkehr:*

> [Domestic tourism] is part of our own economy, it can be influenced by its own people and by its own leadership; it is therefore a factor which can be counted on quite differently from foreign tourism, which depends upon a thousand variables, over which we have no influence. (*Fremdenverkehr*, 1938)

Domestic and foreign tourism within Austria (measured in statistics by the number of overnight stays) rose steadily until 1933. There are some problems with tourist statistics in the interwar period, although an overall upward trend is clear. Gustav Otruba, for example, points out that the growth of recognised tourist sites from 811 (1933) to 1993 (1934) to 2140 (1937) is dubious. In 1933 only those locations which registered over 500 foreign visitors and over 3000 overnight stays had been counted (Otruba, 1978). The Corporate State in particular intervened to promote domestic travel. In the cabinet meeting of 25 May 1934, for example, the hope was expressed that all civil servants would spend their holidays at home [i.e. in Austria], unless there were exceptional circumstances. Encouraged by foreign example (the Italian *Dopolavoro* and the German *Kraft durch Freude* organisations), increasing efforts were invested in keeping Austrian holidaymakers within domestic borders. The incentive was both financial and ideological. As one publication of the *Vaterländische Front* (VF) pointed out, unlike the popular mystery tours, weekend holidays (with special tariffs for members of the VF) where the route was publicised in advance, had an important rôle to fill: the intention of 'awakening the joy in each participant of deepening the knowledge of a specific area of the Fatherland'. The VF, or Fatherland Front, was founded on 20 May 1933 by the federal chancellor Engelbert Dollfuß. It was represented as a 'non-partisan' political organisation intending to unite all Austrian forces loyal to the government. After the dissolution of all political parties, and their replacement by professional or trade groups ('corporations'), the VF became the sole representative of the Corporate State. The financial incentive was particularly important in Austria, because nationals travelling abroad encouraged the problematic foreign currency deficit. The pro-Anschluß publication *Österreichische–Deutsche Fremdenverkehrs–und Reise-zeitung* pointed out that in 1926, France had made 350,000 million Kronen from 70,000 Austrian visitors. To add insult to injury, the article concluded, the French were not even grateful for this foreign influx (*Österreichisch–Deutsche Fremdenverkehrs–und Reisezeitung*, 1926). The tone of the article implies that travelling to France (often identified as the enemy owing to its association with the Treaty of St Germain) constituted a national betrayal.

Prior to the war, Vienna had attracted less international tourism than other European capitals such as Paris or Berlin; the overwhelming majority of visitors came from within the Empire itself and only about 20% from abroad, the majority of whom came from Germany (9%), followed by Russia (4%), Roumania (3%), Britain, France and the USA. During the inter-war period, there was a gradual re-orientation towards visitors from the West, Central Europe and overseas. This also brought a shift of visitors towards the provinces of the west, including the Tyrol, Vorarlberg, Salzburg, Carinthia and East Tyrol, although the capital would always exert a major attraction (Zimmerman, 1991). The presence of foreign visitors offered practical evidence that that Austria merited time and money being spent within her borders. Furthermore, as Graham Saunders has argued, encounters between inhabitants and travellers foster the development of 'new perceptions of each other and of one's own identity, society and culture' (Saunders, 1993: 58). This argument would suggest that tourism drew into the country foreigners who could provide the outgroup to the nation's ingroup, that is, a contrast against which indigenous national identity could be defined. Hans von Hortenau offered the following advice:

> meet the needs and habits of foreigners as much as possible, aim that they should feel at home with you, but while doing so, remain independent, cultivate and protect your Austrian-ness, and above all be proud of it! (Von Hortenau, 1937: 34)

A similar process could take place in the Austrian abroad, permitting the traveller to discover what made home home:

> If a Viennese is in foreign parts, in the most magnificent metropolis, at the most chic health resorts, then he does not deny them his unenvious admiration, and is genuinely enthusiastic about many an achievement, but in a corner of his heart a little bit of homesickness stirs for his Viennese coffee house, which he often misses from the very first day.

Included in a handbook for Austrian tourism, this quotation was also a sophisticated way of introducing the Viennese café as a tourist attraction to the foreign traveller.

However, in Austria it was not always clear cut who constituted a foreigner. Nationals of the former Empire, or of German-speaking Central Europe, were not necessarily constructed as 'other'. In these cases, foreign tourism was perceived as having similar sociopolitical ramifications to domestic tourism – strengthening ties between peoples rather than people. This relates back to the opening issue of the competing solutions for the perceived problem of Austria's viability. So, for example, the lawyer Dr Heinrich Herbatschek, the chairman of the Austro-Czech Organisation, wrote in an article on the ties between Austria and Czechoslovakia that

> the fact alone, that part of Austria's population has its origins in the areas occupied by the present Czech Republic, and the heart still pulls homewards, and on the other hand that many people there have familial, financial, social and other reasons for not wanting to break their connections with Austria ... prove how mistaken those would be who argued 'never again' is a constant. Both states, and particularly both nations which inhabit them, need each other, they cannot exist without interrelationships. (Herbatschek, 1931)

There was a gradual decline in visitors from the Empire, however: thus by 1937/8, only 49% of visitors to Vienna came from the countries of the former monarchy. A quarter of all overnight stays were by tourists from Czechoslovakia, and 8% from Hungary, Yugoslavia 5%, Poland 8%, Roumania 4%, Bulgaria 1%. With a contradictory agenda, but a similar view on the consequences of tourism, the pro-*Anschluß* journal *Beautiful German Austria* argued that nothing would promote the idea of *Anschluß* more effectively than travel:

> I would like to recommend to the Germans whose holidays lead them to the Austrian alpine world, that when they find themselves in the land blessed with beauty ... they should ... consider the thought, this is also part of your Fatherland, this is also referred to in German song, your love of the Fatherland also includes this. (Von Teichmann, 1926)

Publications in favour of an alternative form of existence for Austria, whether *Anschluß* or Federation, nevertheless stressed the diversity and beauty of Austria's assets, and identified what qualities Austria would contribute to an alternative political organisation. In consequence, while challenging the logic of an independent Austrian state, these sources simultaneously defined and valued component parts of Austrian national identity.

The emphasis in the literature on the sociopolitical consequences of foreign tourism should not overshadow its financial implications. The tourist industry was one of the few areas which offered the prospect of substantial foreign currency earnings. In 1935, 6.83 million overnight stays by foreigners were recorded, which brought in 250 million schillings: the first time that income from tourism could cover the unfavourable balance of visible trade (231 million schillings in 1935). The economist Friedrich Hertz had pointed out in the 1920s that the largest positive items on the balance of payments were tourist traffic (244–254 million AS), transit trade (120 million AS) and transit traffic (71.3 million AS). The largest negative item was interest and amortisation on state loans (108.6 million AS) (Hertz, 1925: 62). Over-dependence on a single industry rendered the Austrian economy vulnerable. The income from foreign exchange fluctuated between 307.7 million schillings (its zenith in 1928) and 144.7 million schillings (at its nadir in 1934) (Puchinger, n.d.). From 1932, the industry was badly hit by the depression, and most European countries brought in foreign currency laws (*Devisenbewirtschaftung*). Not surprisingly, the expansion of the tourist industry became a matter of state concern and, as we have seen, after 1933 there was increasing state intervention. The industry featured in economic agreements between states, for example, where quotas of goods were compensated by tourist quotas. Internally, there was the following state support: financial aid for measures which would foster the tourist trade (hotel building, investments); a simplification of relevant laws (on registration, bilateral agreements on visa laws); price controls; improvement of infrastructure and transport possibilities; laws intended to protect spas, landscapes and sites of national interest; education of the population on the importance of tourism to Austria; collating and improving tourist statistics; and cooperation between ministries to foster tourist trade (Bernecker, 1968: 242). The success of these measures would be limited. After the Nazi Bavarian Minister of Justice, Hans Frank, was deported on 15 May 1933, the German Government passed a law to exert economic pressure on Austria (1 June 1933). A tax of 1000 marks was imposed on all German visitors to Austria (the so-called 1000 Mark *Sperre* or barrier). Combined with the effects of the depression, the tax led to a massive drop in visitors to the country. The proportion of German visitors to Austria fell from 32.2% in 1932, to 1.7% in the summer of 1934 (dropping from four million overnight stays in 1931/2 to just over 900,000 in 1935/6) (Otruba, 1978). It proved possible to make up some of the deficit by encouraging domestic tourism and by attracting more American and Western European visitors. These went from constituting 4.8% to making up 12.4% of visitors to Austria (Otruba, 1978). However, the figures for foreign overnight visits never reached even their 1928 level after 1934. The statistics also mask the fact that it was difficult to attract new travellers to areas left destitute by the absence of German hikers – particularly small mountain villages, reliant on passing climbers. For non-industrial areas with few resources other than climatic and scenic attractions, tourism was a rare source of employment and one for which it was difficult to find an alternative.

Political events were not auspicious for the industry. On 25 July 1934, the federal chancellor Engelbert Dollfuß was assasssinated in a failed Nazi putsch. In the cabinet meeting of 30 October 1934, Karl Buresch, the finance minister, argued that the acts of terrorism by National Socialists and the events of July had led to a drop in income from tourism from the predicted 200 million to 100 million. The law of 8 June 1935 was intended to protect the tourist industry and aimed specifically at deterring terrorist activities by National Socialists. The law decreed that anybody who deliberately damaged or endangered tourism on a federal, regional, or local level could be punished by fines of up to 2000 schillings and/or prison sentence of up to six months. It was not until the July agreement of 1936 (11 July 1936), however, by which Austria granted amnesty to Nazi prisoners and committed itself to conducting its foreign policy as a second German state, that the 1000 mark barrier was lifted. Restrictions on travel between the two countries were lifted, and currency relations settled. But, as Otruba points out, the perceived drawing together of the two countries cost Austria the goodwill of many of their newly won Western European visitors (Bernecker, 1968: 246; Otruba, 1981). The agreement failed to bring as much of an improvement as hoped and terrorist activities continued until 1938, when German troops marched into Austria. The *Österreischiche Verkehrswerbung* was dissolved until 1945.

Selling a country to consumers necessitates the construction of a national image, and conversely, as John Urry suggests, 'identity almost everywhere has to be produced partly out of the images constructed for tourists' (Urry, 1995: 165). In a period when Austrian national identity sought a new definition, the interwar tourist trade provided an incentive for self-definition and the fostering of what set Austria apart from her neighbours. As Burkhart and Medlik (1981: 197) argue, it is necessary to create 'an identifiable image of a country's tourist attractions, subsuming to some extent the diversity of attractions within one country into a single coherent image'. The image to which the tourist is to be attracted must first be created, not least in tourist literature. Enticement of the visitor involves both the distillation and generalisation of national identity and the emphases and omissions offer an insight into perceived or idealised national identity. This investigation into the Austrian tourist industry suggests that there are four further broad and related areas through which the relationship between tourism and national identity can be explored. First, there is the relationship between regional and national tourism and the impact of domestic tourism on national cohesion. Second, there is the mutual dependence between the tourist industry and national communication networks and infrastructure. Third, there is the financial incentive which the tourist industry offers to the identification and fostering of 'national' elements. And finally, there is the interaction between domestic and foreign populations which promotes the identification and discussion of national characteristics.

There was little recognition in tourist publications of the negative consequences of tourism on national cohesion. Gerhard Wanner (1985) points out that conservative church circles saw in tourism a threat to morals and behaviour. Tourism could also be resented on economic grounds, as it pushed up prices in key areas, benefitting hoteliers and restaurateurs at the expense of local consumers. There were also tensions between competing constructions of Austrian national identity. Ignaz Seipel, the federal chancellor between 1926 and 1929, complained 'To cultivate our little garden and to show it to foreigners in order to make money out of it are no proper tasks for the inhabitants of the Carolingian Ostmark and the conquerors of the Turks' (Seet, 1947: 323). Adaptations of traditional Austrian art forms to increase their appeal to the tourist were noted and denounced. In the operetta *Axel an der Himmelstür* (*Axel at Heaven's Gate,* 1936), for example, the cast sang a parody of the traditional *Wiener Lied* (Viennese song) which denounced the recycling of ingredients such as the Danube, the Prater and Strauß. As this satire recognised, there was a narrow line between depiction and sterilisation, praise and glorification, reflection and self-stereotyping. What could begin as an exploration of the Austrian character and culture, or the country's historical and geographical heritage, could easily become a pastiche. Nonetheless, in terms of the identity crisis Austria experienced in the interwar period, the rejection of the tourist image required the identification or invention, and defence, of an alternative. And while Austria's viability as a nation is no longer seriously questioned, the images presented in the tourist literature of the interwar period are remarkably consistent with those of the present day.

Acknowledgements

I am indebted to Gerard DeGroot, University of St Andrews, for his committed support of my work. I would also like to thank Claire Carrie, Anthony McElligott, and Peter Yeandle for their discussions and interest. Sandy Grant (Lancaster University) gave up valuable time to offer helpful editorial suggestions. The research on and in Austria would not have been possible without R.G. Peniston-Bird and S.C.E. Peniston-Bird in both the past and the present.

Note

1. I am indebted and grateful to Alfred Slezak, archivist at the *Flugblätter-, Plakate- und Exlibris-Sammlung* of the Österreichische Nationalbibliothek, for his assistance.

References

Arnold, K. (1978) Raumliche Verteilungsmuster im Wiener Fremdenverkehr. *Osterreich in Geschichte und Literatur und Geographie* 22 (Jan.–Feb.), Heft 1.

Bernecker, P. (1968) Die Entwicklung des Fremdenverkehrs in Osterreich. In Hermann Schnell (ed.) *Osterreich – 50 Jahre Republik. 1918–1968*. Vienna: Bernecker.

Bowman, W.D. (1995) Regional history and the Austrian nation. *Journal of Modern History* 67 (4), 873–97.

Brieger, T. (1936) *Wie Werben Wir? Das 1 × 1 der Frembenverkehspropaganda*. Eigenverlag.

Bruckmüller, E. (1984) *Nation Österreich: Sozialhistorische Aspekte ihrer Entwicklung*. Vienna, Cologne, Graz.

Burkart, A.J. and Medlik, S. (1981) *Tourism: Past, Present, Future*. London: Heinemann.

Fremdenverkehr (31 Mar. 1938) Morgenrot fur Osterreichs Fremdenverkehr. 3, Jahrgang 11, 31 March. Vienna.

Fremdenverkehrs-Korrespondenz. Nachrichtendienst für Reiseverkehr, Bäder, Tagungen, Messen und Ausstellungen. Mit den offiziellen Mitteilungen des Österreich-Tschechoschlowakischen Fremdenverkehrssektion. 5 Jahrgang, No. 20/21, 31 August, 1931.

Gedye, G.E.R. (1928) *A Wayfarer in Austria*. London: Methuen.

Hamilton, C. (1935) *Modern Austria as Seen by an Englishwoman*. London and Toronto: J.M. Dent.

Handbuch für den österreichischen Fremdenverkehr (1934) Klosterneuburg, Augustinus Druckerurg, Gewerbeförderungsdienst des Bundesministeriums für Handel und Verkehr / Österreichische Gesellschaft für Fremden-verkehr.

Herbatschek, H. (1931) In *Offizielle Mitteilungen der Österreichisch-Tschecho-slowakischen Fremdenverkehrssektion in Wien u. der Tschechoslowakisch-österreichen Fremdenverkehrs-sektion* No. 5. 10 February.

Hertz, F. (1925) *Zahlungsbilanz und Lebensfahigkeit Osterreichs*. Munich and Leipzig: Duncker & Humbolt.

Jambor, W. (ed.) (1971) *Der Anteil der Bundeslander an der Nationswerdung Osterreichs*. Vienna / Munich: Wedl.

Leer, L. (1927) Burgenlandiche Fremdenverkehr. In Michael Haberlandt (ed.) *Osterreich: seine Land und Volk and Kultur*. Vienna: Verlag für Volks und Heimatkunde.

Otruba, G. (1978) Die grosse Wandlung im Osterreichischen Fremdenverkehr als Folge der Tausend-Mark-Sperre. *Beitrage zur Handels und Verkehrsgeschichte*. Band 3. Graz: Grazer Forschungen zur Wirt-schafts und Sozialgeschichte.

Otruba, G. (1981) Die Folgen des Juliabkommens 1936 für Osterreichs Fremdenverkehr. In *Politik und Gesellschaft im alten und neuen Osterreich. Festschrift für Rudolf Neck zum 60 Geburtstag*. Vienna: Verlag für Geschichte und Politik.

Pelincka, A. (1979) Austriaca – deux fois l'Autriche. Paper presented at Université de Haute-Normandie, February 1979.

Peniston-Bird, C.M. (1997) The debate on Austrian national identity in the First Republic (1918–1938). PhD thesis, University of St Andrews.

Puchinger, E. (n.d.) Unpublished chronology of Austrian tourism. Lower Austria Tourist Board.

Rauhofer, J. (n.d.) *Das Burgenland im Rahmen des osterreichischen Wiederaufbaues*.

Reinalter, E.H. (1933) Osterreichs landschaft. In *Osterreichs illustrierte Fremdenverkehrs und Reise Zeitung* (Nov.). Vienna: Folge 1, 1 Jahrgang.

Rodeck, F. (1927) Wien als Kunststadt. In Michael Haberlandt (ed.) *Osterreich: sein Land und Volk und seine Kultur*. Vienna: Verlag für Volks-und Heimat Kunde.

Saunders, G. (1993) Early travellers in Borneo. In M. Hitchcock, V.T. King and M.J.G. Parnwell (eds) *Tourism in South-East Asia*. London and New York: Routledge.

Seet, P. (1947) Seipel's views on the Anschluss: An unpublished exchange of letters. *Journal of Modern History* 19.

Skalnik, K. (1983) Auf der Suche nach der Indentität. In E. Weinzierl and K. Skalnik (eds) *Osterreich 1918–1938: Geschichte der Ersten Republic* (p. 14). Graz: Styria.

Solvis, S. (1933) *Die Weg zur Neuordnung der oesterreichischen Bundesbahnen*. Vienna: Springer.

Stourzh, G. (1990) *Vom Reich zur Republik – Studien zum Österreichbewußtsein*. Vienna: Atelier.

Urry, J. (1995) *Consuming Places*. London and New York: Sage.

Von Hortenau, H. (1937) *Fremdenverkehr unser Starke*. Vienna: Osterreichische Aufklarungsdienst Heft 3.

Von Teichmann (1926) *Osterreichisch–Deutsch Fremdenverkehrs= und Reise-zeitung*. Vienna: Ost. Dr. U. Verl. Ges.

Wanner, G. (1985) Feldkirchs Fremdenverkehr von 1918 bis 1938, seine Probleme und Einrichtungen. In *Kulturinformation. 100 Jahre Verkehrsverein Feldkirch 1985*. Feldkirch: Rheticus Gesellschaft.

Zimmerman, F. (1991) Austria. In A.M. Williams and G. Shaw *Tourism and Economic Development: Western European Experiences*. London and New York: Belhaven.

Chapter 10

Paradise Lost and Found: Tourists and Expatriates in El Terreno, Palma de Mallorca, from the 1920s to the 1950s

JOHN K. WALTON

This chapter deals with the development of tourism and of expatriate communities on Mallorca during the middle decades of the 20th century, before the advent of what is usually labelled 'mass tourism' from the 1960s onwards. The systematic promotion of tourism on the island began at the start of the 20th century with the establishment of the organisation Fomento del Turismo de Mallorca for this purpose in 1905, following the publication of Bartolomé Amengual's book *La Industria de los Forasteros* (*The Visitor Industry*) two years earlier. These were pioneering initiatives in the Spanish context and it should be emphasised at the outset that tourism was an important feature of the island's economy and society long before the 'boom' that wrought a spectacular transformation from the late 1950s onwards, although this period has been systematically neglected until very recently. The lively early history of tourism on Mallorca was boosted by improved maritime communications after 1910, while the island became a stopover for cruise liners and for long-distance passenger shipping lines in the 1920s and acquired its first air services in 1931, as a summer season developed alongside the older winter residential trade, as in other established Mediterranean locations. Numbers of tourists were still small, however: in 1930 just over 20,000 were recorded in the island's hotels, staying on average for nearly 12 days (a figure greatly boosted by the nearly 600 people who stayed for two months or longer), while there were also nearly 15,000 cruise passengers who came ashore for brief visits. By 1935 the figure for staying visitors had risen to just over 40,000, with a fractionally lower average duration of stay, while the cruise passengers now amounted to over 50,000. By 1935, there were 135 hotels of various levels of comfort on the island, 71 in Palma, the capital, where the cruise liners docked. The tourists who spent time on the island were mainly professional people from northern Europe, retired British (especially Indian) army officers and foreigners with private incomes.

The Spanish Civil War interrupted this modest growth in the tourism of the elite, the comfortably-off and the bohemian, and of the expatriate communities that accompanied it. By the end of the Second World War, Mallorca welcomed increased numbers of tourists but most of them came from the Spanish mainland, in response to the promotion of the island as a honeymoon destination: in 1946, of 61,514 hotel visitors recorded in the official statistics, only 1229 were foreigners. A period of rapid growth followed and, by 1955, the overall total had risen to 188,704. The number of visitors from outside Spain first exceeded the number of Spanish citizens in 1952, after which the gap widened quickly, and the growth in foreign tourism, encouraged by a government that was desperate for tourist revenue to balance the budget and pay for imported essentials and industrial raw materials, inaugurated a period of even more rapid expansion. Speculative development spread beyond its initial core in and around Palma as visitor numbers reached the million mark in 1965, by which time most of the visitors arrived by air, after belated investment in improved air terminal facilities. This is a fascinating story in its own right, now compellingly presented by Joan Buades. But our concern here is with the earlier, formative years of elite tourism in pursuit of various definitions of the Mediterranean paradise. The time span of the chapter covers a transition from dominant literary representations of the island as a Mediterranean 'paradise' of lotus-eating tranquillity to a growing awareness that notions of 'paradise' could take multiple and conflicting forms, from natural simplicity to the ready availability of cheap alcohol and easy sex. A full spectrum of representations was in evidence from an early stage but the balance tilted from the former to the latter as foreign visitors began to return to the islands after the Spanish Civil War, complementing the growing crowds of Spanish honeymooners who had been encouraged during the immediate post-Civil War years. Within Mallorca, the chapter is concerned with expatriates as well as tourists, and the two categories overlap considerably in practice, especially as many visitors returned regularly and for long periods. It homes in on the part of the island where most foreign visitors and residents (not just from Britain) were in evidence: the seaside suburb of El Terreno, a western adjunct of Palma, the island's capital. Before the advent of international tourism on the grand scale across a widening swathe of the island's coastline, which gathered momentum from the 1960s (Buades, 2004: 33–89; Lindo-Webb, 1933: 3, 135; Ripoll, 1994: 80–3), Mallorca's dominant image was 'la isla de la calma', in the oft-quoted phrase of Santiago Rusiñol; but the nature of the experience for visitors and expatriates before this great transformation, a formative period that is generally neglected by students of the island's tourism history, was actually very varied, as different (but intersecting) groups in different parts of the island sought their approximations to paradise in contrasting ways (Rusiñol, 1999).

Paradise means, and has meant, different things to different people: perceptions of it, indeed, might be thought to constitute a touchstone for defining individual and collective cultural values. How might it be defined? One key set of assumptions associates it with the innocence and tranquillity of the Garden of Eden before the 'fall', when the introduction of the tourist gaze began to corrode spontaneity and to introduce the serpent in the form of a new self-consciousness and awareness of the prospect of profit from the display of a subtly transformed everyday self, presenting the irresistible temptations of the fruit of the tree of knowledge of the outside world and the opportunities it offered (Urry, 1995). Another might regard it as a particularly desirable enclave within that world that Adam and Eve were freed to wander, after the fall: a beautiful, 'natural' setting that is nevertheless free to accommodate sin, though preferably with a necessary setting aside of guilt or stress. Another might range far beyond biblical, literary or heavenly associations, and regard paradise as a 'big rock candy mountain' where all pleasures and consumer goods come easily and cheaply, without the need for self-discipline or mundane exertion, and hedonistic pleasures can be indulged without fear of unpleasant consequences. Paradise is of course a highly subjective concept, to the extent that one person's paradise can be another's hell. Should paradise entail going 'back to nature' or to a 'primitive' existence, without the comforts of civilisation or the anonymity of the city? (Sheller, 2003). Or should it entail the maximum access to everything that makes daily living easier and provides gratifications of all kinds? Is it (for example) primarily about nature, cultivation, community or freedom; and how might those tensions be reconciled? What role is actually played, for whom, by easy access to basic resources without the necessity to work?

Writing about another expatriate enclave on Mallorca, the cluster of writers, artists and hangers-on that accumulated in and around the village of Deià, Jacqueline Waldren tells us that such potential conflicts have been reconciled successfully, although her anthropological study recognises tensions both personal and structural. Her study focuses explicitly on 'paradise and reality in Mallorca' and she begins by referring to representations of Deià as 'a paradise imbued with magic and mystery', although she provides no supporting footnote for this quotation. Her more developed working definition draws parallels between Deià and Tangier, St Tropez, Arles, Martha's Vineyard, Tahiti and Goa, where

> a few foreigners who felt they had discovered what they perceived as 'paradise' settled in to pursue the arts... Paradise meant different things to each person, but common themes seemed to include a place that combined nature's bounty, earthly pleasure, social harmony, free will and expression...

Later she offers a different emphasis: paradise is 'an enclosed garden... safe places to play, a place of freedom within set boundaries... the boundaries are clear, the space is known, the people are familiar, the mysteries and fears of a wider world are contained'. She ends her book on an optimistic note, asserting that '[L]ife in Deià has served as paradise for many... For many in Deià, the ideal of paradise and the reality of everyday coalesce'. This might seem an optimistic conclusion, on the basis of evidence provided elsewhere in the book and in other studies and memoirs; and the definitions she uses are problematic, not least in their assumption of separation from the outside world, while the places with which Deià is bracketed are wildly contrasting in scale and culture. In any case, this has been a small minority experience, rendered high-profile by the presence and legacy of Robert Graves, though paralleled in other parts of the island where artistic and literary colonies developed during the inter-war years (Waldren, 1996: x, 1, 250).

My main aim, however, is not to join battle with Waldren, especially in the light of her status as insider (at least to the expatriate community) and anthropologist, but to cast a quizzical gaze on a different and earlier version of an island paradise. This chapter deals with the most numerous expatriate community on Mallorca, with an altogether more worldly and consumerist version of paradise, and the one most closely tied to the mainstream international tourist industry as that developed between the end of the First World War and the start of the Spanish Civil War: the colony of several hundred people who settled in the suburb of El Terreno, overlooking the bay and spreading up the hillside to the west of Palma de Mallorca, and making its own distinctive impact on the social life of the island's capital.

The lure of El Terreno depended in large part, of course, on the more general images of Mallorca that attracted people to the island in the first place, whether they had read or heard about it before arriving or were captivated by it as passengers on the long-distance shipping services that called there. Like other Mediterranean 'paradises', its first incarnation as a site of international tourism was as a winter climatic station for northern

Europeans, but within that framework it acquired a particular reputation for tranquillity, calm and a sense of time standing still. Here is A.S.M. Hutchinson's enthusiastic (if occasionally less than coherent) introduction to Henry C. Shelley's portrait of the island in 1926 (Shelley, 1926: xiii–xiv, xxi–xxii; see also Harrison, 1927: 19–20; King, 1959: 15):

> Majorca… it symbolises, or should symbolise, that there follows it a breathless pause, an enchanted hush… Majorca, as during my stay here I learnt to know her and to love her, was not a real place, it was a dream place: a dream in blue and white… often I sit and dream of her; and if ecstatic pictures will not flow from my pen out of that I do not see what is ever going to make them flow… If any would flee the world and rest their minds and their eyes on peace and beauty, I can conceive nothing that will so exquisitely fill that desire as a stay such as I had… It was not a real life, it was a dream life.

This sense of unreality and detachment from everyday cares is a commonplace in the literature on Mallorca at this time, and indeed earlier (Pemble, 1987: 253). The artist Francis Caron (1939: 1) drew attention to the common perception that time passed slowly in the long silences here or almost stood still:

> The air here is hot, and quite still. It smells of leaves and all sorts of spices, and they say that strangers when they first come to the island are drugged by it. The nights are slower and more spacious than they are at home – and that is because the sky is larger too.

Not only was the island tranquil, it also had beautiful seas and scenery and the people were represented as having an attractive, relaxed, unassertive temperament.

If paradise could not be virgin land, uninhabited on its discovery by the traveller or tourist and, at an extreme, demanding a Robinson Crusoe level of self-catering that would be attractive only to survivalists or people with very high ecological principles, desirous of leaving a minimal 'footprint', it was necessary for the people to be friendly and amenable. Dominant representations of the inhabitants of Mallorca in the 1920s cast them in that role, which was easier to ascribe and work through, with fewer complications and reservations, in an old European setting with none of the heritage of imperialism, slavery, racial stereotyping and economic, environmental and sexual exploitation that complicate the pursuit of paradise in the West Indies or Africa, or even the South Seas. Henry Shelley was typical in regarding them as 'a friendly, even affectionate people', neat and hard-working, honest in business but also shrewd and quick to respond to legitimate opportunity. He emphasised the lack of crime, especially violent crime, and the people's contentment with simple pleasures. He idealised 'the community', which was 'really an object lesson in feudalism at its best... to the detached observer they all seem to constitute one family in which there is the real equality which can only exist when the recognition of worth is based upon service faithfully rendered' (Shelley, 1926: 267–72). The American Frederick Chamberlin, writing in 1927, enjoyed exposing Shelley's mistake in taking a recently-constructed bull-ring at Alcudia to be a remarkably well-preserved Roman amphitheatre but endorsed his views on the temperament of the 'natives', a revealing choice of word. He emphasised the simplicity of life in this setting, the absence of pressure to do unnecessary work, and a relaxed absence of ambition or social competition: 'They *only* want bodily comfort' (emphasis in original), at a very basic level and, moreover, 'In six years, I have seen but three drunken natives'. The Balearics, indeed, were 'the most orderly of all the islands of the Mediterranean, and no thought ever need to be given to any form of disorder or crime' (Chamberlin, 1927: 24, 33, 43, 59, 82–5). Ada Harrison, writing in the same year, also endorsed this picture: 'The Majorcan temperament... is quiet and charming... They have under their Latin affability a solid dependableness and true will to oblige.' She was particularly impressed with the continuing importance of craft occupations, with the leisurely pace of work and attention to detail that matched other aspects of the portrayal; and her perception of the 'almost fabulous gentleness' of the Mallorcans was reinforced by her attendance at a football match in Sóller, where 'the play was so astonishingly polite, the players almost bowing their opponents self-effacingly towards the ball, that the afternoon might have dragged...' (Harrison, 1927: 22, 42, 164–5). Such perceptions matched, and grew out of, a widespread Victorian idealisation of Mediterranean societies in general (Pemble, 1987: chap. 8); but they contrasted sharply with dominant images of another part of the Spanish state that gained an early reputation for hospitality to tourists. Representations of the Basques had many parallels with those of the Mallorquins but a perception of their strength and toughness was always much in evidence, not least in the hard, physical way in which they played football. The people of Mallorca, by contrast, were portrayed in a much more overtly orientalist way, with an emphasis on passive tranquillity which had connotations of Eastern and tropical climes but which was cross-cut by a recognition of 'northern' virtues of hard work, abstemiousness and skills in trade and manufacture (Walton, 2000).

Such perceptions persisted in the 1950s. In 1952 the experienced travel writer Eric Whelpton described the Mallorquins as 'noted for their cleanliness, courtesy and extreme efficiency', as 'honest, moral and "ungrasping"' and as neither censorious nor prudish towards the uninhibited behaviour of Anglo-Saxon visitors, although unaffected by it in their own lives (Whelpton, 1952: 58, 89). Even *Trim*'s worldly-wise guides, published later in the decade, concluded that the distinguishing attraction of Mallorca, over and above climate and scenery, was 'the Majorcans themselves', with their calmness, decency, courtesy, respect, mild manners and abstention from any thought of crime or violence. Extending the orientalist position, the American author argued that his compatriots and other foreigners were drawn to the island because 'in comparison with the Majorcan, any man can be a lion. Any woman in a tight skirt can be a femme fatale. And because the Majorcan, bless him, is too sweet-natured to tell us we're making asses of ourselves' (Trimnell, 1957b: 5–6).

But *Trim*'s version of paradise was predominantly transgressive, a paradise that would be infernal in the eyes of conventional moralists, as he cheerfully pointed out: 'It has been said that the road to hell is paved with *Trim's Guides*. They say that it is so easy to go astray in Palma that any help given in locating booze parlors, saloons, gin mills, pubs and the like, is like haircutting a bald man. They say that *Trim* is a bad influence. But all we do is report the facts of life on this tight little island' (Trimnell, 1957a: 77–8). This last reference was to a particular meaning of 'tight', the one associated with drunkenness and 'apparently referring to the cheapness of drinkables'. *Trim's Guides* were happy to emphasise the cheapness of this 'Mediterranean Tahiti at bargain-basement prices' or 'Land of the Lotus Eaters', especially for cigarettes, alcohol (except beer) and servants, and to offer full guidance around the bars, night clubs and similar establishments of Palma, while pointing out the perils of 'Cognac Gulch', of which more anon, in a jocular way (Trimnell, 1957b: 2, 4, 24–7, 1957a: 1, 14, 55–65). This was not new, as we shall see: these opportunities for debauchery were already in evidence in the 1930s and they were particularly so in El Terreno, at the core of which, around Plaza Gomila, the area that *Trim* labelled as Cognac Gulch was already taking shape in the 1930s, servicing an English, American and otherwise international community of around 500 in the winter as early as the mid-1920s, and greatly augmented by summer tourists and longer-term visitors during the following decade (Chamberlin, 1927: 52). At what point *keif* or hashish became available, no doubt assisted by direct transport links to Morocco, is not clear but Robin King encountered it in the mid-1950s at Puerto de Andraitx. In any case, it is not surprising to find that cocaine was recognised as a commonplace at 'the parties of the more lurid' in El Terreno in 1934. In a way, this matches up with representations of Mallorca as itself addictive, making it hard to leave and impossible not to return to, like the classical land of the lotos-eaters to which it was often likened, although the addictive substance that reinforced the necessity to return was not the consumption of alcohol or narcotics but that of the characteristic spiral pastry called an *ensaimada* (King, 1959: 120–4; *Majorca Sun*, 14 January 1934).

The rather mundane idea of paradise that set store by the cheapness of essentials, a definition that included alcohol and tobacco but also local labour, thereby enabling a limited income to go further than it would 'at home', generated concerns about the possible inflationary consequences of the foreign presence, especially if it tempted the locals into raising their prices and acquiring the acquisitive habits of the consumer society. In 1926, Shelley was amused at the rapidity with which local traders responded to the arrival of British tourist steamers, with a sudden efflorescence of signs advertising 'public house', 'beer and spirits of all sorts', 'jazz band, free' and similar blandishments (Shelley, 1926: 269). Chamberlin noted a year later that servants' wages, prices and expectations about tipping had risen sharply 'since the English colony has increased so rapidly following the War' and that 'the Balearic servant is becoming quite as civilised as those of other lands' and as careless with the employer's money (Chamberlin, 1927: 56–7). Ada Harrison worried that Mallorca had

> lately become one of those places which, the English say, are being ruined by the English. For the army of winterers abroad, who seek sunshine and beauty and advantageous rates of living, have now got it on their list… The island will require some spoiling… But with the best will in the world there is still a risk. A couple of large hotels, however simply constructed and pleasantly filled, cannot be planted down in a tiny antique village without some danger to the inhabitants. It must be our hope that the unturned page of Majorca's history is not to be a record of sophistication and bank-notes… (Harrison, 1927: 16–17)

These rather patronising and hypocritical fears were not realised, however, and what impressed Francis Caron a decade later was the extraordinary cheapness of his basic needs, even in El Terreno (Caron, 1939: 8–9). At the same time, Lady Sheppard commented on the continuing cheapness of rents on the island, although they continued to be associated with conditions that many foreign tenants 'would have considered far too primitive to be accepted anywhere else' (Sheppard, 1947: 122). Paradise here might easily combine a version of the rustic idyll or 'love in a cottage' with a bohemian lifestyle that indulged heavily in drink, tobacco and an intimate sociability focused on a cluster of informal bars and drinking clubs. In this spirit, Whelpton looked back from 1952 on the 1930s as 'the Golden Age, when it was an expatriate's paradise – inexpensive, primitive, but with all the best amenities of life…' (Whelpton, 1952: 89). But even in 1957 *Trim* could propose that here was (almost) the best of all worlds:

> You can buy real Swiss cheese in Palma, and real American hamburgers, and real English tea. The flamenco dancing is real, too, and the bullfighters are the best in Spain. It is all so cheap that you spend all you have, because here you might as well live like a king. On what money it would cost you to survive elsewhere, here you can chaw lotus and hire ostrich-feather fans waved above your annointed *[sic]* and bejewel-ed *[sic]* head. (Trimnell, 1957b: 7)

The extravagance of cheapness enabled long-term visitors, who increasingly came for the summer, and expatriates to construct a version of paradise that combined simplicity with hedonism and lay within the grasp of people with remittances, allowances and unearned income who wanted to try out the life of a novelist, poet, artist or dreamer in this distinctive ambience.

Most of them did so in El Terreno, the seaside suburb that adjoined Palma to the west. It was not a creation of the tourist industry: its villas, gardens and bathing places had developed from the late 19th century as summer retreats for prosperous local and Barcelona families and for the 'indianos' who had returned wealthy from Spain's colonies. Indeed, it retained a strong Mallorquin and Spanish core identity even as the tourists and expatriates became more visible on its streets and occupied more of its houses; and Lluis Fabregas's reminiscences about its history in the first half of the century are focused almost entirely on Mallorquin, Catalan and Spanish personalities, with their sports, clubs, societies and social gatherings in their gardens and in bars, even in that Plaza Gomila which eventually became synonymous with the excesses of the hard-drinking British, Americans and northern Europeans (Fabregas, 1974: 19–20, 27–8 and passim). In its early days, it was readily identified with the island's general image of calm and tranquillity: indeed, Santiago Rusiñol himself took his family to live there from Barcelona and became a well-known figure in the cafés of El Terreno, which he wrote about with witty affection in his seminal *La Isla de la Calma* as 'the Tibidabo of Palma', in allusion to the hill above Barcelona, 'the place where the good bourgeois go to rest in the summer on the money they have been able to make during the winter' (Fabregas, 1974: 35–6; Rusiñol, 1999: 43). The British and Americans moved in alongside this established society from the 1920s onwards.

A.S.M. Hutchinson was enchanted by Henry Shelley's villa there in 1926: 'a dream in blue and white, the lovely little villas, perched one above the other up the heights of Palma and El Terreno' (Shelley, 1926: xii). Gordon West (1929: 63), 'jogging round Majorca' in 1929, thought he detected 'the influence of the English colony' on the 'formal white villas, many of them having beautiful terraces, gardens full of red geraniums, and purple bougainvillea climbing the walls'. Ada Harrison, however, found it 'quite singularly unattractive… El Terreno stretches away in impeccable dreariness along the shore to the west'. She elaborated:

> Only at El Terreno does Palma give evidence of being a resort. El Terreno is a long strip of holiday houses… The mainlanders from Barcelona live in them in summer and the English hire them in the winter… It is not for England in the bungalow period to cast aspersions on any country's architecture, but there is something extremely painful about Mediterranean holiday houses. They have a uniform air of being built of stucco and white cardboard, and attempt to look as sumptuous as they succeed in looking collapsible. El Terreno is an interminable climbing of these, enlivened at intervals by an English book-club, a touch-me-not hotel, and a couple of high-priced English-speaking establishments for disposing of the local needlework. This crop, doubtless innocent enough, is the first from the English seed. (Harrison, 1927: 29–30)

This was a minority view. Lady Sheppard, for example, saw El Terreno in a much more attractive and less uniform light: 'the streets are a gay jumble of modern white-washed houses, many angled and crooked, with perhaps an extra room added haphazard close to the chimney stack' (Sheppard, 1947: 122). *Trim*'s post-war notes on the area in the mid 1950s moved further in a romantic bohemian direction: 'The Montmartre of Majorca. Steep hillside, mostly stairways instead of streets…' (Trimnell, 1957b: 11). For most visitors, El Terreno as a maritime suburban environment was entirely compatible with the vision of paradise that they carried with them. As Lady Sheppard remarked, from the mid-1920s onwards, 'like the rest of the Mediterranean seaboard it had been turned into a summer playground'. This, she thought, affected the nature of the visiting public: 'These torrid and irresponsible sun worshippers bore no relation to the highly respectable – and possibly rather dull – visitors of the preceding six months'. They breached taboos on bodily exposure by wearing flimsy beachwear in the centre of Palma and attracted adverse comment from the locals. The growing numbers of cruise steamers brought more down-market visitors, if for shorter periods, and Lady Sheppard chose to concentrate her fire on a standard British target, the 'red-faced, beer-drinking and perspiring crowds from the Fatherland, who tramped from shop to shop in search of Majorcan straw hats, cheap sandals and local pottery' (Sheppard, 1947: 113–17).

The bar and club society of El Terreno itself became an international melting-pot during these years, with American refugees from Prohibition forming an important nucleus of revellers (Sheppard, 1947: 121). But it was not until the 1930s that the district became more obviously hedonistic and cosmopolitan; and even then it remained an interesting mixture of the respectable and the disreputable, which mingled in the same shops, tea rooms and bars and indeed in the lifestyles of individual residents and visitors. The 1933 edition of James Lindo-Webb's English tourist guide was still dominated by tea-rooms, libraries and shops, headed by the empire of F.G. Short, who had been in on the ground floor in 1917–18 and acted as house, estate and ticket agent, packer and forwarder of goods and garage proprietor, as well as presiding over one of the major social centres in the form of Short's English Tea-Room, Library (5500 books) and Bar. 'When in difficulty or trouble, go to Short's for a house, servant, nurse, doctor, guide, interpreter, motor-car.' His advertisement in the *Majorca Sun*, one of four foreign-language newspapers to be produced in Palma during the 1930s (the others were in English, French and German), promised, 'At Short's Tea Room, El Terreno, you get an English Tea in a charming room… a Book from the Library… a cocktail from Joe's. The Best of Everything' (Lindo-Webb, 1933: 2, 34; *Majorca Sun*, 7 January 1934). This mixture of the respectable and the alcoholic was characteristic of the place and period and is a reminder that, for many, daily life in paradise, whether the visit was temporary or long-term, required a reassuring admixture of the culturally familiar. The services of the Church of England were provided, in the heart of El Terreno, by the Rev. J. de B. Forbes, who lived at the Hotel Victoria. Until it acquired 'new and more suitable premises' in 1934, however, services were held in Short's Tea Room (*Majorca Sun*, 21 January 1934, 22 April 1934). The advertisements in Lindo-Webb's guide put tourists and newcomers in touch with (for example) the English-American Cake Shop and Tea Room, The Treasure Chest ('the popular gift shop of Mallorca'), The Terreno Shop (suits, sweaters, scarves and lingerie, 'hand knitted') and Anne's Dresses, all in Terreno and apparently operated by English speakers, along with hotels in the same district, including one run by Swiss expatriates. There were also local businesses that had adapted to the tourist and foreign resident markets: the San Cristo Bakery offered 'English sandwich loaves, Vienna bread and rolls… French rolls and brioches'; Artiach biscuits were 'made with the best fresh

Spanish products to suit the English taste'; José Homar was the 'premier mattress-maker... Speciality in English mattresses and cushions... Covers and ticking in English style'; and in the town centre the Perfumería Inglesa also offered gifts and souvenirs, while the Antigua Casa Medina addressed what turned out to be a very British set of preoccupations by supplying, 'Every kind of RUBBER GOODS. Hot water bottles; goloshes; waterproof sheets... rainproof knapsacks' (Lindo-Webb, 1933: passim). Here was reassurance on several fronts for those cast adrift in a paradise that might have lacked intimate domestic touches and routines. The advertisements of early 1934 in the *Majorca Sun* show that these services were only part of the story. Here we find additional tea-rooms and tea-gardens, which might, like Lena's Bar–Tea Room, offer both tea and cocktails in an 'intimate' setting; Charles the photographer; Picornell's hairdresser (opposite the English tea room); The Flower Shop, owned and managed by women with English names; 'smart custom made footwear' by Pastoret, also in the heart of Terreno; Beric Couture, a fashion shop on the same avenue, 14 de abril, where so many of these businesses clustered; and a teacher of bullfighting in 15 theoretical and practical lessons. There were German as well as English and American hotels and pensions, and a German lending library and painter advertising even in this English language publication; and this is a reminder that the Anglo-Saxons were only part of the story, as descriptions of bar and club society in the 1930s bring out forcefully (*Majorca Sun*, 7 January 1934).

El Terreno certainly had the sort of middle-class clubs that catered for conventional British middle-class preoccupations: the Bridge Club, the 'Ham and Swiss Cheese Club' whose members were mainly interested in playing poker, the Lawn Tennis Club and the British Association in the Balearic Islands. As befitted the avocations of several members of the foreign colony, there were also regular art exhibitions to attend and discuss. Here it was possible to lead the sort of social life that transplanted the Home Counties to the Mediterranean. But an altogether more cosmopolitan and experimental lifestyle was also accessible, as Francis Caron found. At 'the club' in El Terreno, he met people from Mexico, Cuba and Argentina, and pursued sexual intrigues with young women from California and Java, while sustaining his social life at the Plaza Gomila, 'where every evening there is a great crowd around the bar. I drank vermouth and ate little snails and mussels on toothpicks' (Caron, 1939: 13–14, 28–9, 40, 60, 83). Lady Sheppard also visited the club house, and noted how paradise had been reduced to the international sociability of cocktails and cigarettes:

> Looking round the room, I wondered how many nations were represented there, and how such numbers of people seemed to find their ideal holiday in spending all night, and most afternoons, in a stuffy, smoke-blue atmosphere. Why trouble to come so far, if only an hour or two between getting up at midday and cocktails in the evening, would be spent on the lovely beaches? (Sheppard, 1947: 118–19)

The bars had their own characteristics and habitués, too. Joe's, the original Terreno bar, run by 'a Viennese and a man of the world', was small and quiet, a place for regulars rather than 'casual strangers', with no gramophone or dancing and English the dominant language. The Morisco, by contrast, was 'big, gay, cosmopolitan', with dancing and late opening hours. This, like the club, was a meeting point for locals, Spaniards and a variety of visiting nationalities: 'a babel of English, French, German, Russian, Castilian and Mallorquin'. It was run by 'two debonair Germans'. Lena's bar, in contrast, was more like a restaurant, with 'two nice German boys' as waiters and a Swiss proprietor, the dominant languages being English and German (*Majorca Sun*, 15, 22, 29 April 1934).

There are, perhaps, one or two linguistic hints in this newspaper tour of the bars (itself reflecting an interesting set of priorities) that suggest that an aspect of Terreno as a paradise of exciting and diverse sociability and social opportunity was a toleration of homosexuality that was unlikely to be found in more mundane spaces. Caron suggests that it also offered sexual opportunities to women 'on holiday' from busy husbands: his friend José offered evening excursions for such people, in chauffeur-driven cars. 'The gentleman chauffeurs show the ladies very interesting things indeed – and the moonlight is lovely – and soon they want to go for another educational tour' (Caron, 1939: 83–5). Such versions of sex tourism, which provide a constant undercurrent in the Terreno literature, provide another example of one person's paradise being another one's hell. Gossip could act as the serpent that turned the one into the other where the closed world of the bar or bridge club encountered the wider activities of those who ranged beyond it but depended on its social circle, as Robin King pointed out in a scathing commentary on the expatriate community in the 1950s: 'For the more fashionable and respectable centre of this world is the Bar F— in Palma. Here, between brandies and tit-bits of gossip, somehow the shopping is done; somehow a reputation or two is even more tarnished; somehow more whispers will fly around the island via the bush-telegraph' (King, 1959: 157–9, 171–2).

There are strong hints of the development of such a dysfunctional lifestyle of alcohol ('the Majorcan state of having a brandy just after breakfast...') and gossip in the pages of the *Majorca Sun* of the mid-1930s; but 20 years later, after the interruptions of the Spanish Civil War and the Second World War, these aspects of El Terreno were much further to the fore, especially in the small area around Plaza Gomila that formed the heart of an expanded foreign colony. In 1957 *Trim's Guide* for tourists to Majorca began with the confident statement that 'The promise is not false, for here, truly, is the Land of the Lotus Eaters'. It is full of advertisements for bars and the big night clubs like Jack el Negro's and Trébol that were taking root as the decade became more affluent, for Spain's visitors if not yet for the locals themselves; and its cheerful commentary on Plaza Gomila, complete with classical allusions to the Greek legends, sums up the tensions between prevailing perceptions of paradise and hell, and how the one merged into the other:

> We will not get off [the tram] at Plaza Gomila, the heart of this town [Terreno]; because here we'd never get back on. Gomila is the Buckle on the Cognac Belt. Gritting our teeth, stuffing wax in our ears to drown out the happy cries of the shipwrecked and doomed, the siren song of the hissing siphon bottles, we speed on. As to telling you which saloons in Gomila to patronise, darned if we will. You can choose your own road to hell. (Trimnell, 1957a: 14)

Trim listed 15 places in Palma, most of them in El Terreno, where English was 'really' spoken; and their proprietors covered a spectrum of nationalities from Dutch to Brazilian. Some of the bars specialised in progressive and other kinds of jazz, and Johnny's Bar was 'Palma's only English pub, complete with a dart board and even "shove ha'penny"... Mary Johnson is hostess, and a lovely hostess he is. Naturally, Johnny's is English headquarters and pivot for all action in the Palma area' (Trimnell, 1957a: 38–40). Further research will be needed on the question of whether the 'he' was a printing error or a further illustration of the tolerant sexual liminality of this particular version of 'paradise'.

To what extent developments in Mallorca generally, and in El Terreno in particular, stood out from a broader pattern of 'paradises' where expatriates combined with tourists in search of a touch of idyllic perfection is a matter for further comparative research. What is clear is that in this particular setting the dominant version of paradise, as expressed in published commentaries and guide-books, shifted from peace, nature and the simple life, however compromised by the familiar comforts of domestic civilisation, to hedonism, drink and sensual (sometimes sexual) adventure. The starry silences of the 1920s in El Terreno gave way to the 'crashing din' of Plaza Gomila and the need to find a Bloody Mary on 'the morning after' which came to the fore in the 1950s after a transitional period during the 1930s (Trimnell, 1957a: 60–1). Some, like Francis Caron and Robin King, could try to keep a foot in both camps; the locals mixed with expatriates and visitors at the margins, especially for business purposes, but largely led separate lives. King, however, captured the essence of the matter. He reports an encounter with an American sailor visiting 'Bedrock Bar' in the heart of Plaza Gomila, who described Mallorca as 'a hundred per cent paradise island'. King replied, 'It depends on what you mean by paradise, I suppose'; and he adds that his paradise was different, involving pinewoods, peasant society and a simple life in a fishing village (King, 1959: 173–5). El Terreno had already moved from one kind of paradise to another, each of which would be a hell to those who did not appreciate its charms, before the advent of the great tourist boom that hit Mallorca in the 1960s; and the frontiers between the different versions of paradise, and the hybrids between them, have been steadily shifting ever since.

References

Amengual, B. (1903) *La Industria de los Forasteros*. Palma: Amengual y Muntaner.

Buades, J. (2004) *On Brilla el Sol. Turisme a Balears abans del Boom*. Eivissa: Res Publica Edicions.

Caron, F. (1939) *Majorca: The Diary of a Painter*. London: Cassell.

Chamberlin, F. (1927) *The Balearics and their Peoples*. London: The Bodley Head.

Fabregas, Lluis (1974) *Estampas de El Terreno*. Palma: Caja de Ahorros y Monte de Piedad de las Baleares.

Harrison, A. (1927) *A Majorca Holiday*. London: Gerald Howe.

King, R. (1959) *The Angry Sun: Impressions of a Lotus-Eating Island*. London: Arthur Barker.

Lindo-Webb, J. (1933) *Condensed English Tourist Guide to Palma and Other Places of Interest* (11th edn). Palma: James Lindo-Webb.

Majorca Sun (1931–36) Biblioteca Baleares, Palma.

Pemble, J. (1987) *The Mediterranean Passion: Victorians and Edwardians in the South*. Oxford: Clarendon Press.

Ripoll Martínez, A. (1994) Un repas a l'evolució del turisme a les Balears. In J. Benítez Mairata *et al.* (eds) *Turisme, Societat i Economia a les Balears*. Palma: Emil Darder.

Rusiñol, S. (1999) *Majorca: The Island of Calm*. Palma: Imprenta Politécnica.

Sheller, M. (2003) *Consuming the Caribbean*. London: Routledge.

Shelley, H.C. (1926) *Majorca*. London: Methuen.

Sheppard, Lady (1947) *Mediterranean Island*. London: Skeffington and Son.

Trimnell, R.L. (1957a) *Trim's Majorca Guide*. Palma: Mossen Alcover Press.

Trimnell, R.L. (1957b) *Trim's How to Live in Majorca* (2nd edn). Palma: Mossen Alcover Press.

Urry, John (1995) *Consuming Places*. London: Routledge.

Waldren, J. (1996) *Insiders and Outsiders: Paradise and Reality in Mallorca*. Oxford: Berghahn.

Walton, J.K. (2000) Tradition and tourism: Representing Basque identities in Guipúzcoa and San Sebastián, 1848–1936. In N. Kirk (ed.) *Northern Identities*. Aldershot: Scolar Press.

West, G. (1929) *Jogging Round Majorca*. London: Alston Rivers.

Whelpton, E. (1952) *The Balearics*. London: Robert Hale.

Chapter 11

'50 Places Rolled into 1': The Development of Domestic Tourism at Pleasure Grounds in Inter-war England[1]

HELEN PUSSARD

Introduction: Pleasure Grounds as Domestic Tourism

> All the fun of the fair! All the excitement of the zoo! All the beauty of the country! All the thrill of the sports ground! Coney Island, Whipsnade, Olympia and Alton Towers rolled into one! The complete holiday outing for all the family, without any of the rush and fuss, expense and discomfort of other kinds of holiday jaunt! (Belle Vue (Manchester) Ltd, 1931: 2)

These enticing claims, used to encourage visitors to Manchester's principal pleasure ground in the summer of 1931, highlight the attraction of the day-trip over an extended stay away from home. Prospective visitors would recognise the leisure spaces of the fair, zoo, country and sports ground and the famous places in the entertainment landscapes of England and the USA. Moreover, a day-trip could be enjoyed with minimal disruption to visitors' daily routines and weekly budgets. Ideas of familiarity and convenience have been central, arguably, to the popularity of small-scale domestic tourism. The absence of 'rush and fuss, expense and discomfort', however, has rendered these trips invisible in histories of tourism. As John Benson has argued, 'the day (and part-day) trip/ excursion has always been the most common, as well as the most easily overlooked, form of tourist activity' (Benson, 1994: 83).

This chapter seeks to raise the profile of this kind of domestic tourism by focusing on two leisure sites – Belle Vue in Manchester and the Crystal Palace in south London – that catered for these shorter visits. The term 'pleasure ground' is used to describe Belle Vue and the Crystal Palace as sites that encompassed the shift from the pleasure gardens of the 18th and 19th centuries to the post-war theme park. Pleasure grounds provided a kaleidoscopic range of entertainments: from speedway and greyhound racing to Fascist and Communist rallies; from zoological gardens and museums to the latest fairground rides from America; and from jazz and brass bands to religious meetings of every denomination. The numerous attractions on offer, combined with their proximity to residential areas and links to regional railway networks, ensured a constant flow of local visitors and day-trippers.

The accommodation of both local visitors and day-trippers highlights the difficulties in attempting to define, and situate, sites as either 'leisure' or 'tourist' experiences (Rojek, 1995; Urry, 1990: 2–4). The use of the pleasure grounds by visitors was determined by socio-economic and geographical factors but also by individual preferences. Some residents of Manchester or south London would visit Belle Vue or the Crystal Palace, respectively, once or twice a week. These trips might involve a couple of hours dancing, watching speedway, gambling on the dogs or courting in the woods. In this context, the pleasure grounds constituted part of an everyday leisure experience. For other local visitors and day-trippers from the surrounding counties and regions, however, excursions to Belle Vue or the Crystal Palace might occur once or twice a year. These trips could be considered as tourism, providing a break from daily and weekly routines. Some people travelled much further distances to attend political demonstrations at the sites. Should these visits be equated with work, leisure or tourism? Belle Vue and the Crystal Palace, therefore, elide simplistic definitions of 'leisure' or 'tourism' and point to the multiplicity of meanings that could be attached to sites by visitors.

For the purposes of analysis, however, I have defined the pleasure grounds as domestic tourist sites, catering for a range of leisure experiences. Most trips to Belle Vue or the Crystal Palace can be understood as displaying John Urry's 'minimal characteristics of the social practices' of tourism. The sites were physically separated from work and home, for local visitors and day-trippers, involving the 'anticipation' of 'intense pleasures' and 'landscapes' that were distinct 'from everyday experience' (Urry, 1990: 2–4). Tourism is prefixed with 'domestic' to indicate the proximity, and convenience, of the pleasure grounds to visitors in time and space. The majority of visitors were able to travel to Belle Vue or the Crystal Palace and return home at night. The 'tourist professionals' who organised, managed and worked at the pleasure grounds were similarly drawn from a domestic market (Urry, 1990: 3). The term 'domestic' also highlights the spaces in tourism that *were* familiar to visitors. At pleasure grounds, part of the 'tourist gaze' reproduced the everyday landscapes of work and home, from the industrial mechanisation of fairground rides to mothers doling out bread and tea at picnic tables. Describing tourist activity as 'domestic' illustrates the incomplete break from work and home in leisure provision and consumption. By labelling pleasure grounds as domestic tourist sites, we can approach Belle Vue and the Crystal Palace as both part of, and distinct from, the 'everyday experiences' of work and leisure.

'50 Places Rolled into 1'

Despite their similarities, Belle Vue and the Crystal Palace offer two different models of this kind of domestic tourism in inter-war England. Belle Vue initially opened as a zoological garden in 1836 with a few popular attractions (Nicholls, 1992). Situated in what became the industrial inner suburb of Gorton, as it was absorbed by Manchester's Victorian expansion, the pleasure ground was owned and managed by successive generations of the Jennison family. It grew steadily in size and popularity for most of the 19th century. By 1869, for example, the site housed a music hall, tea room, monkey house, menagerie, museum, lake, bear den, maze, aviary and flower gardens (*Guide*, 1869). The first decades of the 20th century witnessed a slump in attendance at Belle Vue and during the First World War the grounds were used for the war effort. The pleasure ground was eventually sold in 1925 to a newly formed, private company, Belle Vue (Manchester) Ltd, who managed the site until the mid-1950s. The key figure in this venture was John Henry Iles, an entrepreneur who had been involved in amusement parks for several decades. Under this new management, and aided by technological advances in the inter-war years, Belle Vue recovered its position as a key leisure site for the industrial North (Pussard, 1997). The grounds were extended and developed to include an extensive amusement park, enhanced exhibition facilities and new forms of spectator sports.

The Crystal Palace had a rather more impressive launch as the building constructed to house the Great Exhibition of 1851 in Hyde Park, funded by public and private subscriptions (Beaver, 1970). The glass edifice was sold to the Crystal Palace Company and moved to a suburban setting in Sydenham, south London, in 1854. It was intended as a permanent site for education in the arts and commerce, with vast ornamental gardens, fountains and lakes to rival the Palais de Versailles. The Crystal Palace deteriorated towards the end of the 19th century through a lack of financial backing and the legal restriction preventing Sunday opening of the site.

The Festival of Empire in 1911, and the Coronation celebrations in the same year, stimulated a revival of interest. It was not sufficient, however, to relieve the monetary pressure on the Crystal Palace Company and the Duke of Plymouth bought the site in 1911. The Lord Mayor of London established a fund to rescue the Crystal Palace and, in 1913, it was officially bought for the nation. During the First World War, the grounds were used as a naval depot, accommodating around 13,000 sailors. The site reopened to the public in 1920, briefly housing the Imperial War Museum. It was administered by the Crystal Palace Trustees, the majority of whom came from the local authorities of south London. The Crystal Palace retained its educative ethos but introduced new forms of entertainment, under the enthusiastic management of Henry Buckland. The ornamental lake, gardens and ballroom now accommodated boating, speedway and jazz respectively, encapsulating 'all the razz-a-ma-tazz' of the 1920s (Bell-Knight, 1976: 48). The building was completely destroyed by fire in November 1936, after 16 years of mixed public opinion, but parts of the site remained open until its future was decided after the Second World War.

The chequered histories of Belle Vue and the Crystal Palace reveal the diverse origins of, and influences on, domestic tourism. Belle Vue, as a family-run business and entrepreneurial venture in the industrial north, differed greatly from the Crystal Palace, with its imperialist ideals and municipal administration in the suburban south. Both pleasure grounds, however, were part of the changing shape of domestic tourism in England. Domestic tourism became equated not only with short-term visits but, moreover, with an emphasis on combining education with entertainment. Belle Vue and the Crystal Palace were exemplars of this practice and, in this context, are comparable as domestic tourist sites. The pleasure grounds juxtaposed the museums, zoos and gardens of the rational recreation movement with the technology, noise and excitement of amusement parks and dance halls. Day-trippers and part-day visitors came to Belle Vue and the Crystal Palace for political demonstrations and religious rallies, staying on for evening pyrodramas and panoramas. As the 'Home of Amusement and Instruction', therefore, pleasure grounds fulfilled important social, cultural and political roles (Belle Vue (Manchester) Ltd, 1933a: 4).

The expansion of domestic tourist attractions, providing 'amusement' and 'instruction' in varying degrees, accelerated during the inter-war years (Jones, 1986). This chapter explores the qualitative changes that enabled domestic tourism to grow in quantitative terms, becoming an integral part of the leisure and tourist industries. On a quantitative level, pleasure grounds were significant 'players' in the domestic tourist market. There were around one million visitors per annum to the Crystal Palace but individual events at the pleasure grounds also drew large crowds. A Temperance Rally at Belle Vue, for example, was likely to attract around 90,000 visitors in the inter-war years. In monetary terms, the pleasure grounds' expenditure on new attractions and maintenance of the sites absorbed most of their income. The Crystal Palace, however, generated about £80,000 per annum profits only a few years after being declared bankrupt and the Belle Vue circus alone made approximately £125,000 per annum. In qualitative terms, it is apparent from my research on pleasure grounds in the first half of the 20th century that two seemingly contradictory processes were occurring that shaped the development of domestic tourism in England. On one level, the consumer experience at Belle Vue and the Crystal Palace was becoming increasingly fragmented. The accommodation of different types of visitors through different types of attractions led to social stratification based on consumption. This diversifying strategy maximised profits for Belle Vue and the Crystal Palace. Moreover, the resulting commercial hierarchies taught visitors how to be 'tourists', negotiating domestic (and later foreign) spaces through an understanding of difference and display. At the same time, Belle Vue and the Crystal Palace were moving towards uniformity in their overall leisure provision. The owners and managers of pleasure grounds around England were narrowing into a small social group, who controlled a significant proportion of the domestic tourist market. The attractions on offer at the sites often came from commercial transactions within this small group, thus leading to the relative homogenisation of entertainment in domestic tourism.

The diversification of the consumer experience and the increasing uniformity of the attractions have been crucial to the expansion of domestic tourism in the 20th century. The domestic tourist industry became a 'training ground' for tourists at home, with homogenising tendencies. The case studies of Belle Vue and the Crystal Palace, in spite of their different ownership models, support the argument that domestic tourism developed through the processes of fragmentation and uniformity. The following two sections will analyse in more detail these qualitative changes at the pleasure grounds in the inter-war years. We will see that the expression '50 Places Rolled into 1' was an astute summary of the changing shape of domestic tourism in England.

Commercial Hierarchies

The term 'commercial hierarchies' is used to describe the distinctions within the visiting publics at both Belle Vue and the Crystal Palace, based on their consumption of goods and services. The pleasure grounds projected themselves as socially levelling places of interaction, 'domain[s] of democracy' (Belle Vue (Manchester) Ltd, 1928: 3). In part, this was achieved by a set admission fee of 1s for adults on weekdays (children were charged 3d at the Crystal Palace and 5d at Belle Vue), with various reduced prices in the evenings and at weekends. Inside the pleasure grounds' parameters, however, there was a plethora of commercial choices to be made. These public acts of consumption fragmented, and stratified, the consumer body into numerous social groups. Commercial hierarchies, therefore, stimulated profit for the sites and ascribed layers of social meaning to micro-level expenditure.

Commercial choices have been analysed in terms of age, class and gender within historical studies of 20th-century leisure (Davies, 1992; Langhamer, 2000). These social identities were crucial to how visitors experienced Belle Vue and the Crystal Palace. Temporal and geographical distinctions between visitors were also significant factors in the consumption of goods and services. These distinctions often merged, of course, with identities based on age, class and gender. The impact of time and locality, however, is perhaps the most accessible way of understanding the commercial hierarchies produced and consumed at pleasure grounds. The fragmenting of the consumer body into different types of visitors, based on the time/length of their stay and where they had travelled from, diversified the consumer experience at domestic tourist sites.

Lynda Nead has charted the 'temporal zones' that operated at the Cremorne Pleasure Gardens in mid-Victorian London (Nead, 2000). Her research has pointed to the importance of time in understanding how leisure sites continually repackaged themselves for different social groups, in the course of a day and night. At Belle Vue and the Crystal Palace, one highly visible example of commercial hierarchies shaped by temporalities was the catering arrangements. The choice of when, and where, to eat revealed visitors' geographical and social backgrounds. Eating areas were separate but formed part of the 'tourist gaze' at pleasure grounds (compare Urry, 1990: 66–81).

The gates to the pleasure grounds opened between 10.00 am and 10.30 am. In the morning, kiosks around Belle Vue and the Crystal Palace sold snacks that were predominantly bought by day-trippers. Novelty food, such as brazil nuts, was on offer as well as the traditional 'fayre' of English sweets, like toffee. Belle Vue also produced its own ice-cream from an 'Ice-Cream Factory' on site, supplied directly to these small-scale kiosks (Belle Vue (Manchester) Ltd, 1933b: 6).

At lunchtime, local families were catered for in the 'one shilling tea rooms' or hot water rooms where visitors could bring their own picnics.

The hot water rooms seated 3000 visitors at Belle Vue, supplying hot water and crockery for groups and individuals (Belle Vue (Manchester) Ltd, 1933b: 6). Bread, butter, cakes and jams, made in the bakery and kitchens on site, were sold separately. Oral testimonies, on Belle Vue and the Crystal Palace in the inter-war years, highlight the popularity of these rooms with local families who visited the pleasure grounds for the day. One interviewee recalled being taken, with 14 or 15 other children, twice a week to Belle Vue in the summer. Her mother would produce several loaves of bread as they sat at 'large wooden tables' and they would be supplied with tea and water (BBC Radio Manchester, 1982). Situated close to the hot water rooms, 'special' lunchtime deals were consumed by day-trippers. One shilling, for example, would buy you a pot of tea, bread and butter, green salad and fruit cake (Chetham's Library, F.6.1.).

The evening witnessed perhaps the clearest social stratification based on food consumption, as the more expensive restaurants opened. The French Court Café and Grill Room at the Crystal Palace were described as a 'fairyland', with red carpets and an abundance of flowers and silver. These restaurants offered an elevated form of conspicuous consumption. The fireworks at the Crystal Palace were set off so that the final cascade lit up the smarter restaurants. Visitors admiring the fireworks display on the terraces below could watch those eating in the 'fairyland' (Crystal Palace Foundation, 1990: 15, 39). In contrast, cinema-goers bought fish and chips from kiosks as they left the pleasure grounds at the end of the night, to eat on the way out (Crystal Palace Foundation, 1990: 37).

Drinking in the day or evening took place in the pubs located outside the grounds, near the gatehouses at Belle Vue or the low-level railway stations at the Crystal Palace. One interviewee said that he used these pubs to get as 'drunk as a lord' before entering the Crystal Palace! (Crystal Palace Foundation, 1990: 10). There were licensed areas for alcohol consumption in the grounds but the licenses were one of the biggest expenses for the catering departments (Belle Vue (Manchester) Ltd, Accounts Books). The lack of sources on drinking, in general, is indicative of the 'clean fun' image that the pleasure grounds wished to project.

Throughout the day, attendees at meetings and rallies were supplied with food and drink. In demarcated areas, afternoon tea might be served to a local Co-operative Society, and dinner and community singing provided for the Mothers' Union, while those attending the Grocers' Exhibition were entitled to a 1s reduction from the 3s 'Table d'Hote Luncheon' (Chetham's Library, F.6.1). The other group in segregated spaces, who were fed by staff and organised into 'temporal zones', were the animals. Feeding times were advertised in the guides for visitors to watch. In 1931, the afternoon feeding schedule at Belle Vue was as follows: 3.30pm for lions, leopards and tigers; 4.00pm for pelicans; 4.30pm for sea lions; and 5.30pm for the chimpanzee and orang-utan families (Belle Vue (Manchester) Ltd, 1931: 3).

This overview of some of the eating and drinking patterns at Belle Vue and the Crystal Palace indicates the importance of temporalities in constructing commercial hierarchies. Visitors to the pleasure grounds displayed their social backgrounds through their choice of when and where to eat. The conspicuous nature of eating and drinking enabled consumers to distinguish between day-trippers, local families that regularly frequented the sites, courting couples and members of societies. The accommodation of the local clientele alongside day-trippers, in particular, produced differentiated social spaces within Belle Vue and the Crystal Palace. A range of signifiers would indicate visitors' geographical relationship to the pleasure grounds and, thus, contribute to the social stratification of consumers at the sites.

On arriving at the pleasure grounds, modes of transportation were the first signifier of visitors' regional relationship to Belle Vue or the Crystal Palace. The development of coach and car parks allowed day-trippers to arrive in larger numbers. Their presence, therefore, was more conspicuous than the visitors who walked through the outside gates from the local neighbourhoods. The three entrances at Belle Vue gave an indication of where visitors were likely to be travelling from and were advertised as such. The Hyde Road entrance, for example, was the 'most central' and well connected to the city of Manchester. The Longsight entrance served the 'southern parts of the city', whereas the Gorton entrance was for rail passengers from the Midlands (Belle Vue Zoological Gardens, 1912: 1–2). Forms of payment upon arrival also indicated regional distinctions. At the Crystal Palace, day-trippers could present coupons at the turnstiles from Cherry Blossom boot polish to gain a reduced admission fee. On certain days, local visitors could proffer *The Daily Mirror* or *Daily Sketch* to get whole families admitted (Crystal Palace Foundation, 1990: 11).

Once inside the pleasure grounds, visitors made choices about which attractions to patronise depending on the length and nature of their stay. From novelty stalls to sheet music and from Goss china to the moving picture show, additional money was often needed to consume the diverse entertainments on offer. Day-trippers, for example, were more likely to go on the fairground rides. At the Crystal Palace, the Helter Skelter, Merry Maze and Brooklyn Cake Walk were all priced at 3d, whereas the Captive Flying Machine, Wild Animal Jungle and Driveacar were 6d (London Metropolitan Archives, Festivals 1146/75). Local visitors, however, would tend to congregate around the penny-in-the-slot machines. These ranged in content from palm readings to 'what the butler saw' (Crystal Palace Foundation, 1990: 13–14).

The appropriation of the sites by external groups for rallies, meetings and demonstrations created further layers of geographical distinctions in the commercial hierarchies. The National Temperance Fete's Diamond Jubilee, in 1928, had a 'Sale of Work and Fancy Articles' in the Ambassadors Room at the Crystal Palace for attendees (London Metropolitan Archives, Festivals 1148/75). In the same year, the Festival of the London Sunday School Choir sold tickets for its concerts in the Centre Transept for 2s, 1s or 6d (London Metropolitan Archives, Festivals 1147/75). The thousands of spectators to the F.A. Cup finals at the Sydenham site, however, did not necessarily spend money on the entertainments in the evening. One account stated that, instead, the football spectator 'swarms over the West-End with his pockets full of the many football editions' (Leach, 1901: 296).

These commercial hierarchies, structured by temporalities and geographical distinctions between visitors, could also be subverted and transgressed. Spending money was not the only way in which visitors ascribed meanings to their trips to Belle Vue and the Crystal Palace. Oral testimonies highlight the non-commercial uses of the sites that contributed to class, gender and age identities. Temporalities and locality were still significant in these forms of subversion. It tended to be local visitors, familiar with the pleasure grounds from numerous short trips, who were able to breach the 'official' patterns of behaviour. Mothers would hide some of their children in a big silver-cross pram at the admission gate to Belle Vue, to avoid additional payment (BBC Radio Manchester, 1982). Groups of young men would chance the stewards and sneak into the pleasure grounds, jumping over railway bridges or squeezing through the railings. Children would return home from 'various trade fairs' not needing any dinner as they had gorged on 'free samples' all day, much to the annoyance of the stall-owners! (Crystal Palace Foundation, 1990: 43). At the weekend, families from nearby neighbourhoods would promenade around the zoological and botanical gardens as a show of respectability.

As with carnivals, fairs and seaside resorts, pleasure grounds were also places of transgression where the social order of everyday life could be inverted. Some trips to Belle Vue or the Crystal Palace enabled visitors to 'dress-up' and transgress their normal class identities. Eating and drinking were popular forms of courting, for example, at the pleasure grounds. These spaces enabled transgressions to occur, as the following recollection of the Crystal Palace demonstrates:

> Sometimes we would go and have tea in the Mecca Café. Now the Mecca Café was just an ordinary restaurant and you had waitresses which used to wait on you. They were in a Nippy type of uniform, as I remember, like in the Lyons' Restaurants. We used to call them 'Nippies', they were the same sort of thing. We used to be waited on hand and foot, and we used to think we were Lords of the Manor then. (Crystal Palace Foundation, 1990: 15)

Visitors to pleasure grounds in the inter-war years had differing experiences of the sites, depending on when they visited, where they came from and the nature of their trip. Class, age and gender identities were played out through the temporal variations and geographical distinctions made between visitors. These differences were displayed through their choice of transportation, form of entry, catering arrangements and the attractions they visited. Many of these decisions, or inversions, were based on consumption and resulted in commercial hierarchies at Belle Vue and the Crystal Palace. This led to an increasingly fragmented market that catered for a variety of social groups, while the visitors attached their own cultural meanings to activities and entertainments. Diversification enabled the pleasure grounds to maximise their profits, appealing to a range of visitors through the accommodation of multiple social identities. Moreover, domestic tourist sites became 'training grounds', teaching visitors how to read the subtleties of commercial and non-commercial choices. The visual consumption of others was part of the pleasure ground experience. Domestic tourists learnt to interpret displays of difference, through consumption, as signifiers of social and geographical backgrounds. Fragmentation, therefore, was a crucial process in the construction of the 'tourist' as someone who could negotiate these social hierarchies in public spaces. The diversification of markets, based on temporalities and localities, and the emergence of this version of the 'tourist' enabled the domestic tourist industry to develop and expand in 20th-century England.

Commercial Transactions

If the consumption of domestic tourist sites was becoming increasingly stratified, as the previous section has argued, the provision of leisure at pleasure grounds was moving in the opposite direction. A second trend discernible at Belle Vue and the Crystal Palace, therefore, is the move towards uniformity in the production of entertainment. The domestic tourist industry was being expanded and developed in the inter-war years by a relatively small group of owners and managers of leisure sites. The involvement of these 'producers' of leisure in a number of entrepreneurial ventures across England led to the same people (re)producing similar leisure attractions at a range of domestic tourist sites. The commercial transactions between people and places began to standardise what was on offer for visitors. This qualitative shift towards uniformity in the provision of leisure attractions led to a growing homogeneity in the domestic tourist industry. Belle Vue and the Crystal Palace were part of this narrowing in the interest groups and entertainments involved in the production of leisure and domestic tourist practices. The pleasure grounds were accommodating and shaping an increasingly fragmented consumer body through these homogenising processes. The commercial hierarchies and the commercial transactions therefore operated together, enabling the domestic tourist industry to grow in the inter-war years.

In researching the management of pleasure grounds in the first half of the 20th century, it became apparent that a small group of men had business interests not only in Belle Vue and the Crystal Palace but also in a range of leisure sites and attractions in England. The owners, managers and entrepreneurs involved in Belle Vue and the Crystal Palace *were* predominantly men. Miss Alice Hart was the only exception I have found to this trend. She was involved in speedway at Belle Vue during the Second World War and has been accredited with its 'quick recovery' in the post-war period. Referred to as the 'first Speedway lady manageress/ promoter', Miss Alice Hart was given a place on the Board of Directors in the late 1940s as a 'reward' for her hard work (Chetham's Library, F.6.7). A few of these men are well-known figures in the history of leisure, such as William Butlin who sat on the Board of Directors at Belle Vue during the 1940s while his eponymous holiday camps grew in size and popularity (*Manchester Guardian*, 22 February 1947; Belle Vue (Manchester) Ltd, 1948; Ward & Hardy, 1986). Many of the owners and managers, however, have remained shadowy figures that are difficult to identify within the glossy self-publicity of the pleasure grounds. As Peter Bailey has argued in his work on music halls, 'the proprietors have received little attention… compared with that lavished on the performers and the sacred sites of the halls themselves' and this omission needs to be redressed (Bailey, 1998: 81). It is not only the individuals that need to be analysed in greater depth but the *connections* between these men and between leisure sites. These networks facilitated the introduction of new forms of entertainment to England and led to their installation at a number of key domestic tourist sites. The attractions on offer to visitors at leisure sites, therefore, became more uniform across the country during this period, homogenising the leisure experiences of domestic tourism.

There are clear links between particular individuals, new forms of mass entertainment and pleasure grounds that indicate the significance of a small group of men in shaping the leisurescapes of urban and suburban England. D. Buckland-Smith was Publicity Manager of Belle Vue in the late 1940s and 1950s, for example, but had also been involved in the running of cinemas, dance halls and theatres during the inter-war years. He had worked with the Manchester Hippodrome, the Stoll Theatre group, the Ardwick Empire and the Capitol, Apollo and Tatler theatres in Manchester, eventually becoming Chairman of the Press and Publicity Committee of Manchester's Publicity Association (*Manchester Evening News; City and Suburban News*). William Gentle, on the Board of Directors at Belle Vue in the 1920s and 1930s, was Chairman of the Greyhound Racing Association, introducing the spectator sport to Belle Vue and then Manchester's White City (*Manchester Guardian*, 3 September 1948). E.O. Spence was manager of speedway at Belle Vue during this period. It was stated that no one had 'done more to popularise motor-cycling' than E.O. Spence and he was accredited with introducing the coloured lights of the 'electric starting apparatus' that replaced the 'flag-waving method' (*Manchester Football News; Evening Chronicle*). He also became manager of speedway at a number of tracks across the north of England, earning him the titles of 'Speedway Mussolini of the North' and the 'Iron Hand of the Manchester Tracks' (*The Auto-Motor Journal*, 1930).

It is John Henry Iles' involvement in pleasure grounds and amusement parks, however, that provides the strongest indication of the commercial transactions that were occurring between domestic tourist sites. His initial interest lay in the brass band movement after visiting the annual Belle Vue contest in 1898. In 1900, he launched the National Brass Band Contest at the Crystal Palace and founded the weekly newspaper, *British Bandsman*. The contests at Belle Vue and the Crystal Palace became 'arenas where brass band heroes and legends were born' and Iles rapidly established himself as 'the brass band impresario' (Taylor, 1983: 7–8).

By the 1920s, Iles had extended his business domain to fairground rides and it has been claimed, with some hyperbole, that he 'introduced the American Amusement Parks to Europe' (*Who Was Who*, 1967: 567). He supplied a number of fairground rides, such as the Scenic Railway, to the amusement park of the British Empire Exhibition at Wembley in 1924. The attractions from Wembley were either moved to, or replicated at, a range of leisure sites that Iles had investments in, from Belle Vue to Dreamland at Margate. Even in amusement parks or pleasure beaches where Iles did *not* have a direct financial stake, for example at Blackpool or Great Yarmouth, he was listed as a Director of some of the companies formed to franchise fairground rides (National Archives, 1920). From the Caterpillar ride to the Seaplanes, Iles appears to have controlled a significant proportion of fairground rides in leisure sites across England. These mechanised rides were packaged as 'All the way from America' and increasingly marginalised the various sideshows, peep shows and freak shows which had been part of the fabric of pleasure grounds in the 19th and early 20th centuries (*Manchester Guardian*, 24 May 1958). The reproduction of particular commercial attractions at pleasure grounds and parks led to certain rides, for example the Scenic Railway, becoming a standard part of many open-air domestic tourist sites.

I am not suggesting that the emergence of individual entrepreneurs, responsible for new forms of entertainment and leisure activity, was a novel feature of the inter-war period. The history of the leisure industry is full of such men who often became synonymous with the events they organised: Imre Kiralfy's role as 'Britain's premier exhibition organiser' at the Franco-British Exhibition of 1908 and subsequent White City events; Billy Holland's showmanship at Blackpool's Winter Gardens in the late 1880s and early 1890s; Frank Lascelles' imperial pageants from the Crystal Palace to Calcutta; and the Butlin and Pontin holiday camp developments (Greenhalgh, 1988: 90). A shift can be located at this time, however, in the interaction between these men and the leisure sites that constituted the domestic tourist industry. The owners and managers of pleasure grounds often had multiple business interests in the expanding leisure industry. Particular entertainments, from speedway and greyhound racing to national brass band contests and American fairground rides, were introduced to several key leisure sites as a result of these connections. The 1920s and 1930s, therefore, witnessed the widespread incorporation of new forms of leisure at pleasure grounds, beaches and parks through the commercial transactions of a small group of men. This resulted in the relative homogenisation of attractions on offer at sites across England. It is a trend that has continued to shape domestic tourism throughout the 20th century if we consider, for example, the influence of the Tussaud's group on contemporary domestic tourist activity.

Conclusion

The pleasure grounds of the inter-war period provide historians with the opportunity to explore the mechanics of a growing domestic tourist industry. Combining 'amusement and instruction' in a vast array of attractions and amusements, Belle Vue and the Crystal Palace appealed to a wide range of local visitors and day-trippers from nearby cities, counties and regions. The success of these sites in the 1920s and 1930s can be mapped on to the progressive rise in the standard of living in England or on to the development of companionate leisure within a smaller nuclear family, providing 'clean fun' for everyone. The pleasure grounds were certainly packaged as democratic, popular and wholesome forms of leisure. These explanations, however, do not examine the shifts *within* the production and consumption of entertainment that shaped the development and expansion of the domestic tourist industry.

This chapter has argued that two processes were in operation at pleasure grounds that represent the ways in which domestic tourism was evolving in the 20th century. On one level, the consumer experience at Belle Vue and the Crystal Palace was becoming increasingly diversified. Temporal and geographical distinctions in the consumption patterns of visitors produced differentiated social spaces within Belle Vue and the Crystal Palace. These hierarchies encouraged visitors to read micro-level expenditure and behaviour as displays of difference. Pleasure grounds, therefore, became training grounds where visitors learnt to be tourists, negotiating social hierarchies in familiar and unknown spaces and places. This fragmenting of experience occurred at precisely the moment when the owners and managers of leisure sites around England were narrowing into a small social group. The commercial transactions between these men, and between leisure sites, led to a move towards uniformity in the forms of entertainment on offer.

The expression '50 places rolled into 1' describes the processes of, and interconnections between, the diversification of the consumer experience and the homogenisation of entertainments at pleasure grounds. The familiarity of particular fairground rides, attractions and spectator sports, as they became standard to many domestic tourist sites, provided visitors with a safe and known environment. This produced reassuring landscapes in domestic tourism through which the complex figures of the discerning consumer and novice tourist could emerge. Belle Vue and the Crystal Palace, therefore, housed not only an eclectic mix of attractions on one site but also the embryonic features of the post-war tourist industry.

Note

1. The expression, '50 places rolled into 1', is taken from an interview with Phil Moss, a musician and bandleader at Belle Vue from the 1930s to the 1950s: Roy Nicol Video Productions, 1995.

References

BBC Radio Manchester (1982) Out and about – Belle Vue. North West Sound Archive, Clitheroe, ref. 1982.6710.

Bailey, P. (1998) *Popular Culture and Performance in the Victorian City*. Cambridge: Cambridge University Press.

Beaver, P. (1970) *The Crystal Palace 1851–1936. A Portrait of Victorian Enterprise*. London: Hugh Evelyn.

Bell-Knight, C.A. (1976) *The Rise and Fall of the Biggest Ever Glass Container*. London: Bell-Knight.

Belle Vue (Manchester) Ltd (1931) *Belle Vue Summer News*. Manchester.

Belle Vue (Manchester) Ltd (1928) *Official Guide*. Manchester.

Belle Vue (Manchester) Ltd (1933a) *Official Guide*. Manchester.

Belle Vue (Manchester) Ltd (1933b) *Have Some Fun at Belle Vue Zoological Gardens*. Manchester.

Belle Vue (Manchester) Ltd, Accounts Books November 1934–October 1935 (Archives, M491/8274). Manchester: Local Studies Unit.

Belle Vue (Manchester) Ltd (1948) *Dance Little Lady*. Manchester.

Belle Vue Zoological Gardens (1912) *Official Guide*. Manchester.

Benson, J. (1994) *The Rise of Consumer Society in Britain 1880–1980*. Harlow: Longman.

Chetham's Library, Belle Vue Zoological Gardens, Nicholls Collection, miscellaneous tickets, F.6.1. Manchester.

Chetham's Library, Belle Vue Zoological Gardens, Talbot Collection, F.6.7 (1978) Belle Vue Aces, *Golden Jubilee Meeting*. Manchester.

City and Suburban News, 28 September 1956.

Crystal Palace Foundation (1990) *The Perfect Playground. Childhood Memories of the Crystal Palace*. London.

Davies, A. (1992) *Leisure, Gender and Poverty: Working-Class Culture in Salford and Manchester 1900–1939*. Buckingham: Open University Press.

Evening Chronicle, 3 April 1930.

Greenhalgh, P. (1988) *Ephemeral Vistas. The Expositions Universelles, Great Exhibitions and World's Fairs, 1851–1939*. Manchester: Manchester University Press.

Guide to the Belle Vue Zoological Gardens (1869) Manchester.

Jones, S.G. (1986) *Workers at Play: A Social and Economic History of Leisure 1918–1939*. London: Croom Helm.

Langhamer, C. (2000) *Women's Leisure in England 1920–60*. Manchester: Manchester University Press.

Leach, H. (1901) Football London. In G.R. Sims (ed.) *Living London* (Vol. 1). London: Cassell.

London Metropolitan Archives (1928) 43.5 (CRY), Crystal Palace Programmes, Festivals 1146–8.

Manchester Evening News, 27 September 1956.

Manchester Football News, 4 April 1929.

Manchester Guardian, 24 May 1928, 22 February 1947, 3 September 1948.

National Archives (1920) BT31 32415/16642, Margate Scenic Railway Ltd.

Nead, L. (2000) *Victorian Babylon: People, Streets and Images in Representations of London*. New Haven, CT: Yale University Press.

Nicholls, R. (1992) *The Belle Vue Story*. Altrincham: Neil Richardson.

Pussard, H. (1997) 'A mini-Blackpool': Belle Vue and the cultural politics of pleasure in inter-war Manchester. MA thesis, University of Manchester.
Rojek, C. (1995) *Decentring Leisure. Rethinking Leisure Theory*. London: Sage.
Roy Nicol Video Productions (1995) *The History of the Belle Vue Zoological Gardens. Volume One – Your Memories*. Manchester.
Taylor, A.R. (1983) *Labour and Love: An Oral History of the Brass Band Movement*. London: Elm Tree.
The Auto-Motor Journal, 1 August 1930.
Urry, J. (1990) *The Tourist Gaze*. London: Sage.
Ward, C. and Hardy, D. (1986) *Goodnight Campers! The History of the British Holiday Camp*. London: Mansell.
Who Was Who 1951–1960 (1967) Vol. 5. London: Black.

Chapter 12

Public Beaches and Private Beach Huts – A Case Study of Inter-war Clacton and Frinton, Essex

LAURA CHASE

Introduction

Serried ranks of beach huts form a striking visual component of many English seaside resort towns, introducing elements of a miniaturised suburbia into a maritime landscape. In larger resorts, they contrast with the more urban presence of the Pier and its garish amusements. Jointly, these built environments have helped to give the seaside resort an iconic status as a timeless symbol of escape and as a hybrid of the natural and the artificial, the naughty and the restrained. These oppositional characterisations are epitomised by the comic seaside postcard, where images of release and rejuvenation vie with those of discomfort and restriction. Similar tensions also characterised the division of resorts into the seemingly fixed categories of popular and select, with the artificial and the naughty seen to be in the ascendant at the popular resort, and the natural and the restrained at the select resort. This chapter will explore these tensions by focusing on the relationship between changing social practices and the use and appearance of beach spaces at the Eastern English resorts of popular Clacton and select Frinton. The period selected is the inter-war years, a time when seaside resorts were at the forefront of setting new fashions, changing social practices and creating new leisure spaces (Chase, 1999; Walton, 2000).

Tourism studies has produced a 'rise and fall' narrative of the seaside resort which smooths over many of these complexities (Agarwal, 2002). The example of beach huts illustrates the limits of this narrative in that they continue to retain their popularity in what is meant to be the 'decline' phase of the seaside resort. Beach huts in places such as Frinton, Southwold and Whitstable, for example, are much in demand and seen as status symbols for both urban style setters and those who have inherited a hut from the previous generation. This continuing appeal of the beach hut warrants examination. I suggest that while they are clearly predominantly private spaces, their clustering, visibility and access gives them a element of conviviality for their users, if not for the general public, which links them to public places such as parks and private 'third places' such as cafés and bars. These are the sorts of places identified as increasingly important in the cyber age. When beach-hut users position their deck chairs outside their huts, they move themselves into the public realm, becoming both flâneurs and objects of attention for the flâneurs passing by. They also continue to embody the display of cultural capital and they communicate messages of self-sufficiency and quaintness, which contrast with the perceived tawdriness of the commercial section of popular resorts.

Their continuing appeal, however, is set within an ever-changing context. Cultural theory has a tendency to subsume differences between resorts over time, under an overall categorisation of the English beach as a 'pleasure zone' that has now largely lost its particular powers to please (Urry, 1990, 1997). This reflects an approach that is theoretically led, rather than following on from empirical work. The concept of liminality, for example, is useful in highlighting the symbolic content of seaside activities and rituals, and their importance in defining class hierarchies, but ignores the ways in which the seaside resort was not a liminal zone at all times and for all people (Shields, 1991). The transitional zone between land and water was a place where pleasure and sexuality were both restrained and given an outlet but these intersected in different ways in different times and places. It is an examination of the specific *constraints* on liminality and the 'tourist gaze' that best explains the differences between resorts and the evolving development of built environments and social practices.

I will accordingly focus on the changing social and leisure practices which defined the use of the beach huts and the evolving architectural influences that defined their style. Additionally, I will address the ways in which beach huts shaped and were shaped by perceptions of class and national identity.

From Bathing Machines to Beach Huts

The original ancestors of the beach hut were bathing machines, which were relics of the era of bathing as a medical ritual. The machines housed bathers as they were pulled by horses or winches from the shore into the water for a brief immersion, ensuring privacy and modesty. The machines, however, were only tolerable in the context of a medicalised ritual rather than a pleasurable one. Although bathing machines became merely quaint anachronisms once shed of their function, their forbidding interiors initially had associations with the sea as a place of shocks and discomfort, harking back to the era of the sea as 'territory of the void' as described by Corbin, prior to its transformation by the Romantic imagination into a site for the sublime (Corbin, 1994).

The rationale behind bathing machines ceased once mixed bathing and bathing costumes for men became common by the turn of the century. An earlier 19th century discourse had succeeded for a time in sanitising the practice of men bathing naked. While this practice was at odds with Victorian morality, it arose in the context of bathing as a health ritual, and not as a licentious activity. As John Travis observed in his examination of English sea-bathing, costumes were considered to prevent men from receiving the full benefit of having salt water next to their skin. He also notes that wearing bathing drawers was regarded as a sign of effeminacy (although women bathers were wearing flannel gowns rather than drawers). Many men only reluctantly accepted the requirement to accept an imposition upon their masculine prerogatives and Travis comments that nude bathing continued to the end of the 19th century, albeit in a marginalised fashion, and only died out before the First World War along with the belief that exposure of bare skin to salt water was good for health (Travis, 1997: 13).

The practice of nude bathing did not lead only to a requirement for men to wear costumes; it also led to the creation of separate bathing areas for men and women. The ascendancy of Evangelical attitudes to recreation provided the initial moral arguments for local authorities to impose bathing bylaws and segregated bathing areas in the 1850s and 1860s. As Travis notes, however, local authorities often failed to enforce these regulations in an effort to keep all sections of their market happy, particularly since it was often wealthy patrons who preferred to bathe in the traditional manner. The occasional day-tripper incurred prosecution by the local authorities but enforcement was not consistent.

By the end of the century, with most men willing to wear costumes, the moral arguments had shifted to place the focus on the unsuitability of segregated bathing for family holidays. Additionally, bathing had lost many of its medical connotations and had become a more hedonistic pastime. Swimming became more popular and, by the turn of the century, was practised by increasing numbers of men and women, meaning that boundaries of segregated bathing areas were more frequently crossed. Commercial pressure to accede to this demand for mixed bathing facilities thus led to the widespread repeal of segregated bathing regulations by the turn of the century.

In spite of the changes in bathing practices, bathing machines still lingered on in most resorts until after the First World War, with many fixed on shore for use as changing facilities. In Frinton, for example, bathing machines were available for hire until the First World War, and several remained on the beach until 1925, when they were scrapped and replaced by six beach huts. Tents served as a transitional form of changing facilities, and photographs of Edwardian beaches show tents, bathing machines and huts all sharing the beach. Local authorities preferred to invest in structures more solid than a tent, so unlike continental resorts, tents gradually diminished on English beaches after the First World War.

In terms of its place in forming and reflecting British identity, the beach hut can also be viewed as a little colonial outpost, on the boundary between the manmade and natural worlds. In Frinton, beach huts were permitted primarily for those with residences in the town. Of course, many Frinton visitors and residences had colonial connections themselves and would have been familiar with the bungalows and huts found in different forms throughout the Empire. Anthony King's history of the bungalow finds the first English examples at the select resort of Westgate and Birchington, along the Kent coast in the 1870s (King, 1984). While these late Victorian bungalows are differentiated from beach huts by their isolation, they did establish the principles of bridging the natural and the manmade, bringing domestic spaces to the edge of the sea. By the inter-war years, the bungalow was seen to be a sign of unwanted ribbon development rather than as an accessory dwelling for the leisured classes. By then, however, the beach hut had taken over from the bungalow as the approved site for communing with the sea. It had also come to serve a wide range of domestic functions, including shelter, catering, including the all important cup of tea, and the display of objects and interior design skills, surrounding the otherwise relatively anonymous beachgoer with a number of indicators of social status and lifestyle preference (Theroux, 1983: 68–70, for acerbic comment on chalets).

The beach hut is but one of the temporary building types found at the beach, which includes railway carriages, as at Shoreham, shacks and chalets, found at settlements around the coast including Jaywick, not far from Frinton, and then in post-war years, the caravan (Ward & Hardy, 1984). There are many physical similarities between the original chalets at Jaywick and the huts at Frinton but the beach hut is distinguished from its chalet cousins by the social tone signifiers discussed later and by the fact that they were not allowed to be used for overnight accommodation. In this respect, they can be seen as adult Wendy houses or doll's houses – by miniaturising the scale of domestic life, an element of play and fantasy is introduced. The beach hut symbolised a miniaturised suburbia, domesticating the seafront and deflating connotations of either fear or the sublime. This domestication also meant that the presence of the beach hut signalled ownership by groups of select individuals rather than unrestricted public access: beach huts were rarely found singly. The uniform appearance of their serried ranks communicated control and order, particularly when paint colour choices were strictly limited, as in Frinton, as opposed to the more festive palette permitted at resorts with artistic pretensions such as Southwold. Unlike the earlier terraces of the Georgian seaside resort, however, this uniformity retained distinct individual boundaries for each owner rather than subsuming them under a collective grandeur.

Accommodating Swimmers at the Inter-war Beach

Links made to the image of popular and select resorts were perceived at the time, not just in retrospect, and can be seen in contemporary debates about how Councils should respond to the demand for bathing facilities:

> Clacton tradesmen have protested against the Council erecting more beach huts… They will constitute a most serious nuisance, especially from a sanitary point of view…They are a spoliation of our great asset, namely a free and uninterrupted front. When people engaged the huts they made a sort of private preserve of the ground around them and if there was a public footpath near, people were given the impression they were not allowed to use it…. people bring their own food, no trader revenue… Visitors to the huts would be given the prerogative of becoming Lords of the Manor for the time being… but… the beach was the privilege of all who visited it. (*Clacton Times*, 16 November 1929)

Clacton Urban District Council's overall priority thus remained to support the provision of public bathing facilities, viewing it as a component of the public infrastructure required to attract visitors. In 1919, the Council sent out an enquiry to other seaside resorts concerning their public bathing facilities. Of the 18 replies received, only three towns had provided baths and/or a pavilion (Clacton UDC, Improvements Committee, 26 May 1919). The Council saw this result as an opportunity to outstrip the facilities of its rivals and opened the East Cliff bathing chalets in 1922.

Clacton policy-makers were, however, swayed by the promise of extra income which beachfront development such as beach huts could generate, which they attempted to reconcile with the perceived inappropriateness of transforming the front of a popular resort by introducing a quasi-private area. An attempt to introduce more beach huts in 1931 was greeted unenthusiastically by the local Chamber of Commerce:

> In Clacton we cannot compare our town with a place like Frinton. Where Frinton gets one visitor, we get a hundred in the season. We want our front for the enjoyment of the people; we do not want any particular individual to have the right of our front. Where they say 'I rent this and this is my property'. When those people are sitting in the huts they will feel, if you walk in front of their hut you are importuning on their property. (*Clacton Times*, 17 January 1931)

The *Graphic* agreed, editorialising that it was

> to be deplored that Chamber of Commerce advice on huts had been treated so off-handedly by the Council ...Each one will be sure to be the nucleus of family and friendly gatherings, which as we know by experience, will prove to be nothing but a stumbling block and hindrance to promenaders. ...These huts will inevitably lead to an increase in the mackintosh bathing and as a natural consequence our bathing pitches will become obsolescent. (*Clacton Graphic*, 7 February 1931)

The term 'mackintosh bathing' now requires elaboration, since it was an alternative to changing in either private huts or public chalets. The term arose to describe the practice of bathers arriving at the beach in swimwear covered by a mackintosh (or more probably a beach wrap) and bypassing council-owned changing facilities. Mackintosh bathing ran contrary to council regulations that sought to enforce the use of council-owned bathing facilities. These restrictions originally largely affected working-class visitors who could not afford the charges for the changing facilities and costume and towel rental. Day-trippers would adapt by rolling up their stockings or trousers and go for a paddle instead. Those who contravened the restrictions could be cautioned by the Beach Inspector, although enforcement does not appear to have been vigorously pursued.

Mackintosh bathing increased in the 1920s in response to more relaxed attitudes to seaside attire, the growing fashion for sun-tanning and the addition of new leisure fashions to the holidaymaker's wardrobe which they wished to display. The *Clacton Graphic's* 'Clacton Chatter' column observed in 1930:

> The bathing public are already deleting the bathing tent from their programmes and proceeding from their apartments ready for their dip covered with the now popular bathing wrap, and thus saving

themselves and depriving the Council of a source of revenue. (*Clacton Graphic*, 23 August 1930)

The increase in mackintosh bathing posed a dilemma for Clacton Council. To permit it would entail a loss of revenue to the Council from changing facilities but to forbid it would discourage visitors and harm its reputation as a forward-thinking resort. Discussion on the subject was couched in commercial rather than moral terms, with concerns about possible indecency overshadowed by worries about loss of revenue to Council-owned facilities. The Council reluctantly removed restrictions on mackintosh bathing in 1930, feeling under pressure from competition from other resorts that permitted it.

In Frinton, where the Council was less concerned with generating revenue from its limited number of public changing facilities, although more concerned with preserving social tone, it was noted in 1930 Council minutes that mackintosh bathing was allowed 'consistently with the observation of decency' (Frinton UDC, General Purposes Committee, 25 March 1930). This suggests that popular resorts had to work harder than select resorts at imposing restrictions and enforcing them, since select resorts could rely on a greater degree of shared norms. Eastbourne Corporation, an example of a larger resort resisting popular status, sought to enforce its 'no hut no bathe' rule in 1930, and dispatched police in lorry-loads to take the names and addresses of hundreds of mackintosh bathers (Everritt, 1980: 41). Eastbourne's policy, however, was the exception rather than the rule, and by the end of the inter-war period bathing was at last largely unrestricted in practice by local authorities at English seaside resorts, even where byelaw restraints lingered on in theory.

Making Bare Limbs Modest

The decrease in bathing restrictions accompanied dramatic changes in bathing fashions. In 1919, a dip in the sea normally entailed renting an ill-fitting costume that unflatteringly covered both men and women from the neck to the knees, changing in a tent or chalet and a prompt change back into everyday clothes following a swim or paddle. Photographs of the English beachfront prior to the 1920s show no acknowledgement in the user's attire that they are in a distinctive public space. Victorians and Edwardians did not feel the need to acquire specialised clothes to mark a special environment.

By the 1920s, a new consumer market had been created for beachwear which took advantage of new man-made textiles, changing social mores and the alliance of health with sun-tanning. Lansdell's study of seaside fashions notes: 'The bathing costumes of the 1920s for both men and women showed almost year by year, an increase in the amount of skin exposed and a decrease in the weight and amount of fabric used' (Lansdell, 1990: 63). The extent of this dramatic transformation, however, was limited both by the English climate and by the clear boundaries still remaining in social behaviour. Photographs of the seaside in the inter-war years tend to show the great majority of beachgoers wearing their everyday clothes when not in the water. Leisurewear and abbreviated swimwear became accepted in principle but its actual purchase and use was the province of trendsetters with sufficient disposable income, particularly the nascent youth market. Seaside towns, seeking to encourage the growth of this market, were willing to encourage the spread of the new fashions as part of their efforts to project a modern image. In 1930, for example, Clacton's local newspaper noted that

> bathers of both sexes were allowed to wear what they like at Clacton...the principal seaside resorts have now accepted modern ideas in relation to the type of bathing suits to be worn this season. While this country is not prepared, and rightly to accept Continental fashions, we are willing to recognise and permit the wearing of multi-coloured suits, and in many instances the low cut 'sun back' is also allowed...the modern generation realise the wisdom of wearing garments which are not only more in keeping with the present trend of fashion but freely admit the ultra-violet rays so beneficial to health...We must not, nor do we wish to, emulate Continental resorts by permitting men to appear only in shorts, and ladies in suits without legs, but this country is now sufficiently broadminded to accept new fashions in such moderation as will be beneficial to the wearers. (*Clacton Graphic*, 17 May 1930)

During the next decade, Clacton became broadminded enough to accept men in shorts and ladies in suits without legs as well, with the perceived health benefits of ultra-violet rays providing the medical rationale for the acceptance of otherwise overly daring 'Continental' styles. New boundaries were swiftly set so that prevailing behaviour remained within the bounds of decency and decorum.

This change in norms and public discourse helps explain why the increase in the display of bare flesh at the seaside did not greatly heighten the seaside's reputation as a liminal zone, where social norms could be relaxed and even transgressed. While some aspects of a liminal image emerged more strongly in the inter-war years, with the heyday of the comic postcard and the development of the 'dirty weekend' image for

Brighton, in most respects the beachfront was characterised by continuing efforts to control and direct activities that might offend against prevailing standards. By the time bathing regulations had changed in the wake of social practice in the latter half of the inter-war years, disrobing on the beach and abbreviated bathing costumes were conventional rather than disruptive and thus no longer offended against prevailing standards. Relaxations in the regulations were viewed as common-sense measures to meet popular demand:

> The problem of dress today at the seaside is not what one should wear, but what one can dispense with without incurring the wrath of authority. The change of sentiment regarding clothes is defended in the cause of health...No one – that is except for a few fanatics – would like to see those frumpish and foolish dresses of a decade ago. Generally speaking sensible and comfortable holiday dress of today goes to show a sensible advance. (*Clacton Times*, 12 August 1933)

Thus, the skimpier costumes were seen as 'sensible' and any opposition to them the province of a few 'frumpish and foolish fanatics'. The new fashions were part of a discourse which integrated swimming and sun-tanning with health, hygiene and progress, essential characteristics of the 'modern' inter-war resort image. This discourse often took the course of giving seaside towns feminine characteristics, in contrast to 'masculine' inland industrial towns. In this discourse, the female beachgoer projected confidence and vitality, clouding other comic postcard images of the passive bathing beauty. Writers such as Alison Light and David Matless have also observed this moral landscape in the countryside, which was also defined in feminine and domestic terms such as the rose-covered thatched cottage (Light, 1991; Matless, 1998: 9). Light argues that this was part of an overall trend to a 'feminised' notion of Englishness developed in inter-war years and resulting from the destruction of the heroic masculinity of the First World War. These metaphors of femininity were used to create spatial distinctions as well, with the seaside and countryside contrasted with urban industry, corruption and pollution. Seaside-resort image-makers frequently linked their towns with qualities of both femininity and modernity, which demarcated them as places for the 'new kinds of social and personal opportunity offered by changing cultures of sport and entertainment' (*Clacton Times*, 25 June 1932). These opportunities were facilitated by increases, for women in particular, in disposable income and physical freedom.

These changes affected bathing and fashion, so that previously unacceptable dress and actions were brought within the realm of propriety.

Contemporary commentary redefined the exposure of bare skin accordingly: 'Clacton belles with that poise of jolly independence and unawareness which makes bare limbs modest and is the natural grace of English girls' (*East Coast Advertiser*, 17 July 1925). Subtle class distinctions also complicated a simplistic ahistorical view of the female bather, providing different contexts for fashions sweeping through both Clacton and Frinton.

Frinton's conservative social structure and behaviour codes apparently adjusted easily to the new fashions:

> There are sand girls at Frinton who could compete successfully with any bronzed beauty of Palm Beach. Regardless of complexion, they have allowed the sun to burn them deep brown – and the sun has heaps of opportunity. For if Frinton is strict about stalls on the beach, it has no objection to lolls on the front. So the bathing girls dry themselves in the sun on the sands, or sit before their huts – still in bathing costume – and drink tea. And here and there, you see a young mother in bathing costume and bath robe pushing her brown baby in a perambulator, with the nurse at the side.

In this example, the bronzed beauties retain such social markers as beach huts and servants to legitimise both their behaviour and the newspaper's voyeuristic discussion of it.

Quiet Respose versus Gay Allurements

These changes in social practices had clear implications for the spaces demanded at the inter-war resort, creating a demand for both the domestic-scaled beach hut and for public spaces for the new consumers. For popular resorts, the priority among these was for spaces to clearly promote fluid mass movement and to proclaim public status. Clacton accordingly preserved the area next to the Pier, where most visitors would have congregated, for public spaces such as formal gardens and facilities such as the Band Pavilion. The market for beach huts provided by middle class residents and visitors, meanwhile, was catered for on the West Beach. The huts in West Clacton shared a similar character with those at Frinton's neighbour, Walton-on-the-Naze, a popular resort abounding in beach huts. In both cases, the beach hut can be seen as the signifier of the 'family resort' characterised by repeat visitors, an intermediary category to either the select resort or the popular resort catering to day trippers. Walton's family resort status was confirmed in the inter-war years by the active August Visitors Society, a group of regular neighbouring beach-hut users from the East End of London, who organised annual social and sporting events.

The nuances of actual use and regulation of beach huts are thus important to an understanding of how they influenced social tone. In Frinton, the owner of a beach hut was constrained by Council restrictions designed to control development, thereby maintaining social tone. While the beach huts themselves were owned privately, the Frinton local authority owned the land underneath the huts. A particular restriction that set Frinton apart from other local authorities was that hut owners were required by Council byelaws to be Frinton residents. The Council gradually relaxed its residency requirements, providing a few non-residents' sites in 1919 and a few more in 1920 when demand slowed. The policy, however, to refuse non-resident applications was tightened up again later in 1920 when resident demand picked up, and residency requirements were not again lifted until 1974. The residency requirements heightened the focus on gradations of social tone, since the ones reserved for the best houses accordingly had the most prestige. A local resident recalled:

> Before the war, according to where you lived in the town, you were allocated to a certain area. The dividing line was the main street. If you lived on the west side of the main street you went on the low wall, which was the posh section, and if you lived on the east side you went on the east wall, which wasn't quite so posh. (Mr R. Tomkins, interview with author)

The Council retained an active role in preserving the character of the huts, of which there were around 600 by the 1920s. In the 1910s and 1920s, the Council passed regulations governing the naming of the huts (preferably after the owner's main residence); requiring regular hut maintenance; requiring Council approval for hut designs; and recommending that all huts be painted white with black roofs. The Council and Frinton residents thus worked together to ensure that the beach huts contributed to a select social tone, contributing to the huts' evolution from a bathing accessory to a shore-bound icon symbolising the resort hierarchy.

The beach would initially seem to be defined clearly as a public space but, as the previous discussion illustrates, varying assumptions about ownership, along with actual ownership itself, link perceptions of spaces as public or private to perceptions of whether they are select or popular. The key point here is that many distinctions creating select or popular social tone were not prescribed by statute or explicit demarcations. A distinction between commercial and non-commercial activities on the seafront was one of these important unspoken considerations, which arose from the legacy of rational recreation and the priority placed on the acquisition of cultural capital amongst the bourgeoisie. 'Commercial' implied activities that required minimal effort on the part of a consumer in search of stimulation while 'non-commercial' activities such as sports or enjoying nature were felt to require greater physical or mental involvement, albeit concealed by the restraint in actions and emotions associated with an exclusive and conservative resort. 'Commercial' was perceived in the context of crowds, urbanity, fads, transgressive behaviour and artifice, all qualities antithetical to a select resort. An 1894 brochure promoting Frinton defined its audience clearly:

> We are not speaking to those who want to take town and all its gaieties to the sea-side with them. To such, the main charm is absent, for Frinton is essentially quiet and reposeful. Bands and niggers, and all the gay allurements which are so attractive to the tripper, are conspicuous only by their absence. (Anon, 1894. 'Niggers' refers to the beach entertainers known as 'nigger minstrels')

Economic activity was cloaked by this quiet and repose but not absent. Unlike the constant flow of coins at Clacton pier, the price of leisure at Frinton was more discreetly obscured in the large upfront costs required to join the golf or tennis clubs or to buy a house and its associated beach hut.

The division of public/private and commercial/non-commercial spaces at the seafront was neither fixed nor static. The use and control of spaces on the beach was contested, whether it involved the nature of permitted activities, the types of structures that could be erected, or the kinds of public behaviour that would be tolerated. Some activities such as bathing became less regulated over time, while others, such as commercial activity, became more regulated and spatially concentrated. The local authority was usually at the centre of these conflicts, whether in its role as guardian of public order and morality, municipal entrepreneur, image-maker or rate collector.

By the inter-war period, differences between select and popular resorts in the types of available leisure activities were well established, with commercial ones predominating in popular resorts and activities perceived as non-commercial predominating in select resorts. In the popular resorts, this process was accompanied by a concentration of commercial activities into prescribed areas, along with their increasing regulation. This concentration in a town such as Clacton was intended to further its attempts to capture a wide spectrum of the potential market and provide appropriate environments for both working- and middle-class holidaymakers. It also served to direct revenue away from itinerant hawkers and entertainers to Council-run services and the Pier.

While the link between social tone and types of seaside activities had been clearly made before the inter-war period, this link was significantly transformed during this period by the expansion of consumerism and commercialised leisure and related changes in the workforce and economy (Perkin, 1981). Leisure activities for the middle and working classes were increasingly defined by a commercial and popular culture realm outside the parameters of the 19th century discourse of rational recreation.

Victorian and Edwardian seaside resorts were noted for the cacophony produced by roving pedlars, musicians, and entertainers. These activities were gradually rationalised and consolidated, both spatially and organisationally, in a manner similar to other forms of popular entertainment such as music halls or sport (Bailey, 1986; Lowerson, 1993). This process was set under way earlier on in Clacton than in other popular resorts such as Southend, since its core area was initially under the unified control of the steamboat company. Their restrictive covenants provided that 'summer shops, bazaars, small amusements and cafes were contained within the commercial core of the town and not allowed on the sea-front' (Gayler, 1965: 150). Photographs of Clacton Beach in the 1890s, however, do show a number of stalls and pitches for pierrots, ice-cream vendors, photographers and novelty merchants. Over the next 30 years, these activities were largely moved to the Pier, Council-run kiosks or town centre locations. The Council played a key role in this process and gradually increased its control over seafront enterprises (with the notable exception of the privately run Pier).

A key moment in this consolidation and sanitising of commercial activity was the demolition of the shops in Pier Gap in 1914 and their replacement by formal gardens and a Venetian Bridge. Pier Gap led into the Pier entrance and thus provided a key focal point for the seafront, shaping the first impressions of disembarking steamboat passengers. The sharply sloping Pier Gap was too steep to clean with dustcarts and was felt to offend the sensibilities of the better class of visitors due to the smell of fish, the noise of 'the little shop proprietors, some of them Italian, worrying visitors to buy' and 'the shrimp heads, shells, bones and so on that were dropped every day along with cigarette packets, chips, old newspapers etc.' (Jacobs, 1986: 21; *East Coast Advertiser*, 2 January 1926). The old Pier Gap thus compromised images of hygiene, social respectability and Clacton's pride in being a purpose-built seaside resort rather than an expanded fishing village. The new Venetian Bridge and formal gardens, epitomising rational planning, aesthetic refinement and an absence of commercialism, were felt to be in line with the Council's policy to 'attract a different class of people' and to create a 'place without whelk stalls and rattletrap affairs' (*East Coast Advertiser*, 8 August 1925). The influence of the old Pier Gap, however, was considered to have had a long-lasting detrimental effect on Clacton's social tone. Eight years on, a local paper bemoaned: 'The town has a bitter experience of the cockle stalls and the shops of the old Gap, the stigma of which is still to some extent being lived down' (*East Coast Advertiser*, 2 September 1922).

The Council's efforts to restrict commercial activity to approved businesses in approved areas were challenged by itinerant hawkers and pedlars who wandered into areas of the seafront that would have otherwise been free of a commercial presence. The beach was expected to be a zone for non-commercial relaxation and the Pier and the town proper the appropriate zone for settled, respectable, ratepaying commerce.

In 1928, Clacton Council decided that regulating demand through licensing was the best way forward and this seems to have been successful in limiting hawking. The decline in hawking is also likely to have been influenced by increases in the number of Council kiosks, greater consumer sophistication and the low profit margins of seasonal itinerant trading. The zones of non-commercial activity that were created on Clacton Beach by these trends, however, were insufficient to ensure Clacton's appeal to the upper end of its target market. The Pier, continuously expanding in the inter-war period, instead emerged as the dominant focus for the Clacton seafront and put images of commercial activity to the fore.

Frinton Council had a far less ambiguous view of commercial activity. It was seen to be totally inappropriate for a select seafront and limited by restrictive covenants. The Council reinforced this policy for public land by refusing requests to carry out any activities on the seafront that could be considered remotely commercial or damaging to social tone.

Enforcement of a select social tone at Frinton was, however, primarily a matter of convention and shared values. On the beach, for example, during the inter-war years, there was a Beach Inspector to enforce regulations but the nanny, a key figure in forming upper-class British identity, also had a high profile on the Frinton inter-war seafront. A Frinton resident recalled of his childhood that 'we had a nanny and we used to spend virtually every day at the seafront…the nannies ruled the roost down there' (Mr R. Tomkins, interview with author). This would have been particularly true during the month of June, when upper-class parents sent their toddlers and babies off to Frinton while they travelled. Frinton acquired a particular niche catering for the children of the well-to-do or with parents living abroad. The extent of the market for facilities for wealthy and expatriate children is testified by the existence of *Wheeler's Indian Guide to British Resorts and Schools,* published during the inter-war years as an aid for those seeking to make their leave arrangements and provide for their children. An advertisement for the Glenvar School in Frinton stressed that 'children of officers and Indian Officials are especially welcomed', particularly since doctors had recommended Frinton as being suitable for children from tropical countries because of its bracing air and sunshine. Certain hotels such as the Cedars specialised in accommodating nannies and their charges, during the month of June in particular. Older children, also tended by the 'nanny brigade', followed in July once school was out.

The nannies at Frinton were there as part of their job, rather than strictly for pleasure, and part of that job would have been to ensure the absence of behaviour deemed inappropriate in the presence of small children. Their presence would have reinforced the perception of the beach and beach huts as domestic zones, curtailing the freedom granted by the anonymity of the crowd and public spaces. The transposition of private domestic practices to a public space blurred boundaries between public and private in the process of setting other boundaries of social tone. As in an urban public park, the presence of large numbers of nannies with high quality, expensive baby equipment and provisions communicated the absent economic and social influence of their employers and allowed them to control the space immediately around them: to 'rule the roost'.

Conclusion

The association of beach huts with a select social tone means they have been defined in opposition to commercial recreation. The discussion has thus focused on the sorts of environments and experiences they exclude as well as those they signify. The domestic scale of the beach huts has been contrasted with the crowds and stimulus associated with commercial areas of the seafront and Pier.

The evolution of the beach hut from bathing machine to home away from home has illustrated how functional spaces can be saturated with social and cultural significance over time. In this process, beach huts have become part of the tourist landscape and experience but they also become part of the everyday landscape for their regular users. I think it important to consider tourist spaces across the spectrum of users, since their roles in defining place image are so very contingent on whether the experience of the space is one-off or regular, in addition to the variables of class, ethnicity and gender. Work on tourism has tended to focus on the experiences of the short-term and intermittent tourist rather than that of the regular visitor, and the former's demand for spectacle and the out of the ordinary. Seaside spaces such as the Pier or the Winter Garden require judgement on this scale of the extraordinary, and are currently found to be wanting, but the beach hut also requires evaluation as a site for everyday life. For regular hut-users, the significance of the beach huts lies in their incorporation into regular summer rituals of domesticity and strictly defined social interaction, thereby reinforcing notions of class and national identity.

References

Agarwal, S. (2002) Restructuring seaside tourism: The resort cycle. *Annals of Tourism Research* 29, 25–55.
Anon (1894) *A New Watering Place*. Frinton.
Bailey, P. (ed.) (1986) *Music Hall – The Business of Pleasure*. Milton Keynes: Open University Press.
Chase, L. (1999) The creation of place image in inter-war Clacton and Frinton. PhD thesis, University of Essex.
Clacton Graphic and East Coast Illustrated News (1920–38).
Clacton Urban District Council (1919–39) Full Council Minutes.
Clacton Urban District Council (1903–38) Improvements and Entertainments.
Corbin, A. (1994) *The Lure of the Sea: The Discovery of the Seaside 1750–1840*. London: Penguin Books.
East Coast Advertiser and Clacton News (1919–27) thereafter, *Clacton Times and East Essex Gazette* (1927–39).
Everritt, S. (1980) *Southend Seaside Holiday*. Chichester: Phillimore.
Frinton Urban District Council (1901–34) and Frinton and Walton Urban District Council (1934–39) General Purposes Committee Minutes.
Gayler, H.J. (1965) The coastal resorts of Essex: Their growth and present day functions. MA thesis, University of London.
Jacobs, N. (1986) *The Sunshine Coast, Bygone Clacton, Walton, Frinton and District*. Lowestoft: Tyndale and Panda.
King, A. (1984) *The Bungalow: The Production of a Global Culture*. London: Routledge and Kegan Paul.
Lansdell, A. (1990) *Seaside Fashions 1860–1939*. Princes Risborough: Shire Publications.
Light, A. (1991) *Forever England: Femininity, Literature and Conservatism between the Wars*. London: Routledge.
Lowerson, J. (1993) *Sport and the English Middle Classes 1870–1914*. Manchester: Manchester University Press.
Matless, D. (1998) *Landscape and Englishness*. London: Reaktion Books.
Perkin, H.J. (1981) *The Structured Crowd*. London: Routledge.
Shields, R. (1991) *Places on the Margin*. London: Routledge.
Theroux, P. (1983) *The Kingdom by the Sea*. London: Hamish Hamilton.

Travis, J. (1997) Continuity and change in English sea-bathing, 1730–1900: A case of swimming with the tide. In S. Fisher (ed.) *Recreation and the Sea* (pp. 8–35). Exeter: University of Exeter Press.

Urry, J. (1990) *The Tourist Gaze*. London: Sage.

Urry, J. (1997) Cultural change and the seaside resort. In G. Shaw and A. Williams (eds) *The Rise and Fall of British Coastal Resorts* (pp. 102–11). London: Mansell.

Walton, J.K. (2000) *The British Seaside: Holidays and Resorts in the Twentieth Century*. Manchester: Manchester University Press.

Ward, C. and Hardy, D. (1984) *Arcadia for All*. London: Mansell.

Wheeler's Indian Guide to British Resorts and Schools (1931–37). London: Wheeler.

Chapter 13

'The Most Magical Corner of England': Tourism, Preservation and the Development of the Lake District, 1919–39

CLIFFORD O'NEILL

The inter-war years were a transitional period in the evolution of the Lake District as a tourist centre. Throughout the period the holiday industry still displayed many of the characteristics that had emerged in the later-19th and early 20th centuries as a result of the railways (Marshall & Walton, 1981; Walton, 1991; Walton & McGloin, 1981; Walton & O'Neill, 2004). The area remained an up-market holiday destination, capitalising on the scenic attractions and literary connections that, in 1937, led E.M. Forster to describe it as 'the most magical corner of England' (Forster, 1937: 46). A string of lakeside resorts, headed by Windermere and Keswick, provided accommodation and respectable entertainment for these visitors in hotels and guesthouses, although the more 'adventurous' tourists stayed in the rural cottages and farmhouses thought to offer a more authentic taste of Lakeland life. The railways, which delivered visitors to Windermere, Keswick, Lakeside and Coniston, continued to be the main source of supply for the holiday industry. Alongside these continuities, however, the district also had to come to terms with changes that presaged the salient trends of the years after the second World War. The development of automobile-based tourism and the burgeoning growth of the outdoor movement presented a range of challenges to the holiday industry in Lakeland. In addition, the district also faced a variety of environmental pressures that generated an increasing clamour for the preservation of the fragile landscape which sustained the tourist trade.

The overall structure of the holiday industry in the Lake District in the inter-war years showed few changes from that established prior to the First World War. The district catered for a relatively small, niche market composed of those who wished to contemplate the scenery, partake of outdoor activities and savour the artistic associations. Statistics on the size of the market are limited but the 1921 census does give some indications. The June census of that year captured the visitors to Lakeland and allows comparisons of the Lakeland resorts with other holiday centres. Windermere had 1286 visitors, Keswick 1277 and Ambleside 578. These figures were dwarfed by those published for Blackpool, which had 25,807 visitors, and by those for more genteel resorts such as Southport (4751) and Harrogate (4511). The June enumeration took place before the height of the summer season but the relative figures still demonstrate the restricted nature of the holiday market in Lakeland (Walton & O'Neill, 1993).

Similar differences are observable in local newspaper estimates of excursionist numbers at summer weekends and bank holidays. Details for Lakeland as a whole do not exist but figures for Windermere and Keswick enable comparison with the seaside resorts. The *Westmorland Gazette* gave seasonal totals of 39,000 for the number of Sunday excursionists arriving at Windermere in 1929 and 38,000 for 1930. The highest claim made for a particular day was for a holiday crowd of 15,000 at Bowness on Whit Monday 1928, a figure which included residential holidaymakers and coach trippers as well as excursionists. For Keswick, 8000 visitors attended the bank holiday gala of 1920. These numbers pale in comparison with totals for the popular coastal resorts. Blackpool in the 1930s claimed figures of half a million visitors on a busy summer Saturday (*Cumberland and Westmorland Herald*, 7 August 1920; Walvin, 1978: 124–5; *Westmorland Gazette*, 2 June 1928, 20 September 1930). Such comparative statistics confirm that the Lake District catered for a more exclusive and much smaller market of visitors than that of the rapidly expanding seaside centres.

Topping the visitor profile of the Lake District at this time was a mix of international plutocrats, wealthy manufacturers and members of the higher professions. These visitors often enjoyed the luxurious trappings and tea dances of the large resort hotels or took residence at the district's villas and cottages. The reminiscences of the daughter of a Newcastle industrialist contain glimpses of their lifestyle, giving details of the garden parties, lake regattas and car-borne excursions that constituted the 'gay life' at White Cross Bay on Windermere. Those with a purer taste for the fells stayed at the hostelries and farmhouses scattered across the valleys. The Woolpack hotel in Wasdale boasted visitors such as William Beveridge and Maurice Hewlett, whilst nearby Wha House farm entertained the novelist Israel Zangwill and the artist, Colin Phillip. More mundane members of the middle classes also partook of the farmhouse experience that, according to G.D. Abraham, offered 'interesting opportunities for studying the dalesmen's ways and means of living'. Oral testimony provides a vivid insight into this process for a family who 'enjoyed' the earth closets and occasional lack of hot water of a farmhouse holiday at Nibthwaite (Ambleside Public Library, Respondents BC, AD, BS; Abraham, 1913: 9). This established market remained relatively constant in the inter-war years, providing some security against the economic vicissitudes of the period.

Other segments of the holiday market were more vulnerable to the fluctuations of the inter-war economy and local newspapers frequently contained laments about the state of trade in the district. Such comments had particular relevance to the fortunes of the boarding houses, apartments and small hotels that proliferated in Windermere, Bowness, Ambleside and Keswick. These establishments drew their clientele from the lower middle classes – the clerks, teachers and small businessmen – and from the more affluent members of the working classes who took their annual holidays in the district and enjoyed its outdoor attractions. This sector appears to have been under considerable pressure in the inter-war years, with custom declining not only because of prevailing economic uncertainties but also as a result of changing patterns of holiday-making. Census figures show a decline in the number of lodging-house keepers in all of the resorts between 1921 and 1931, although there are some problems of interpretation associated with these figures (O'Neill, 2001: 69–70).

At the lower end of the profile were the thousands of trippers who came on the excursion trains from Lancashire, Yorkshire and the Northeast. These visitors made 'honeypots' of the main resorts on summer weekends, congregating around the lake shores and forming queues for the various vessels that allowed them to take to the waters of Windermere, Coniston, Ullswater and Derwentwater. They also provided much of the clientele for the motor coach tours that criss-crossed the district on multi-lake tours and enabled a relatively whirlwind appreciation of its charms. Although Lakeland was still not exactly a playground for the common man, the working-class trippers nevertheless made a significant contribution to the tourist economy. Indeed, in times of recession, the district felt the adverse effects of unemployment and short-time working in the industrial areas. As one Lakeland newspaper put it in 1931, 'there was never a truer saying that when the cotton trade is bad, the season at the lakes is poor' (*Westmorland Gazette*, 1 July 1931).

For the most part, these descriptions of the main characteristics of the holiday industry in Lakeland would hold just as true for the years before the First World War. To some extent, the deployment of the internal combustion engine had merely reinforced existing means of enjoyment of the district. Motorised versions had replaced horse-drawn tours of the lakes and the motor engine had added just another means of enjoying their waters (Abraham, 1929; *Westmorland Gazette*, 15 April 1922). We should not over-emphasise continuity, however, as the region had to adjust to other effects of the development of motor transport, to changing leisure preferences and to the evolution of more interventionist attitudes to the management of the environment by government. This combination of factors created an agenda of change and controversy in the district, as those interested in the tourist trade sought to reconcile the different demands for enjoyment, entertainment, tranquillity, exploitation and preservation. It is time now to explore this agenda.

The upmarket nature of the tourist market in Lakeland meant that the region soon faced the effects of the spread of car ownership amongst the affluent after the Great War (O'Connell, 1998). The rise of the automobile had major implications for the spatial-temporal pattern of tourism in the Lakes. Both hotel and boarding-house sectors had prospered from the relatively long-stay holidays that had become the norm for most of the area's staying visitors. The mobility offered by the car threatened this system, as visitors could now opt for touring holidays, making shorter stays at a number of different locations. Statistical evidence of this trend is difficult to attain but it was a salient aspect of contemporary commentary on the local tourist industry. Observers noted this change by the early 1920s, with even the editor of the *Blackpool Gazette* remarking that in the Lake District 'the modern visitor stays no length of time' whilst contrasting this with the 'old stately way of taking a month at the Lakes' (*Blackpool Gazette*, 17 July 1924).

As the period progressed, complaints about this trend were recurrent features of the local newspapers. In 1925 a commentary on the summer season at Keswick worried about 'flying visits' to the district, expressing anxiety about how the 'weekend habit seems to be growing amongst those who holiday in the Lake District, and this has been developed by the motor car, as has the holiday tour' (*Westmorland Gazette*, 10 October 1925). In the 1930s, disquiet at these changed circumstances intensified, prompting a nostalgia for the 'old days before the advent of the fast car and luxurious coaches'. According to the hoteliers, even the foreign visitors seemed to have succumbed to the short-stay holiday. This prompted a member of the local resorts' federation in 1936 to condemn bitterly the 'ten-minute American hustlers' who rushed through the district and then spent the night in Harrogate (*Westmorland Gazette*, 16 June 1936).

Criticism was also levelled at the new tendency of car-based day trips and 'motor picnicking', which further seemed to ensure that 'boarding-house keeping will soon become a thing of the past' (*Westmorland Gazette*, 16 July 1927). Similar complaints focused on the motor coaches that had added to the opportunities for people to come on day trips to the Lake District, when perhaps beforehand their occupants might have opted for a staying holiday in the boarding houses. In 1925, according to one source, an average of 30 to 40 coaches visited Keswick each day in the summer season. The coaches came from Morecambe and Blackpool in the Northwest but also from the Northeast, from the Midlands and some from the South (*Westmorland Gazette*, 10 October 1925). The vulnerability of the boarding-house sector to the trend for day trips increased further in 1932 when the London, Midland, Scottish railway introduced weekly contract tickets, which allowed visitors to make daily journeys to the region and then return home each night (*Westmorland Gazette*, 15 October 1932).

The growth of the outdoor movement added to the problems of the boarding-house sector. The desire to be close to nature generated a craze for hiking in the inter-war period that brought with it a demand for alternative and cheaper modes of accommodation (Howkins & Lowerson, 1979; Taylor, 1997; Walker, 1985). Camping developed steadily in the area (although to nothing like the extent seen in the years after the Second World War), as farmers sought to supplement their income by catering for this new source of business (for example *Penrith Observer*, 11 June 1935; *Westmorland Gazette*, 29 July 1922, 8 August 1925, 11 April 1931, 3 April 1937). The period also saw a rise in the number of holiday hostels in the area. The Co-operative Holiday Association and its sister organisation, the Holiday Fellowship, continued its policy of buying and converting buildings for this purpose (Leonard, 1934). The main source of expansion, however, came with the formation of the Youth Hostels Association in 1930. By 1931, four YHA hostels were open in Lakeland, a figure which had increased to 12 by 1935. The number of visitors to these hostels grew rapidly through the decade. Statistics for the total of bednights in the hostels show and increase from 12,000 in 1932 to 72,640 in 1938 (O'Neill, 2001: 94–6).

These developments generated anxiety in the traditional accommodation industry about unfair competition regarding rates and cheap prices. The boarding-house sector in particular felt the pinch of this competition and blamed the campsites and hostels for contributing to their economic woes. In 1932, for instance, the threat to 'the proprietors of small boarding houses' by the emergence of impromptu campsites in Borrowdale was brought to the notice of Cockermouth Rural District Council. Guesthouse owners also insisted that far from catering solely for a young generation who would not have stayed in their establishments, the Youth Hostels also took from the former group's target clientele of older, more affluent people. In 1934, Kenneth Spence, on behalf of the regional council of the YHA, denied these charges, pointing out that the hostels brought many new people to the district who would often use the guesthouses on the frequent occasions when the hostels were full. His words failed to pacify the guesthouse owners, however, as demonstrated later in 1934, when an irritated boarding-house keeper from Grasmere published his desire to remove the local Youth Hostel and the 'tents and caravans that desecrate one of Lakeland's most beautiful valleys' (*Westmorland Gazette*, 27 August 1932, 20 October 1934, 6 October 1934).

Such cries of frustration, of course, could do little to stop the trends that were changing the shape of Lakeland tourism. Yet these changes did not threaten wholesale alteration of the nature of the visiting public. For all the laments about 'ten-minute hustlers' and 'the restless, step-on-it motorist who has eyes to see yet sees not', the car-borne visitors, hikers and campers still came to the district to enjoy similar experiences to those engaged in by the traditional long-stay visitors (*Westmorland Gazette*, 3 July 1937). Both private and public investment, therefore, sought primarily to secure and develop the traditional attractions and activities that had established the area as a holiday destination. Those involved knew full well that the area flourished as a contrast to the vulgar pleasures of the seaside and consequently eschewed the forms of entertainment associated with the latter, believing that 'amusements and beauty of surroundings are not compatible'. One local newspaper summarised the perceived superiority of the cultural and aesthetic experience available in the Lake District when it commented that 'although from the sea front of Morecambe the hills which look down upon Windermere can be seen in the distance, from the shore of Lake Windermere one cannot even imagine Morecambe' (*Lakes Express*, 2 October 1928; *Westmorland Gazette*, 5 April 1919).

The local councils sought to enhance the attractiveness of their respective resorts, although ambitious public initiatives in this field faced several restrictions. The small populations of the Lake District resorts meant that the councils lacked the sizeable incomes from the rates available in the larger seaside resorts. Concern about excessive council expenditure was also a constant factor in the economic climate of the period and both Windermere and Patterdale witnessed the formation of ratepayers' organisations in the 1930s (*Westmorland Gazette*, 14 January 1933, 18 March 1933, 7 March 1936). The composition of the resort populations also accentuated the pressures on the councils, for most of the resorts had a number of wealthy offcomers who were more concerned about the resorts' residential amenity than about the development of the tourist trade (Ward, 1948: 214; Westall, 1991). In the face of these constraints, the resorts tended to be cautious in their attempts to boost the tourist trade in the region.

Such caution can be seen in the attempts by the councils to expand public access to the shores of the lakes that were their prime tourist assets. The costs of purchasing such prime land often encouraged the councils to cooperate with preservationist organisations or sympathetic individuals. Keswick UDC, for instance, had the National Trust to thank for the 'nationalisation' by 1929 of almost all of the Keswick side of Derwentwater, as the *Keswick Reminder* put it. Similarly, the Lakes UDC gained control of Jenkins' Field on the shore of Ullswater through a donation from a private individual. At Windermere, the council in 1927 raised the purchase price of an area of the glebeland partly through public subscription and partly from a donation by the National Trust. Public subscription secured a further two acres of land on the lakeshore in 1937, whilst in 1938 the council obtained ownership of part of the bed of the lake through a private donation (CCRO Kendal, WSUD/L, Minutes of Lakes UDC, 27 May 1937, 28 September 1938; *Keswick Reminder*, 12 July 1929; Open Spaces Committee, 9 June 1936, 9 March 1937, WSUD/A, Windermere UDC, Health and Pleasure Grounds Committee, 13 July 1937; *Westmorland Gazette*, 18 June 1927).

The maintenance of already existing public access in their respective areas also concerned resort councils and the inter-war years saw them engaged in a number of footpath disputes with private landowners. Members of the councils recognised that these paths and walkways were important parts of their tourist portfolio and doggedly defended them against closure, just as they had done in the 19th century. Keswick UDC, for instance, fought a long battle to keep open a footpath to Castlerigg near the town in the face of an attempt by the owner to close it. At Windermere, the council tried to purchase land in Elleray Wood in 1924 in order to secure extra footpaths to the Orrest Head beauty spot near the town, as the landowners had closed the permissive routes through the wood. The most bitter dispute broke out at Ambleside in 1924 when estate trustees closed a footpath to Stock Ghyll waterfalls. Outraged council members, convinced that the footpath was public, instructed their surveyor to break the locks on the gate to the footpath and ceremonially walked its length. This remarkable action involved the council in a court case that in the end determined that the footpath could be considered public on account of long usage by the community. The council's lawyer cannily stressed the traditional use of the path by local farmers but also emphasised its extended history as part of the town's tourist space (CCRO Carlisle,

SUDK/1/1/17, 3 September 1924, 13 November 1924; CCRO Kendal, WSUD/A, Minutes of Ambleside UDC Highways and Sewers Committee, 25 April 1924, 7 May 1924, 1 April 1925; SUDK 1/1/18, 7 October 1926; *Westmorland Gazette*, 3 May 1924, 20 and 27 December 1924, 4 April 1925).

Another form of tourist space in the resorts were the pleasure grounds that entertained both the local and the visiting public through the provision of rational, orderly recreations. Their development in the inter-war years was the product of both public and private initiatives. In Keswick, for instance, the urban district council relied on a private trust to extend Fitz Park pleasure ground in the town. In Windermere and Ambleside, the councils proved more active. In 1928, Ambleside council assumed control of White Platts pleasure ground, which had been opened in 1923 after a public subscription led by local businessmen gathered together in the town's Advertising Association. The council provided more facilities and later extended the park by taking over the site of the local sheep fair. Although this last action upset local farmers, it demonstrated fully, as the local newspaper noted, that the council 'realised that the trade and prosperity of Ambleside so essentially depended on visitors'. At Windermere, the council took over Queen's Park and assumed the running of Bowness recreation ground but proceeded slowly in developing the Glebeland as a pleasure ground because of costs (Bott, 1994: 114–15; CCRO Kendal, WSUD/A/9, 11 December 1929, 1 October 1930; *Westmorland Gazette*, 6 July 1929, 1 October 1930; WSUD/W, Health and Pleasure Grounds Committee, 12 August 1930, 26 September 1930, 10 March 1936).

The pleasure gardens and lakeside paths added to the ambience of the resorts, which the local councils zealously guarded in order to avoid any unpleasantness or vulgarity that compromised their upmarket reputation. This ambition involved the councils in policing behaviour in the resorts. Windermere UDC, for instance, urged the police to contain the rowdiness of trippers near the lakeshore at Bowness, where 'unsightly dancing' and 'racing for beer' prompted one councillor to describe Sunday afternoons as 'something like the Lancashire Wakes'. The vigilant councils also controlled business initiatives that threatened the orderly atmosphere or attractive surroundings that were the lifeblood of the resorts. Ice-cream vendors, mobile fish and chip vans, ticket 'touts' for the charabanc firms and various other traders and smallholders received short shrift from resort leaders determined, as at Windermere, not to let their towns take on the prospect of a 'penny bazaar' (O'Neill, 2001: 141–6).

As we have seen, the lakes were the resorts' greatest assets and the councils were determined to ensure appropriate activity in their vicinity.

Safety, congestion, speed and noise were all issues that occupied the councils as they sought to define proper use of the lakes. The conduct of the boating community, for instance, was a matter of concern in both Windermere and Keswick. At Keswick, the UDC, angered by the scruffy appearance of 'hutments and boxes' and by a build-up of refuse and empty petrol cans, sought to control the physical appearance of the boat-sheds and landings on Derwentwater. It also warned the boatmen about boisterous touting for custom in 1924 and threatened to take away the licenses of some accused of bad language and touting in 1927. In Windermere, the council restricted the boatmen's activities to defined areas. In 1933, the boatmen themselves formed an association in an attempt to regulate the competition for clients on the shore of Bowness Bay. Such measures seem to have worked to some extent but occasional complaints from visitors about touting (and fighting) still reached the ears of the councillors (CCRO Carlisle, SUDK 1/1/20, 3 April 1930, 7 March 1929; SUDK 1/1/17, 1 May 1924; SUDK 1/1/19, 7 July 1927; *Westmorland Gazette*, 18 July 1931, 1 August 1931).

Safety on the lakes also attracted the attention of the town councils, a concern which reflected the increasing number of motor-powered craft on the lakes. The councils took it upon themselves to monitor the condition of the boat landing stages and deal with the problems of congestion around them. Windermere council initiated a range of measures, delineating time limits for loading and unloading and building a new pier to accommodate the motor boats. Its counterpart at Ambleside repaired a number of landings at Waterhead on Lake Windermere whilst seeking new agreements with the owners of moorings and landings to ensure greater safety. Keswick council took similar actions and used its licensing system to restrict the number of boats on Derwentwater. Excess speed also raised concern, causing Windermere UDC to operate a speed limit of six miles per hour in Bowness Bay to ensure safety in this most crowded part of the lake (CCRO Carlisle, SUDK/1/1/15, 4 May 1922, 6 July 1922; CCRO Kendal, WSUD/A, Highways and Sewers Committee, 13 and 28 October 1920; *Westmorland Gazette*, 3 September 1921, 18 February 1922, 18 August 1923, 28 June 1924).

The noise of the motor boats also provoked controversy in the district but the stances of the resort councils differed on this matter. At Keswick, members of the UDC sought to reduce the impact of the motor boats on the peace of Derwentwater. Soon after the First World War, they insisted that motor boats must have silencers fitted on their engines, whilst the protection of Derwentwater's serenity was another factor behind the councils curtailment of the number of boats allowed on the lake. At

Windermere, however, a more liberal approach to the use of motor boats on the most popular of the lakes had the potential to divide the community. The council itself, which had a significant raft of trades people and businessmen who wished to promote tourism, had proved not to be averse to noisy intrusions on the lake. Just before and after the Great War, the council had allowed companies to operate flying boat journeys from the lake, whilst water carnivals and motor-boat racing were recurrent features by the 1920s (CCRO Carlisle, SUDK/1/1/15, 8 May 1919, 5 June 1919, 3 July 1919, 6 May 1920; O'Neill, 2001: 117, 131; Walton, 1991: 31–2).

In 1926, however, the council sanctioned the use of the lake for powerboat racing and also applied to host the prestigious Duke of York trophy race in 1927. The arrival of the large powerboats, with their more powerful engines, generated considerable disquiet in the local community, particularly amongst its wealthier members who had come to the area to enjoy its repose. A petition containing the signatures of 150 residents and 60 non-residents expressed alarm at the council's 'breach of guardianship' of the lake for 'sordid commercial reasons'. Tellingly, the petitioners stated that the 60 non-resident signatures demonstrated the concerns of the visiting public. The petition prompted an angry reaction from some councillors, who, in a barbed criticism aimed at resident wealthy offcomers, argued that only five out of the 150 local people named on it made a living from the tourist trade. They added that it was time that people recognised the need to 'entertain the multitudes' who came to the resort. Councillors certainly seem to have acted on this message. Although they failed to get the Duke of York trophy, they allowed hydroplane events on the lake in 1928 and hosted Henry Seagrave's fatal attempt on the world water speed record in 1930. On Windermere, it can be seen, the interests of tourism did not always coincide with the interests of those who wished to preserve the serenity of the Lake District (*Westmorland Gazette*, 18 October 1924, 18 and 25 September 1926, 28 August 1926, 2, 9, 23 and 30 October 1926, 23 June 1928, 3 May 1930, 21 June 1930).

Worries about speed and congestion arose not only with regard to the lakes but also from Lakeland's ambivalent relationship with the automobile. We have already seen that whilst the car and the motor coach had increased the accessibility of the district, it had affected the pattern of holidaymaking in ways that troubled the holiday industry. In an area renowned for tranquillity, fresh air and pleasant surroundings, the physical impact of the vehicles also presented challenges to the nature of the holiday experience. The resorts encountered problems soon after the end of the Great War, as increasing numbers of cars and coaches prompted anxieties about safety and obstruction. Grasmere, Ambleside and Keswick councils all implemented control measures, providing car parks and banning charabancs from certain roads. At Keswick, the council closed the key road to Derwentwater to heavy traffic in 1922. The authorities at Windermere acted in similar fashion, restricting vehicles from standing on Bowness Promenade (CCRO Carlisle, SUDK/1/15, 3 June 1920, 2 September 1920; CCRO Kendal, WSUD/GM/43, 7 June 1921; SUDK/1/16, 7 December 1922; *Westmorland Gazette*, 27 March 1930; WSUD/GM/44, 7 November 1932, 4 January 1933, 1 May 1933; WSUD/A, Highways and Sewers Committee, 6 April 1921, 6 July 1921, 4 August 1926, 1 December 1926).

In their attempts to deal with the automobile, the councils faced problems with local trades people who were afraid of driving trade away from the towns. In 1921, 79 traders petitioned Keswick council protesting about parking restrictions on cars in the Market Square in the town. Another petition arrived in 1930 from Lake Road traders who wanted the prohibition of heavy traffic lifted. Unrest also surfaced in Windermere where a councillor sympathetic to the traders announced in 1925 that the town was 'losing trade on account of this constant annoyance of the motorists'. By 1926, the council had relented a little and allowed parking on parts of the promenade whilst also securing land for a car park near Bowness Bay (CCRO Carlisle, SUDK/1/16, 2 June 1921; SUDK/1/20, 4 July 1930; *Westmorland Gazette*, 28 June 1924, 6 June 1925, 1 August 1925, 9 October 1926).

The tension between efforts to protect the resorts from congestion and to promote trade from tourism was particularly apparent in the debates that developed over bypass proposals for Ambleside and Keswick. Westmorland County Council first considered a bypass for Ambleside in 1926 and in 1928 Ambleside UDC supported the scheme 'because the annoyance caused by vibration and noise due to heavy motor traffic was driving visitors away'. A strong reaction from local businessmen, worried about the effect on trade, persuaded the council to rescind its decision, however. Similar arguments reappeared in 1938 when the county council tried again. Opponents of the scheme feared that a bypass would make Ambleside a backwater and the ferocity of the opposition persuaded the County Council to withdraw (*Westmorland Gazette*, 11 December 1926, 20 October 1928, 26 March 1938, 2 April 1938; *Lakes Express*, 16 October 1928).

Bypass proposals for Keswick ignited an even fiercer altercation in the late 1920s and 1930s. Cumberland County Council's original idea engendered a favourable initial reaction from Keswick UDC. The council's belief that a bypass would alleviate the noise and fumes which alienated visitors received support from the Council for the Preservation of Rural England (CPRE). Commercial traders in the town responded negatively, however, and presented a petition with over 200 signatures against the proposal. A local newspaper summed up their views when it commented that Keswick 'makes a living out of tourism. It is imperative that visitors should be brought directly to the town'. The UDC consequently withdrew its support for the bypass but was then involved in a series of disputes through the 1930s as the County Council tried to rationalise road provision in Cumberland. In 1934, the UDC resisted another County Council initiative by organising a plebiscite of ratepayers that revealed a massive majority against the proposed loop road. Even as late as 1939, the two authorities were still locked in dispute over the question of a bypass, although by this time the UDC enjoyed the backing of the preservation societies against some aspects of the proposal (Rural History Centre, University of Reading, CPRE Archives, CPRE 38/3, correspondence 1930–9; *Penrith Observer*, 11 February 1930; CCRO Carlisle SUDK/1/1/20, 3 September 1931, 8, 22 and 29 May 1934; SUDK/1/1/21, 7 June 1934).

The involvement of the CPRE early in the Keswick dispute indicates that preservation and exploitation are closely linked themes in the tourism history of the Lake District. Preservationist opinion was keen to protect the landscape from unsuitable industrial development but also to curb the excesses of the tourist industry itself. Not surprisingly, a host of preservationist organisations emerged in the inter-war years seeking to defend this landscape. The National Trust had already fulfilled this function before the First World War but after the war it was joined by the Society for Safeguarding the Natural Beauty of the Lake District (SSNBLD) in 1919, by the CPRE in 1926 and by the Friends of the Lake District (FLD) in 1934. These societies maintained complex relationships with tourism interests in the Lake District, sometimes cooperative, sometimes antagonistic, as they sought to define notions of appropriate development in the area (O'Neill, 2001: 148–70).

Transport developments provided excellent examples of how tourism and preservation interests could both combine and conflict in the Lake District. The inter-war years saw a number of schemes to improve the region's communications network in order to improve accessibility and boost tourism. A succession of financially precarious proposals for road improvements over Lakeland passes such as Wrynose, Hardknott and Styhead perturbed preservationist opinion in the decade after the First World War. The schemes, seeking to make West Cumberland more accessible, imperilled the solitude of the more remote areas of the district and provoked furious criticism from the amenity societies and outdoor organisations.

Those interested in the commercial development of the Lakes were more ambivalent, however.

A suitable example of this ambivalence came in 1923 when representatives of Lancashire, Westmorland and Cumberland County Councils and a number of local councils met to consider the arguments for and against a proposed road over Hardknott and Wrynose Passes, which would have improved access between Langdale, Eskdale and Wastwater. They listened to the pro-road argument that 'accessibility is the keynote of success to places of health and pleasure', whilst also bearing in mind the preservationist counter-argument that such an incongruous development would harm the beauty that attracted the tourist in the first place. The dynamic tension between these two arguments, which could divide those concerned with tourism development, was apparent in the 50/50 split in the final vote. The lack of a majority sidelined the scheme but the closeness of the vote indicated clearly that key players in the tourism trade did not always believe in the inviolability of the mountain fastness (*Westmorland Gazette*, 27 January 1923).

Further road proposals saw the rehearsal of the same arguments regarding tourism promotion and the defence of solitude. A classic example was Cumberland County Council's audacious bid in the mid-1930s to construct roads over a number of the passes in order to promote economic development and alleviate unemployment in West Cumberland. The council justified its request for grant aid from the Special Area Commissioner by arguing that it was trying to make 'some of the finest scenery in Britain a paying proposition'. Some Keswick hoteliers remained unconvinced that this would be the result, with one asserting that the roads would put 'the Lake District in danger of losing its greatest charm – its beauty, solitude and peacefulness'. The County Council failed in its application for grant aid but used its own money to build a road over Honister Hause, much to the annoyance of the amenity societies (Murdoch, 1984: 164; *Penrith Observer*, 22 January 1935).

Most of the road proposals of this period failed not only because of environmental considerations but also because they rested on shaky economic foundations. They were reliant on financial contributions from various local authorities at a time when economic orthodoxy called for cutbacks in public expenditure. This same combination of preservationist opposition and financial shortcomings accounted for the failure of plans for a light railway from Windermere to Keswick in the early 1920s. The scheme proposed to link five lakes and the resorts of Windermere, Ambleside, Grasmere and Keswick. Its proponents knew that similar plans had met with protests from amenity campaigners in the late-19th century and therefore sought to stress its environmental friendliness. They promised a line that would avoid obtrusive banks and bridges and, because of its electric-petrol engines, generate little noise or smoke.

Initial reactions to the initiative were mainly sceptical. Some resort leaders in Ambleside were in favour of the scheme but opinion in Grasmere and Keswick remained uncommitted. Preservationist spokesmen, led by Gordon Wordsworth, grandson of the poet, attacked the proposal as a desecration of the landscape and also exposed its weaknesses. The line was to cross public roads at 12 points with the inevitable consequence of unsightly bridges or level crossings. He also questioned the economics of the scheme, demanding to know the costs of rolling stock and pointing out the likely paucity of demand for the railway in the winter months. These inherent financial uncertainties persuaded both the Lake District County Councils against the scheme, decisions they reiterated when a revised scheme reappeared in 1923. Without their backing, the scheme faded away (O'Neill, 2001: 216–20).

The intricate relationship between preservation issues and tourism development observable in transport questions surfaced in other landscape controversies in the period. The proposed introduction of electricity pylons to the district engendered a cacophony of protest in the late 1920s and 1930, particularly in the Keswick area. Local opponents of the Central Electricity Board's plans formed an Anti-Pylons Committee to campaign for the cables to be placed underground. The membership included local hoteliers worried that placement of the pylons in the area would offend the sensibilities of the more refined visitors who constituted the more lucrative long-stay holiday market. A long struggle ended in victory for the protesters but the provision of electricity from the National Grid in various areas of Lakeland remained a controversial subject well into the 1950s (Berry and Beard, 1980: 46–9; *Keswick Reminder*, 14 June 1929; Luckin, 1990: 102–9).

Similar sentiments, which fused the protection of landscape and tourism interests, arose in the defence of Ullswater from pollution by the Greenside lead mine and in the campaign against the Forestry Commission's proposals for afforestation of parts of the Lake District (O'Neill, 2001: 198–209; Sandbach, 1981: 125–32; Symonds, 1936). To the preservationist organisations, however, the area's landscape seemed under almost permanent attack from what H.H. Symonds sarcastically called the 'the swirling tide of "progress"' (Symonds, 1936: 1). Increasingly, therefore, they clamoured for more powerful regulatory controls which would enable a balance between suitable development and the defence of beauty in the district. Initially, the societies had high hopes of the Town and Country Planning Acts of 1919 and 1932 but problems stemming from the inadequacies of these acts, from the reluctance of local authorities to bear the compensation costs involved and from landowners' opposition to planning controls delayed these initiatives in Lakeland. Although Windermere and Keswick initiated planning schemes and regional schemes developed in South Lakeland, North Lonsdale and Cumberland, progress was frustratingly slow. By 1939, only the South Lakeland scheme had gained government approval (O'Neill, 2001: 262–83).

The bureaucratic obstacles and retarded development of town and country planning in Lakeland persuaded many interested in its protection to opt for the creation of a National Park in the district. Early declarations in the period subtly argued the need for an overall controlling authority. G.M. Trevelyan, for instance, proclaimed in 1926 that such an authority would not ossify the area. He stated that 'no-one wants to restore the remoteness and solitude of Wordsworthian Grasmere' but maintained that the district could only maintain its character if 'a portion of the beauty can survive the departure of the solitude'. The formation of the Friends of the Lake District in the 1930s saw the campaign for a National Park develop more impetus. This organisation denounced the ineffectiveness of existing planning controls and proposed a local committee with the power to apply a more exigent form of regulation over the whole district. A National Park Commission would provide central government funding to cover the compensation costs to landowners that had impeded the application of previous planning legislation. These measures, they claimed, would preserve open access to the fell country and protect its beauty 'to the great benefit of the whole tourist industry'. The scheme thus hoped to place environmental protection and the development of tourism in a new regulatory context that would be advantageous to both (Friends of the Lake District, 1937; *Westmorland Gazette*, 1 May 1926).

The Friends of the Lake District's vision for the area came to (partial) fruition in 1951 with the creation of the National Park. It would be foolish to argue that the Park was solely the product of events in the inter-war years. The effects of war, of socialist notions of central planning and of post-war austerity all had their part to play in the eventual composition of the National Park. It would be equally foolish, however, not to acknowledge that the creation of the Park was a recognition of the myriad pressures placed upon the Lake District in the inter-war years. These years had indicated that the district needed to come to terms with the impact of new forms of tourism and with increasing challenges to the landscape from industry, transport and various public utilities. The National Park was an attempt to apply a management framework that would permit an integrated approach to the issues of preservation and development that had been so starkly revealed in the decades between 1919 and 1939.

References

Abraham, G.D. (1913) *Motor Ways in Lakeland*. London: Methuen.

Abraham, G.D. (1929) *Motoring in the English Lakeland*. Keswick: Methuen.

Ambleside Public Library, Ambleside Oral History Society, interview collection, various respondents.

Berry, G. and Beard, G. (1980) *The Lake District: a Century of Conservation*. Edinburgh: J. Bartholomew.

Blackpool Gazette, 17 July 1924.

Bott, G. (1994) *Keswick: The Story of a Lake District Town*. Keswick: Cumbria County Library.

Cumberland and Westmorland Herald, various issues.

Cumbria County Record Office (CCRO), Carlisle, SUDK, Minutes of Keswick UDC.

Cumbria County Record Office (CCRO), Kendal, WSUD / A, Minutes of Ambleside UDC; WSUD / L, Minutes of Lakes UDC; WSUD / W, Minutes of Windermere UDC.

Forster, E.M. (1937) Havoc. In C. Williams-Ellis (ed.) *Britain and the Beast*. London: J.M. Dent.

Friends of the Lake District (1937) *Make the Lake District a National Park*. Ambleside.

Howkins, A. and Lowerson, J. (1979) *Trends in Leisure, 1919–39*. London: Social Science Research Council.

Keswick Reminder, 14 June 1929, 12 July 1929.

Lakes Express, various issues.

Leonard, T.A. (1934) *Adventures in Holiday Making*. London: Holiday Fellowship.

Luckin, B. (1990) *Questions of Power: Electricity and Environment in Inter-war Britain*. Manchester: Manchester University Press.

Marshall, J.D. and Walton, J.K. (1981) *The Lake Counties from 1830 to the Mid-Twentieth Century*. Manchester: Manchester University Press.

Murdoch, J. (1984) *The Discovery of the Lake District*. London: Victoria and Albert Museum.

O'Connell, S. (1998) *The Car in British Society: Class, Gender and Motoring, 1896–1939*. Manchester: Manchester University Press.

O'Neill, C. (2001) Visions of Lakeland: Tourism, preservation and the development of the Lake District. PhD thesis, Lancaster University.

Penrith Observer, various issues.

Rural History Centre, University of Reading, CPRE Archives.

Sandbach, F. (1981) The early campaign for a national park in the Lake District. In R. Kain (ed.) *Planning and Conservation*. London: Mansell.

Symonds, H.H. (1936) *Afforestation in the Lake District*. London: Dent.

Taylor, H. (1997) *A Claim on the Countryside*. Edinburgh: Keele University Press.

Walker, H. (1985) The popularisation of the outdoor movement, 1900–1940. *British Journal of Sports History* 2 (2), 140–53.

Walton, J.K. (1991) The Windermere tourist trade in the age of the railway, 1847–1912. In O.M. Westall (ed.) *Windermere in the Nineteenth Century* (2nd edn). Lancaster: Centre for North-West Regional Studies.

Walton, J.K. and McGloin, P.R. (1981) The tourist trade in Victorian lakeland. *Northern History* 17, 153–82.

Walton, J.K. and O'Neill, C. (1993) Numbering the holidaymakers: The problems and possibilities of the June Census of 1921 for historians of resorts. *Local Historian* 23 (4), 205–16.

Walton, J.K. and O'Neill, C. (2004) Tourism and the Lake District: Social and cultural histories. In D.W.G. Hind and J.P. Mitchell (eds) *Sustainable Tourism in the English Lake District* (pp. 19–47). Sunderland: Business Education.

Walvin, J. (1978) *Beside the Seaside*. London: Allen Lane.

Ward, E.M. (1929, reprinted 1948) *Days in Lakeland, Past and Present*. London: Methuen.

Westall, O.M. (1991) The retreat to Arcadia: Windermere as a select residential resort in the late nineteenth century. In O.M. Westall (ed.) *Windermere in the Nineteenth Century*. Lancaster: Centre for North-West Regional Studies.

Westmorland Gazette, various issues.